"Paul Foster has edited an excellent collection of essays on some key figures of the pre-Nicene Church. Teachers of the period will find this an invaluable volume, both for the quality of the essays and for the particular selection of figures included. In English this collection has no equal."

Lewis Ayres, Bede Chair of Catholic Theology, Durham University

"This is a thoroughly reliable, appreciative introduction to the formative perspectives of early Christianity by a well-chosen team of experts. Early Christianity used to be taught in a scholastic kind of way as if it had fossilized completely. The contributors to this volume all understand early Christianity as a time of creative ferment, when innovations were extended and at times withdrawn in a way both like and unlike today. This account of tentative progress is an excellent foil for those wrestling with the changing church today."

Iain R. Torrance, President, Princeton Theological Seminary, Princeton, NJ

"This fine series of essays provides an accessible and up-to-date introduction to twelve key figures who helped to shape the development of mainstream Christianity before the age of Constantine. *Early Christian Thinkers* will be a valuable aid in the study of this formative period of church history."

Christopher A. Beeley, Walter H. Gray Associate Professor of Anglican Studies and Patristics, Yale Divinity School

"In *Early Christian Thinkers*, Paul Foster has assembled a team of world-renowned scholars to give us a refreshing look at the lives and influence of twelve pivotal figures of early Christianity. From Justin, Irenaeus and Theophilus, to Perpetua, Origen, Gregory Thaumaturgos and Eusebius, this masterful collection deals with history, sociopolitical relationships, theology, apologetics, lives, martyrdom, in short, as Frost calls it, 'the intellectual legacy and cultural heritage' of a faith and a new people that sprung from that little-known region of Galilee to bring God's good news of salvation to all. Arranged in a meaningful chronological order, *Early Christian Thinkers* will be used in colleges and seminaries to open up for its readers the multifacet...   appreciation not only of their subject b...   ...e scholarship ought to be done in the ser...   alike."

George Kalan...   or of The Wheaton Center for Early Christi...

"This splendid volume has encouraged its authors to construct twelve fine chapters about early Christian theologians. The project's genius emerges both from the high-level manuscript studies in the introductions and the well-written summaries concerning what is known of the theologians' lives and thoughts. The pithy comments will stay with us all. Fellow specialists will turn to this book for the state of many questions; undergraduates can see what patristics has been and is now becoming. A rare combination of features which we should find together more often."

FREDERICK NORRIS, Professor Emeritus of World Christianity, Emmanuel School of Religion

"'Where can I find the current state of scholarly opinion on such and such patristic figure?' This is a question frequently confronting serious teachers and scholars who are not content to fall back on the golden oldies of patristic scholarship. . . . IVP Academic's *Early Christian Thinkers* is the place. These essays provide a succinct account of contemporary scholarly views on major, as well as less familiar, figures from the second to early fourth centuries (e.g., Justin, Theophilus of Antioch, Eusebius of Caesarea) by the guild's top scholars who know how our understanding of these figures has developed over the last fifty years. *Early Christian Thinkers* will be a resource valuable to professionals as well as students seeking a snapshot of the writers whose lives and thought shaped how early Christians understood and lived out the gospel."

J. WARREN SMITH, Associate Professor of Historical Theology, Duke Divinity School

Early Christian Thinkers

The Lives and Legacies of Twelve Key Figures

EDITED BY **Paul Foster**

IVP Academic

An imprint of InterVarsity Press
Downers Grove, Illinois

InterVarsity Press
P.O. Box 1400, Downers Grove, IL 60515-1426
Internet: www.ivpress.com
E-mail: email@ivpress.com

InterVarsity Press® is the book-publishing division of InterVarsity Christian Fellowship/USA®, a movement of students and faculty active on campus at hundreds of universities, colleges and schools of nursing in the United States of America, and a member movement of the International Fellowship of Evangelical Students. For information about local and regional activities, write Public Relations Dept., InterVarsity Christian Fellowship/USA, 6400 Schroeder Rd., P.O. Box 7895, Madison, WI 53707-7895, or visit the IVCF website at <www.intervarsity.org>.

Unless otherwise noted, Scripture quotations are translated by the author or are taken from the translations of the relevant early Christian figure.

ISBN 978-0-8308-3937-7

Printed in the United States of America ∞

 InterVarsity Press is committed to protecting the environment and to the responsible use of natural resources. As a member of Green Press Initiative we use recycled paper whenever possible. To learn more about the Green Press Initiative, visit <www.greenpressinitiative.org>.

Library of Congress Cataloging-in-Publication Data

Early Christian thinkers: the lives and legacies of twelve key
figures / edited by Paul Foster.
      p. cm.
   Includes bibliographical references and index.
   ISBN 978-0-8308-3937-7 (pbk.: alk. paper)
   1. Theology—History—Early church, ca. 30-600. 2.
Theologians—Biography. 3. Church history—Primative and early
church, ca. 30-600. I. Foster, Paul, 1966-
   BT25.E27 2011
   230.092'2—dc22
   [B]

                                                    2011006929

P	19	18	17	16	15	14	13	12	11	10	9	8	7	6	5	4	3	2	1
Y	27	26	25	24	23	22	21	20	19	18	17	16	15	14	13	12	11			

Contents

Contributors

Prof. Timothy David Barnes taught in the Department of Classics at the University of Toronto from 1970 to 2007; since 2008 he has been attached to the University of Edinburgh as an Honorary Fellow in Divinity and in Classics. His most important publications relating to early Christianity are *Tertullian: A Historical and Literary Study* (Oxford: Clarendon Press, 1971; 2nd edn with postscript 1985); *Constantine and Eusebius* (Cambridge, Mass.: Harvard University Press, 1981); *The New Empire of Diocletian and Constantine* (Cambridge, Mass.: Harvard University Press, 1982); *Athanasius and Constantius: Theology and Politics in the Constantinian Empire* (Cambridge, Mass.: Harvard University Press, 1993); *Ammianus Marcellinus and the Representation of Historical Reality* (Ithaca: Cornell University Press, 1998); *Early Christian Hagiography and Roman History* (Tübingen: Mohr Siebeck, 2010). He has recently completed *Constantine: Dynasty, Religion and Power in the Later Roman Empire*.

Prof. J. Patout Burns is the Edward A. Malloy Professor of Catholic Studies at Vanderbilt Divinity School. He is the author of *The Development of Augustine's Doctrine of Operative Grace* (Paris: Études Augustiennes, 1980) and *Cyprian the Bishop*, Routledge Early Christian Monographs (London: Routledge, 2002).

Prof. Everett Ferguson is Professor of Church History Emeritus and Distinguished Scholar in Residence at Abilene Christian University. Among his numerous publications are the books *Backgrounds of Early Christianity* (Grand Rapids, Mich.: Eerdmans, 1987; 3rd edn, 2003) and *Baptism in the Ancient Church: History, Theology, and Liturgy in the First Five Centuries* (Grand Rapids, Mich.: Eerdmans, 2008). He has served as president of the North American Patristics Society, from which he received the Distinguished Service Award for more than thirty years of service.

Dr Paul Foster is Senior Lecturer in New Testament language, literature and theology in the School of Divinity at the University of Edinburgh. He is author of *Community, Law and Mission in Matthew's Gospel*, WUNT II.177 (Tübingen: Mohr Siebeck, 2004), *The Apocryphal Gospels – a Very Short Introduction* (Oxford: Oxford University Press, 2009) and *The Gospel of Peter: An Introduction, Critical Edition and Commentary* (Leiden: Brill, 2010).

Prof. Judith L. Kovacs is Associate Professor in the Department of Religious Studies at the University of Virginia. She is author of *The Church's Bible: 1 Corinthians Interpreted by Early Christian Commentators* (Grand Rapids, Mich.: Eerdmans, 2005) and co-author (with Christopher Rowland) of *Revelation: The Apocalypse of Jesus Christ*, The Blackwell Bible Commentaries 1 (Oxford: Blackwell, 2004).

Her current research project is directly related to Clement of Alexandria and will result in a monograph entitled *Contending for the Legacy of Paul: Clement of Alexandria and the Valentinian Gnostics*.

Prof. Rebecca Lyman is the Samuel Garrett Professor emerita at the Church Divinity School of the Pacific, Berkeley, California. She is the author of *Christology and Cosmology: Models of Divine Activity in Origen, Eusebius and Athanasius*, Oxford Theological Monographs (Oxford: Clarendon Press, 1993).

Dr Denis Minns is formerly lecturer in patristics at Blackfriars, Oxford, and now Prior of St James' Priory, Glebe, New South Wales. He is co-author with Paul Parvis of *Justin, Philosopher and Martyr: Apologies*, Oxford Early Christian Texts (Oxford: Oxford University Press, 2009) and author of *Irenaeus: An Introduction* (2nd edn; London: Continuum, 2010).

Dr Paul Parvis is an honorary fellow in the School of Divinity at the University of Edinburgh. He is co-author with Denis Minns of *Justin, Philosopher and Martyr: Apologies*, Oxford Early Christian Texts (Oxford: Oxford University Press, 2009), as well as writing the study 'Justin: Philosopher and Martyr: The Posthumous Creation of the Second Apology', in S. Parvis and P. Foster (eds), *Justin Martyr and His Worlds* (Minneapolis, Minn.: Fortress, 2007) 22–37.

Dr Sara Parvis is lecturer in Patristics in the School of Divinity at the University of Edinburgh. She is the author of *Marcellus of Ancyra and the Lost Years of the Arian Controversy 325–345*, Oxford Early Christian Studies (Oxford: Oxford University Press, 2006), and has co-edited (with Paul Foster) *Justin Martyr and His Worlds* (Minneapolis, Minn.: Fortress, 2007).

Dr Rick Rogers is a lecturer in the Department of History at Eastern Michigan University. He is author of *Theophilus of Antioch: The Life and Thought of a Second-Century Bishop* (Lanham, Md.: Lexington Books, 2000). He specializes in the traditions of Near Eastern origins (Judaism, Christianity and Islam) and his current research focuses on the common roots and history of the Abrahamic Religions, and on inter-faith dialogue.

Prof. Michael Slusser was chair of the Department of Theology and professor at Duquesne University, Pittsburgh, Pennsylvania, until his retirement in 2006. He was the translator of *St. Gregory Thaumaturgus: Life and Works*, Fathers of the Church 98 (Washington, DC: Catholic University of America Press, 1998).

Prof. Dr Ulrich Volp is Professur für Kirchen- und Dogmengeschichte in the Evangelisch-Theologische Fakultät, Johannes Gutenberg-Universität Mainz. His publications include *Tod und Ritual in den christlichen Gemeinden der Antike*, Supp. VigChr 65 (Leiden/Boston: Brill, 2002), and *Die Würde des Menschen: Ein Beitrag zur Anthropologie in der Alten Kirche*, Supp. VigChr 81 (Leiden/Boston: Brill, 2006).

Acknowledgements

The chapters all appeared originally in the *Expository Times* and are reproduced by permission:

Chapter 1 Paul Parvis, 'Justin Martyr', *Exp Times* 120.2 (November 2008), 53–61.

Chapter 2 Paul Foster, 'Tatian', *Exp Times* 120.3 (December 2008), 105–18.

Chapter 3 Denis Minns, 'Irenaeus', *Exp Times* 120.4 (January 2009), 157–66.

Chapter 4 Rick Rogers, 'Theophilus of Antioch', *Exp Times* 120.5 (February 2009), 214–24.

Chapter 5 Judith L. Kovacs, 'Clement (Titus Flavius Clemens) of Alexandria', *Exp Times* 120.6 (March 2009), 261–71.

Chapter 6 Everett Ferguson, 'Tertullian', *Exp Times* 120.7 (April 2009), 313–21.

Chapter 7 Sara Parvis, 'Perpetua', *Exp Times* 120.8 (May 2009), 365–72.

Chapter 8 Rebecca Lyman, 'Origen of Alexandria', *Exp Times* 120.9 (June 2009), 417–27.

Chapter 9 J. Patout Burns, 'Cyprian of Carthage', *Exp Times* 120.10 (July 2009), 469–77.

Chapter 10 Ulrich Volp, 'Hippolytus', *Exp Times* 120.11 (August 2009), 521–9.

Chapter 11 Michael Slusser, 'Saint Gregory Thaumaturgos', *Exp Times* 120.12 (November 2009), 573–85.

Chapter 12 Timothy D. Barnes, 'Eusebius of Caesarea', *Exp Times* 121.1 (December 2009), 1–14.

Introduction

PAUL FOSTER

The significance of early Christian ideas

The period from the mid second century, when Justin Martyr wrote his defence of the Christian faith, until the beginning of the fourth century, when Eusebius presented a somewhat triumphalistic account of church history, was a period of both theological creativity and challenge for this emergent religious movement. While group members shared a common devotion to the person of Jesus, the basis of such piety and worship required further definition. It was during this period that numerous thinkers wrestled to formulate an intellectual account of the faith. In part, this was motivated by a desire to understand better the nature and basis of the Christian belief system. However, at other times the motivations were more pragmatic. These included the very real challenge of adjudicating between competing perspectives and interpretations concerning matters of faith, the need for the regularization of leadership and ecclesial structures, as well as addressing pastoral concerns such as the rehabilitation of lapsed believers. As the early Christian movement developed from being a loose confederacy of scattered yet like-minded communities into a more coherent Empire-wide institution, albeit still officially proscribed until the beginning of the fourth century, there was a pressing need to bring consistency of practice to this growing faith-system. This involved both searching for a meaningful expression of core beliefs and negotiating a broad and workable consensus concerning the correct system of governance for the burgeoning movement. A number of its most prominent thinkers in the period covered by this book, AD 150–330, sought to resolve issues such as these.

Within the time span covered by this volume it is possible to identify significant developments of thought. These developments were often either built on previous insights or shaped by pressing new circumstances. Therefore, the writings and impact of each of the 12 figures discussed here reflect the way in which these early Christians, while being rooted in their own cultural contexts, made innovative contributions towards developing Christian thought, theology and piety. Consequently, while these figures must be understood within their own historical situations, they also left lasting legacies which have shaped the subsequent history of Christianity. Many of their ideas were formative for later expressions of Christian theology. Although it may be debated whether these enduring contributions were positive or negative, the discussions in this book seek to describe the life, theology and contribution of each of the figures within the broader stream of the development and evolution of Christianity.

The impact of the Christian movement on subsequent Western culture is well known, and this alone justifies an investigation of the development of its intellectual origins and earliest institutional developments. However, what is sometimes overlooked is the way in which early Christianity itself drew upon, modified and transmitted already existing intellectual ideas. The role of tradition, the place of argumentation, the canonization of texts, the control of dissident voices and the management of a widespread voluntary association are all issues that find precedents in religious and political systems that were in existence before Christianity's spread. Yet the way in which these ideas are combined and developed in the first few centuries of the movement resulted in the structural and intellectual framework that would create the space in which the medieval notion of Christendom could come to fruition. While it would be too much to claim that all these later developments can be traced to trajectories initiated by figures in the second to fourth centuries, there is undoubtedly much continuity and many ideas can be identified *in nuce*. However, theological creativity did not cease at the beginning of the fourth century. Therefore, while many beliefs found more precise expression in later centuries many can still be recognized in embryonic form in the first few centuries of Christianity. Thus the 12 figures under study in this volume reflect the intellectual legacy and cultural heritage of a faith that transformed itself from being a messianic sect originating in the backwater of Galilee into a group that proclaimed a universal salvation and in the process shook the religious fabric of the Empire.

The 12 figures under discussion

Justin, apologist, philosopher and martyr, stands at a temporal and intellectual crossroads in the history of early Christianity. In reality historical eras do not open or close as perfectly discrete units. Like a number of the so-called Apostolic Fathers with whom he overlaps in temporal terms, Justin shares a primitive ecclesiology and an undeveloped scriptural canon. However, he represents one of the first major attempts to place Christian thinking on an equal footing with the élite philosophies that were part of the education of the intellectually privileged in the second-century Roman Empire. In his treatment of Justin, Paul Parvis notes the way in which Justin challenged the prevailing philosophical systems of his own day with a muscular and robust presentation of Christian thought. Moreover, Justin's life is seen as providing a snapshot of the international and multicultural nature of life in the Roman world. Parvis traces Justin's life from birth in Flavia Neapolis of Syria Palestina, via his intellectual growth in Ephesus, then on to the imperial capital where as leader of a 'school-church' he sought to articulate the intellectual credentials of what was originally a Jewish messianic movement. This agenda came to fullest fruition in Justin's apologetic writings. Controversially, but plausibly, Parvis argues that Justin's commonly titled *Second Apology* was in fact not a work independent of the *First Apology*. Rather he sees it as being the assemblage of out-takes from an initially longer version of the *First Apology*. Thus, according to Parvis, the so-titled *Second Apology* may be viewed as a posthumous creation of Justin's disciples, who reassembled the out-takes into a separate document soon after the martyrdom of their teacher. Paradoxically, Parvis argues that the success of Justin's influence can be measured by the quick disappearance of his works. Justin's pioneering work as an apologist was taken up by successors in the replication and expansion of that literary genre. Perhaps it would not be too great a claim to suggest that the modern theological sub-discipline of apologetics ultimately finds its origin in the second-century figure of Justin who, without any sense of contradiction, both wore the philosopher's mantle and yet died the martyr's death.

The second figure to be discussed in this volume was himself a pupil and disciple of Justin. Like his teacher, Tatian was not a native of Rome, although he fell under the tutelage of Justin in the capital. Unlike his teacher, however, Tatian would not be remembered as a representative of orthodoxy by later church figures. This is probably due to his later association with the Encratite movement in the Eastern region of the Empire, and perhaps also because he did not undergo the legitimating fate of martyrdom. Nonetheless, his one complete surviving work, *Oratio ad Graecos*, which adopts the apologetic genre used so effectively by Justin, was distinct in not addressing members of the imperial household (like previous Christian apologies) but was addressed more broadly to 'the Greeks'. However, Tatian had in view a particular branch of Greek culture: its philosophical schools. With brash confidence and enthusiasm he ridiculed the self-perceived superiority of the philosophers. Both Plato and Aristotle are parodied and mocked. Moreover, Greek learning is claimed to be indebted to other cultures and consequently baseless in its critique of barbarian thinking, and the Christian conception of divinity is argued to be superior to that contained in philosophical accounts. While the *Oratio* is Tatian's only complete surviving work, he is perhaps more famous for a work that survives only partially in fragments and citations. His unified combination of the four Gospels, known as the *Diatessaron*, was an attempt to present a continuous and harmonized text of these accounts of the life and death of Jesus. The challenge which this text presented to the emergence of the fourfold Gospel canon should not be underestimated, especially in the Syrian Church. While Tatian may not have been the innovator of Gospel harmonies, his combination of the four Gospels into a unified narrative was undoubtedly the most influential of such harmonies. Tatian's legacy is difficult to assess. Setting aside the later assessment of him as a heretic, his association with both Justin and Encratite theology reveals much about the fluidity and diversity of early Christianity. His impact through the *Diatessaron* shaped Syriac Christianity for several centuries after his death, and in response it may have helped to crystallize the eventual decision to accept a fourfold Gospel canon rather than a single harmonized narrative.

Although perhaps as little as a decade or two separates Justin and Tatian from Irenaeus, the differences in their respective theological outlooks and responses to internal dissensions within the Christian movement is fully apparent. Fully cognisant of this shift in mindset, Denis Minns presents Irenaeus as a crucial figure in the early history of the development of Christian doctrine. This remarkable development in Christianity between the early 150s and Irenaeus' own time is highlighted through investigation of six key theological themes in his writings. These are Irenaeus' discussions concerning: (1) the nature of 'heresies' and the way he formulates responses to deviant teaching; (2) the role of 'tradition', with a rebuttal of claims of preservation of strands of secret traditions in other branches of Christianity; (3) the development of the concept of 'the measuring rod of truth' – in effect this was a claim that those who knew the central tenets of faith could correctly gauge the truth claims of others; (4) the plan of salvation, which functions to affirm the unity of the Old and New Testaments; (5) the idea of 'recapitulation', viewed as a salvific summing-up of the cohesive divine plan of salvation primarily in the person of Christ; and (6) Trinitarian and Christological thought, which in embryonic ways anticipate later creedal statements. In essence Irenaeus' contribution was to attempt to articulate a coherent theological structure for Christianity. Minns also notes that the different ways in which Irenaeus articulates theological concepts such as the 'sin of Adam' or the 'economy of salvation' means that he has much that is fresh and invigorating to offer to contemporary theology.

Theophilus of Antioch was a contemporary of Irenaeus, and like Irenaeus he was a bishop, Christian writer and defender of the faith. While his surviving writings, three documents collectively known as *To Autolycus*, are generally seen as belonging to the genre of the apology, Rick Rogers argues that they do far more than offer a robust defence of the faith. He suggests that they should be examined as protreptic literature going well beyond merely defending the faith to promoting a world and life view. In essence the writings are seen as an invitation to participate in Christian life and the way of salvation. Theophilus offers his readers what is in some ways an idiosyncratic form of 'logos-Christology'. Thus, he portrays the logos 'as a literary personification of God, who provides salvific *nomos*' (p. 66). Because of Theophilus' apparently anomalous theology, he is often seen as being somewhat of a misfit in the stream of emergent orthodoxy, yet this does not mean his perspectives should be adjudged heretical. Rather, as Rogers suggests, 'it might be better to say that Theophilus was a heterodox theologian, who upheld the conservative Christianity of Antioch' (p. 66).

With Clement of Alexandria, the focus of the volume shifts not only centuries but also continents. While these differences need to be acknowledged they should not be overplayed, since in many ways they are artificial boundaries. The city of Alexandria was certainly not a provincial backwater but, as Kovacs notes in her study, it was perhaps the most lively and stimulating city in the Roman Empire. While little is known of Clement's life, Kovacs observes that the reference to Clement as 'blessed presbyter' (p. 69) suggests that he held an official position within the church. This is an important observation, for it provides some insight into the relationship between the intellectual branch of Christianity in a catechetical school in Alexandria and its wider worshipping community. Discussing Clement's writings, Kovacs concentrates on his primary trilogy of the *Exhortation*, an invitation to Christian life, the *Instruction*, a treatise addressed to new believers on the Christian way of life, and the seven books of his *Miscellanies*, which is his most advanced work of theological reflection. As Kovacs presents it, Clement's legacy is multifaceted. He combined advanced philosophical learning with the Christian message to produce a more rationalistic understanding of faith. Moreover, he provides readers with the first written records of Christian theology from the intellectual powerhouse of Alexandria. Thus Clement opens up new vistas on both the intellectual and geographical landscape of the early Church at the beginning of the third century.

Like his near contemporary Clement, Tertullian provides a North African perspective on early third-century Christianity in North Africa. However, in many ways, it is here that the similarities stop. Everett Ferguson recognizes Tertullian as being the principal propagator, if not creator, of theological Latin. Moreover, he was a strident critic of Roman Christianity, an outspoken opponent of heresy, yet also himself suspected of being a schismatic. Ferguson presents a potted version of Tertullian's life, which notes the recent scholarly tendency to question whether his association with Montanism did indeed indicate that he went into schism from mainstream Christianity. Tertullian's prolific literary output, spanning the period 193–217, reflects his skill as a forensic orator. Ferguson groups the generally accepted corpus of 31 surviving works into three categories: (1) apologetic writings – mostly against paganism; (2) anti-heretical and doctrinal writings; and (3) moral and disciplinary writings – both orthodox and those influenced by Montanism. It is noted that Tertullian's writings proceed along rationalistic lines, and that he is influenced by Irenaeus in his portrayal of Christ's work as recapitulation. His impact touched later ancient authors as well as providing resources for modern theologians. In relation to the former, his high evaluation of martyrdom not only shaped the ethos of the North African church, but also became part of later controversies which required resolution. For modern theologians, his stance against Christian participation in warfare has been seen as a resource for pacifist theologies. According to Ferguson, however, the best way to understand Tertullian is as a rhetorician of his own age, who wrote employing varying techniques to win those arguments in which he was involved.

Perpetua is indeed the 'odd woman out' in this male-dominated list of 12 figures, yet this is not solely due to her gender. She is the only figure among the 12 who did not leave extensive theological writings. However, fragments of her prison diary survive in a composite document. Her inclusion among other figures is not due to an attempt to embrace the feminist agenda for its own sake, or to feign some other type of 'trendiness'. Rather, Perpetua represents a 'lived-out' theological commitment, which resulted in the ultimate demonstration of commitment to her religious beliefs. Therefore, as Sara Parvis notes in her discussion, while Perpetua may not have been the greatest theologian of the early Church, she does nevertheless provide a rare insight into the genuine and characteristic theology of the more general Christian population. Parvis seeks to rescue Perpetua from what she characterizes as 'pop-Freudian psychological analysis' (p. 106), which labels Perpetua as a neurotic and wilful suicide. Instead Perpetua is seen as having a simple, but not simplistic, theology that finds its centre in the experience of a relationship with the divine. Perpetua's spirituality stems from a sense of belonging to a charismatic church, enriched with visions, miracles and prophecies. Consequently, the recovery of her voice reminds modern readers of the vibrancy and spiritual immediacy that attracted many to faith in the early Church.

The contrast between Perpetua and the next figure discussed in this book, Origen, perhaps exemplifies the diversity and breadth of the early Christian movement in antiquity. In her introduction to Origen, Lyman emphasizes the range and volume of his literary output. Origen's life reflects a Christian ancestry coupled with a consistent and deepening commitment to God. His father was arrested and eventually martyred around 203, and the adolescent Origen was zealous to join his father, but was thwarted by his mother hiding his clothes. Whether the description of his self-castration is a later slander or reflects an ascetic practice, there is little doubt that Origen was attracted by ascetic disciplines. However, it is the prolific range and sophisticated nature of his writings that created his lasting legacy for the Christian movement. Lyman groups Origen's writings into three categories. First, scriptural writings including commentaries and homilies, as well as his mammoth work of textual criticism, the *Hexapla*, a six-column edition of the Old Testament text with columns for the original Hebrew, a transliteration into Greek characters, and recensions of the Greek translation due to Aquila, Symmachus, an unattributed recension and that of Theodotian. The second category utilized by Lyman deals with Origen's philosophical theology as outlined in his work *On First Principles*. Here it is noted that Origen's aim was to expound apostolic teaching in philosophical terms with reference to cosmology, anthropology and eschatology. In the third category, Lyman groups together Origen's *Contra Celsum* which in many ways represents the pinnacle of the genre of the apology, along with his treatises *On Prayer* and *On Martyrdom*, both of which are addressed to those inside the community of faith. In terms of his legacy, now as in the centuries following his death, Origen is an elusive figure to categorize. Therefore, Lyman notes that 'he breaks rather than fits our categories in his adventurous orthodoxy and spiritual intellectualism' (p. 124). Yet, perhaps it is this very elusiveness which is Origen's legacy, coupled with the reminder that the Church impoverishes itself when it stigmatizes those it fails to fully understand.

The fifth character with a North African connection is Cyprian of Carthage. He was a contemporary of Origen, and an episcopal leader who negotiated difficult theological and social problems in the aftermath of the Decian persecution. In his chapter, J. Patout Burns notes that Cyprian, bishop of Carthage, had to deal with a church split over the process necessary for reintegrating those who had committed apostasy in the face of persecution, as well as simultaneously reining-in the confessors who claimed the right to pronounce forgiveness for such apostates. It is noted that Cyprian was a surprise but popular choice as bishop of Carthage. This wealthy aristocratic rhetorician had been a Christian only for two years when the laity overrode objections of the majority of presbyters and chose him as bishop. Within two years Cyprian found himself confronted with one of the most intense periods of persecution, instigated by Emperor Decius in December 249. Cyprian wrote a number of treatises, of which perhaps the most pastorally pressing and structurally significant for the Church was entitled *On the Lapsed*. In addition, a corpus of 82 surviving letters associated with his term in office reflect detailed information on the practice of Christianity in North Africa in the mid third century. Burns notes that the range of theological issues addressed by Cyprian is indeed narrow compared to that of his predecessor Tertullian. However, this is due to the fact that 'his theology developed in response to conflicts over practice within the church' (p. 131). The ongoing contribution of Cyprian revolves around his development of a theology of the unity of the Church as a universal communion. He also emphasized the episcopal college's role in maintaining the unity and holiness of the Church. Although the Donatist controversy of subsequent centuries served to emphasize the problems inherent in Cyprian's conceptions, his ecclesiological theory provided the basis for the institutional episcopal structure of the Western Church.

With Hippolytus of Rome the focus shifts from North Africa back to the imperial capital. While he overlapped in time span with Origen, his death occurred perhaps two decades prior to those of Origen and Cyprian. Ulrich Volp assembles some of the fascinating details of the life of Hippolytus. He was a presbyter in Rome at the turn of the third century. However, his poor relations with a succession of bishops of Rome may well illustrate the unstable and somewhat insignificant nature of that office in the early part of the third century. Hippolytus' apparent leadership role in the church in Rome, while simultaneously being a fierce opponent of Calixtus who was elected bishop in 217, has led to Hippolytus sometimes being labelled as the first 'antipope'. Historical anachronism aside, Volp notes that if this were true then he would be the 'only ever canonized antipope' (p. 141)! One of the many strengths of Volp's study is his up-to-date survey of the so-called 'Hippolytan question', which tries to sift the genuine works from the spurious ones attributed to his Roman presbyter. In response to this question of authentic authorship, three ancient catalogues of his writings are surveyed. One is contained in the writings of Eusebius, another preserved by Jerome and, intriguingly, a third in the form of an inscription discovered in 1551 'on an ancient statue of a figure, probably female, which the Roman community somehow connected with Hippolytus after his death' (p. 143). The document known as the *Apostolic Tradition*, which is attributed to Hippolytus, is a liturgical text which gives detailed instructions concerning the orders for Eucharist, baptism and ordination. Volp notes that the prayer texts which it preserves have experienced something of a resurgence in usage in the twentieth century both in Roman Catholic and some Protestant churches.

As Michael Slusser makes clear, Gregory Thaumaturgos suffers from an identity crisis, due to often being misidentified as one of his more famous Cappadocian namesakes. The Gregory in question, the so-named 'wonderworker', was bishop of Neocaesarea on the border of Cappodocia and Pontus during the 250s and 260s. The sources for his life, as described by Slusser, are references in Eusebius' *Historia Ecclesiastica*, Rufinus' expansions to that history, and in the writings of Jerome. Other references appear to be at least partially dependent on these earlier sources. Slusser discusses more recent revisionist and minimalistic readings of these sources in relation to reconstructing Gregory's life. After careful evaluation he rejects this sceptical approach. Assessing Gregory's theological contribution, it is noted that he had a deep grounding in Scripture. His *Metaphrase on Ecclesiastes* argues for 'conversion from the world to the philosophical life' (p. 166). In terms of Christological outlook, Gregory is presented as understanding Christ 'more as the divine Logos than as the human Jesus' (p. 168). However, the categorization of his Christology as docetic is resisted. Instead Slusser argues that Gregory can be more correctly understood as anticipating kenotic conceptions. Furthermore, Gregory is seen as urging a type of piety which is its own reward, and finds its realized paradisiacal vision in leading the life of philosophy in unity with the divine. Noting the elusive nature of the figure of Gregory and the fragmentary evidence concerning him, Slusser asks a question that reminds readers of the paucity of ancient sources: 'How many like him have vanished completely from our ken?' (p. 172).

It is due to the last figure treated in this volume that even more like Gregory have not disappeared from our sight. Eusebius of Caesarea rightly deserves the title of 'the Church's first historian'. In his magisterial study of Eusebius, Timothy Barnes not only treats Eusebius as a collector of Christian traditions but also more fundamentally sees him as an influential figure who shaped the ecclesiastical politics of his own day. Barnes divides his study into five sections: (1) Eusebius' life before he became a subject of Constantine; (2) what is known about his participation in ecclesiastical politics after Constantine's conquest of the East in 324; (3) a discussion of the date, context and contents of Eusebius' extant writings, usually with a brief bibliography of modern scholarship relevant to each work; (4) Eusebius' theological views and his interpretation of human history; (5) an extensive bibliography. Each of these discussions not only challenges consensus positions but often shows that the evidence points more compellingly to alternative answers. Barnes rails against the tendency in twentieth-century scholarship to neglect Eusebius' biblical commentaries, which he argues provide the deepest insights into the thought and habits of mind of Eusebius. The dominant classification of Eusebius' writings into six categories is seen as being intrinsically flawed. Consequently, Barnes offers a new classification of the Eusebian writings with extensive supporting discussion. The discussion of 'Eusebius on God in History' reveals the idiosyncratic nature of his reading of the origins of the Christian religion. Without doubt this is a challenging and provocative discussion of Eusebius and the issues surrounding the reconstruction of his life, the interpretation of his writings and the description of his theology. Barnes presents many compelling lines of evidence to support his arguments and there is little doubt that this provocative reading will generate many fresh discussions and responses in Eusebian studies.

The ongoing value of studying early Christian history

The cast of characters assembled in this volume is indeed a motley crew. It is highly debatable whether they would have seen eye-to-eye on a number of issues, or whether they would have felt comfortable in each other's company. Yet in many ways that is what makes this selection of early Christian figures so fascinating, because in a very real sense their diversity represents much of the complex dynamic of early Christianity from the mid second century to the beginning of the fourth century. In no way can early church history be represented as either irenic or unproblematic. In fact, quite the opposite is true. One must remember those who were deemed by either contemporaries or later authorities to be suspect of heresy (figures such as Tatian or Origen included in this volume) contributed in a real way to the development of Christian thinking. Thus, the 12 figures discussed are of value for contemporary study not only because of the historical lessons they teach but also perhaps more importantly because they provide ongoing insights into the manner in which robust doctrinal, ecclesiological and ideational differences can be negotiated.

What these 12 do not provide, however, is a template or exact pattern by which modern church disputes can be resolved. Their culture is not ours, their modes of thinking cannot be simplistically transported to the modern era, and their pre-scientific world-view is no panacea for people living in a post-Enlightenment age. Yet, notwithstanding these obvious differences, these figures do provide resources and options that can be brought to the table of modern ecclesiological debates and disputes. Both failed options and successful solutions from antiquity can direct and shape modern responses to contemporary issues. Any simplistic attempt to impose old solutions onto new situations is actually a failure to take seriously the energy and creativity of the 12 figures discussed in this book. They themselves were not happy with stock answers. Rather, they challenged their own contemporary conventions, they pressed theological boundaries and they were willing to integrate the best insights of the wider philosophical, cultural and political ideas into the formation of a robust Christian faith. Their belief system was not a hermetically sealed entity, but instead saw that the God of all creation had spread wisdom in all aspects of society, both Christian and non-Christian. So if they leave modern readers with one overarching legacy it is this: a call to engage one's intellect in the fullest pursuit of truth, in the confident hope that honest enquiry is always of the highest benefit for Christian faith.

1

Justin Martyr

PAUL PARVIS

Introduction

Justin is an early Christian figure who is very much of his own time, yet his ideas and intellectual legacy transcend temporal confines. He does not represent just a snapshot of the Christianity of Rome in the mid-second century, but was a courageous figure who challenged the prevailing philosophical systems of his own day with a muscular and robust presentation of Christian thought. Rather Justin, leader of a 'school-church' in Rome, is a key figure in the early development of Christianity. Some of the ideas he offered remain central to Christian thinking.

In the manuscript tradition of his works, Justin is almost invariably called 'the holy Justin, philosopher and martyr'.[1] Those two epithets – philosopher and martyr – reflect in different ways the two most enduring aspects of his legacy, but they do not represent the whole man or even the whole of his achievement. Indeed, in some ways they mask it, for they do not adequately reflect the imagination and the courage it took for a Christian in that world to cross boundaries, to move out and address the dominating structures, political and cultural, of the outside world. We will try to come to terms with the scale of that achievement by following the wandering course of Justin's life.

Flavia Neapolis

Justin introduces himself as 'Justin, son of Priscus, son of Baccheios, from Flavia Neapolis of Syria Palestina' (*1 Apol.* 1).[2] That phrase reveals – as it was meant to – a lot about his identity. To begin with, he is writing in Greek, but his own name and that of his father are Latin. He is a Roman provincial, from the province known as Judaea until its name was changed by Hadrian as a part of his policy of trying to crush Jewish identity in the terrible aftermath of the Bar Kokhba revolt of 132–35.

---

[1] Indeed, he is already called 'Justin, philosopher and martyr', by Tertullian (*Adv. Valentin.* 5), writing scarcely more than a generation after Justin's death.
[2] References to Justin's works – the *First* and *Second Apology* and *Dialogue with Trypho* – are given as *1 Apol.*, *2 Apol.*, and *Dial.*; editions and translations are listed in the bibliography.

Flavia Neapolis was, as its name implies, a new city (*nea polis*), a Roman foundation, Greek-speaking and pagan. It was built very near the site of the ancient biblical city of Shechem, and from it Justin would have looked up to Mt Gerizim, where the Samaritans had for centuries observed the Passover sacrifice. But within Justin's own lifetime a pagan temple, dedicated to Highest Zeus, had been built on one of the twin summits of the mountain by the Emperor Hadrian.[3]

Thus the world Justin comes from is that of a Greek-speaking pagan in the Roman-dominated world of the High Empire. When he presents himself in those terms he is addressing the Emperor Antoninus Pius, Hadrian's successor, who was on the throne from 138 to 161. Otherwise there are very few fixed points in the chronology of Justin's life. The date of his birth can be worked out only roughly and indirectly. His *Dialogue with Trypho*, to which we will turn in a moment, is a literary account, written up much later, of a debate with a learned Jew who was 'a Hebrew of the circumcision and a fugitive from the war that has just ended' (*Dial.* 1.3). That takes us back to the end of the Bar Kokhba revolt in 135. And at some stage before that, Justin had been converted to Christianity. His birth, then, can hardly be later than 110, and probably not much before the turn of the century, since, as we will see, he was active as a teacher in Rome until his martyrdom around 165. More than that we cannot say.

On to Ephesus

Justin himself has given us an account – of sorts – of the intellectual journey that brought him to Christianity (*Dial.* 2.3–8.1). It begins with a brightly coloured little narrative of his passionate and frantic quest for philosophical truth (2.3–6). He first tried a Stoic teacher, but after some time decided that 'nothing further was coming to me about God' (Stoics were materialists of a sort and more concerned with ethics than with metaphysics).

He next approached a Peripatetic – that is, an adherent of the philosophical school descended from Aristotle. He was a shrewd man, but after a few days asked for a fee, which Justin regarded as a very unphilosophical thing to do. So Justin moved on again. His next stop was a Pythagorean, but the Pythagorean insisted on his pupils being familiar with music, astronomy, and geometry, and Justin was unwilling to spend the time these preliminary studies would have required.

Finally – and he thought successfully – he found

a wise man and one prominent among the Platonists, who had recently come to stay in our city ... And the intellection of immaterial things greatly lifted me up, and the contemplation of the forms gave wings to my understanding, and within a short time I thought that I had become wise. (2.6)

---

[3] A coin (of Trebonianus Gallus) showing the temple on the top of Gerizim appears as Plate 2 in Sara Parvis and Paul Foster (eds), *Justin Martyr and His Worlds* (Minneapolis, MN: Fortress, 2007).

But then Justin encountered a mysterious old man by the seashore, who told him about the Hebrew prophets.

What are we to make of this story? It has been read in a wide variety of ways. There are, at one end of the spectrum, those who take it simply and straight-forwardly, at face value. And there are, at the other end, those who point out that a tale of philosophical quest among various schools was a commonplace in the second century[4] and conclude that the whole story is simply a literary fiction, telling us much about Justin's aspirations and the way he wished to package himself, but virtually nothing about his biography.

The question is of some importance. The straight-forward, face-value reading supports the picture, often drawn, of a Justin who is intellectually sophisticated, philosophically acute, and attuned to the current debates of the schools. The latter reading coheres with the picture of a Justin out of his depth in his fumbling attempts to engage with the Greek philosophical tradition. The truth probably lies somewhere in the middle. The philosophical quest described in the *Dialogue* is not a simple slice of autobiography and is not presented as such. It is after all a tale told by a character in a dialogue, even though the character is Justin himself. On the other hand, the stylized nature of the narrative does not mean that it has no foundation at all. We need to see the humour in it and to realize that it is shaped by the sympathetic amusement with which Justin now looks back on the misdirected enthusiasm of his youth.

Justin, in any event, came to package himself as a philosopher. At the beginning of the *Dialogue*, Trypho recognizes him as such by the way he is dressed (*Dial.* 1.2), for in Justin's world the popular philosopher was a stock character, easily recognizable as such on a street corner or in the pages of comedy by his uniform – a rough woollen cloak, beard, wooden staff.

But the Justin of the *Dialogue*, though dressed as a philosopher, is really a spokesman for a very different tradition. The long and rambling debate that ensues between Justin and Trypho, spread out over two days, centres on the interpretation of the Jewish scriptures, the books that make up our Old Testament. Though Trypho is supposed to be a refugee from Judaea, the debate, conducted in Greek, is concerned exclusively with texts in Greek. Indeed, Justin can deploy two different types of Old Testament text. Normally and by preference he invokes the Septuagint but, because he is aware of accusations that its readings have been falsified by Christian alterations, he can also use, for purposes of argument, a more literal version, related to the Jewish revision of the Septuagint known to modern scholars as the *kaige* version.[5]

---

[4] The case is well put by J. C. M. van Winden in his valuable commentary on these chapters, *An Early Christian Philosopher: Justin Martyr's Dialogue with Trypho, Chapters One to Nine*, Philosophia Patrum 1 (Leiden: Brill, 1971).

[5] The classic demonstration of this was an article by Dominique Barthélemy, 'Redécouverte d'un chaînon manquant de l'histoire de la Septante', *Revue Biblique* 60 (1953), 18–29. See the thorough and incisive survey by Oskar Skarsaune, 'Justin and His Bible', in *Justin Martyr and His Worlds*, 53–76.

And the argument proceeds through the careful collection and collation of texts and a detailed examination of word usage.

All this happens in an impeccably Greek setting. The conversation takes place in a ξυστός, a covered walkway attached to a gymnasium (*Dial.* 1.1 and 9.3). That gymnasium was probably in the great city of Ephesus,[6] the heart of the Roman province of Asia on the Aegean coast of Asia Minor. But the characters, for all their Greek dress and Greek manner – Justin, in his opening salvo, even quotes Homer – are passionately concerned with a style of exegetical argument that we might call rabbinic in its methods and aims. It has in fact been argued that Trypho's contributions, when pieced together, are not the disconnected responses of a straw-man opponent, but rather represent a serious argument in touch with contemporary Jewish thought.[7]

Thus, somewhere along the line – somewhere between Flavia Neapolis and Ephesus, as it were – Justin has been in close contact with a Christian scribal tradition akin to that often hypothesized as the context in which Matthew's Gospel emerged. Oskar Skarsaune suggests, more specifically, that one of the voices we hear in Justin's work 'is the voice of Jewish Christians addressing their fellow Jews in the distressing years immediately after the Bar Kokhba revolt' and adds that 'nothing . . . excludes the possibility that Justin got his fundamental theological "education" in Palestine', perhaps among 'the Gentile Christians who occupy Jerusalem after the revolt'.[8] Moreover, this 'school' was concerned not just with texts of our Old Testament but also with newer, Christian material. It has, for example, been shown that Justin worked with a harmony of Matthew, Mark, and Luke containing at least sayings of Jesus.[9]

Rome

Justin's *Dialogue* ends abruptly: he has to leave because he has a ship to catch (*Dial.* 142). We might imagine that he was on his way west, to Rome, for that is where he turns up next and where he would eventually end his life. In the mid-second century the population of Rome was probably very near a million (at a time when the population of the Empire as a whole was

---

[6] At least, so Eusebius says (*Historia Ecclesiastica* 4.18.6). The text of the *Dialogue* that has come down to us makes no mention of place, but does suffer from various lacunae and is clearly damaged or abridged at the beginning.

[7] See Timothy J. Horner, *'Listening to Trypho': Justin Martyr's* Dialogue *Reconsidered* (Leuven: Peeters, 2002).

[8] Oskar Skarsaune, *The Proof from Prophecy. A Study in Justin Martyr's Proof-Text Tradition: Text-Type, Provenance, Theological Profile*, Supplements to Novum Testamentum 66 (Leiden: Brill, 1987), 371 and 373. This is a book of fundamental importance for Justin's use of the Old Testament.

[9] Arthur J. Bellinzoni, *The Sayings of Jesus in the Writings of Justin Martyr*, Supplements to Novum Testamentum 17 (Leiden: Brill, 1967). The question of whether Justin also knew John's Gospel has been much debated, but the argument that he did is quite compelling. See Skarsaune, 'Justin and His Bible', 67–68.

scarcely more than sixty million), and its wealth and power acted as a magnet attracting from all corners of the Mediterranean world those with careers to make or ideas to sell.

The church Justin encountered there would have been rapidly growing, predominantly Greek-speaking, and drawn, in substantial part at least, from immigrant communities from the East.[10] It would also have been fragmented, almost cell-like in structure. Separate house-churches or school-churches, each under its own presbyter or teacher, would have met all over the city, drawn together on linguistic or regional or theological lines. The structure into which these separate groups fit would have been fairly loose, though there would appear to have been at the least a regular meeting of all the presiding presbyters, the chairman of which may have been the 'overseer' (ἐπίσκοπος), the one whose name entered the lists, drawn up by at least 160, of bishops of Rome.[11] Each of these separate communities would have been a centre of study, instruction, and worship. Justin seems to presuppose that converts, for example, are prepared and baptized in separate groups and then brought together for a common eucharist (*1 Apol.* 61.2–3, 67.1). Justin must have made his living as just such a teacher.

'A certain woman' and her marital troubles

A vivid light is shone just for a moment on what it was like to be a Christian in Rome by a nasty little incident that happened around the year 153 and that was destined to have long-term repercussions for the whole Christian church. Someone Justin refers to only as 'a certain woman' (γυνή τις) was converted to Christianity from what, Justin is anxious to stress, was a life of licentiousness, for she and her husband had engaged in oral and anal sex and been involved in drunken revels and other (unnamed) vices with the slaves and hired servants (*2 Apol.* 2.4, 7). Eventually she was forced to divorce him (under Roman law either party could dissolve the marriage), being unwilling to 'share bed and board' (2.6) any longer with such a man.

In retaliation her happily pagan husband denounced her to the authorities as a Christian. She then filed a petition to the Emperor – the detail here will be important to our story – asking that her case be put on ice until she had time to sort out her affairs, a petition which the Emperor granted (2.7–8). The husband, blocked on that front, next denounced the teacher who had instructed her in the faith and whose name was Ptolemy. Ptolemy was eventually brought before the Urban Prefect, Q. Lollius Urbicus, and sentenced to death as a Christian. Two Christian bystanders in court, one named Lucius and the other unnamed, protested and were condemned in their turn (2.9–20).

---

[10] See the important study by Peter Lampe, *From Paul to Valentinus: Christians at Rome in the First Two Centuries*, tr. Michael Steinhauser, ed. Marshall D. Johnson (London: T&T Clark, 2003).

[11] Lampe, who regards the list as a retrospective creation, is unduly sceptical here (Lampe, *From Paul to Valentinus*, 403–407).

In order to understand what is going on here it is important to realize that until the middle of the third century there was no specific law or imperial edict prohibiting Christianity. However, the governor of a province or the Urban Prefect in Rome could exercise enormously wide discretion in taking cognizance of complaints and punishing malefactors. Since at least the time of Pliny's correspondence with Trajan in 110,[12] it had been normal to punish Christians for the name alone, that is, for the mere profession of Christianity, without the need specifically to prove their complicity in any crimes associated with the name. It was of course assumed that there were such crimes, for there was an urban myth, widely held in the second century, that Christians routinely engaged in cannibalism (eating babies) and incest (promiscuous sex with whoever could be grabbed in the dark, including mothers and sisters) – or 'Thyestean banquets' and 'Oedipean intercourse'. But until the mid-third century, there was no such thing as general or Empire-wide persecution. Outbreaks were local and sporadic, triggered by natural disaster or inter-communal tension or, as in the case of γυνή τις, personal animosity.

The woman's response is important. The family clearly had money, so she would have brought a sizeable dowry with her into the marriage. In Roman law the dowry passed under the control of the husband for the duration of the marriage but had to be returned to the woman on its dissolution. In petitioning for the case to be suspended until she sorted out her affairs γυνή τις was, therefore, in effect forcing her ex-husband to choose between the money and his desire for revenge, since the matter could not proceed until he disgorged the dowry.

What she submitted to the Emperor was a petition, βιβλίδιον in Justin's Greek. It was a normal part of Roman administrative procedure that ordinary folk could approach a provincial governor or even the Emperor himself and submit a petition (*libellus* in Latin, βιβλίδιον in Greek) asking for legal clarification, administrative intervention, redress of grievance. The official would 'subscribe' the document (*subscribere* in Latin, ὑπογράφειν in Greek) – that is, literally, write his answer underneath – and then post it up (*proponere*, προτιθέναι) in a public place. That is the procedure γυνή τις used to frustrate her husband. And that is the procedure Justin would use to change the face of Christian theology, for he decided to respond to this savage little, local persecution by submitting a petition of his own.

The *Apologies*

What Justin did was to hijack this normal Roman administrative procedure and turn it into a vehicle for articulating and disseminating the message of the Gospel. About the year 153 he produced a document that begins, as normal petitions do, with the name of the recipient (in this case the Emperor and his sons) in the dative and the name of the petitioner ('Justin, son of

---

[12] Pliny the Younger, *Epistulae* 10.96, with Trajan's response in 10.97.

Priscus, son of Baccheios ...') in the nominative.[13] He then makes a request, using the normal verb found in petitions (ἀξιόω), here a request for a change in legal procedure, so that Christians be tried on specific charges rather than for the name alone (*1 Apol.* 4). And the document concludes, as many of the *libelli* found among the papyri do, with the citation of (an apparent) legal precedent, Hadrian's rescript to the Proconsul of Asia, Minicius Fundanus (68.6).[14] Moreover, he asks the Emperor to 'subscribe (ὑπογράψαντας) what seems good to you and to post up (προθεῖναι) this petition (βιβλίδιον)' (*2 Apol.* 14.1).

The work is, then, a petition, but a distinctly odd one. For one thing, it is something like fifteen times the length of a normal petition to the Emperor. For another, Justin has supplemented his simple petition with a long presentation of who Christians are. There is an account of how they live, drawing on a harmonistic summary of the ethical teaching of Jesus, perhaps originally arranged for catechetical purposes. Then there is a long explanation of Old Testament prophecy and an attempt to demonstrate its fulfilment in Jesus and in the church. And finally there is an account of how Christians worship, with an explanation of baptism and eucharist. In other words, Justin has turned a *petition* into an *apology*. That is the decisive move that Justin makes, and we will return to its significance in a moment.

But first we must note that the position is complicated by the fact that we have, or appear to have, not one *Apology* but two. The authentic works of Justin – the *Dialogue* and the *Apologies* – are transmitted in but a single manuscript of independent standing, Parisinus graecus 450, in the Bibliothèque Nationale in Paris. It was completed, the scribe tells us, on 11 September 1364.[15] It presents a shorter text, entitled 'Apology on behalf of Christians', and a longer one, called 'Second Apology'. But because the shorter text contains a number of back references to things that are actually found in the longer document, they have been reversed ever since Grabe's edition of 1700–1703, so that the 'Second Apology' of the manuscript is what we always

---

[13] The date can be fixed within fairly narrow limits by the address to Antoninus Pius and his adopted sons. The year 153 in particular – or perhaps 154 – is suggested by the fact that the undistinguished Lucius Verus – still 'a private citizen in the imperial house' as he is called in his semi-fictional biography (*Scriptores Historiae Augustae*, 'Verus' 2.11) and so strictly speaking having no place in a petition – seemed then to be entering public life.

[14] The authenticity of the rescript has been often discussed. In a careful study Denis Minns concludes that it is authentic, but did not have the meaning Justin hopefully attaches to it: Denis Minns, 'The Rescript of Hadrian', in *Justin Martyr and His Worlds*, 38–49.

[15] There is also a manuscript, of identical contents, copied from Par. gr. 450 in Venice in 1541 and once in the private collection of Sir Thomas Phillipps of Middle Hall near Cheltenham (Claromontanus 82). It was for a number of years on loan to the British Museum, but has now been withdrawn for private sale. However, as a direct copy of the Paris manuscript, it has no independent value for the establishment of the text. For a discussion of the manuscripts, see the introduction to the critical edition of the *Apologies* by Denis Minns and Paul Parvis, *Justin, Philosopher and Martyr: Apologies*, Oxford Early Christian Texts (Oxford: Oxford University Press, 2009). (Manuscripts of later works, falsely attributed to Justin, are numerous.)

know as the *First*, and the short text it calls simply 'Apology' is what we know as the *Second*.

The relation of the *Second* to the *First* is a long-standing and rather tedious problem. There are three main theories – that there was really only one, artificially chopped in two by an officious scribe (as suggested by F. C. Boll in 1842); that there are indeed two *Apologies*, as the manuscript presents them; and that there is one *Apology* with an appendix or supplement added some time, perhaps a very short time, later (first propounded by Grabe in 1700).

But none of these well-rehearsed theories is without problems.[16] So Denis Minns and I have tried to suggest[17] as an alternative that the *Second Apology* is, in effect, out-takes or clippings from the cutting-room floor. On this theory, Justin kept revising the original petition, cutting out things deemed no longer to be relevant and reworking some of his earlier arguments. He would also have had to hand some supplementary materials – notes for street-corner debates, memoranda on how to respond to likely objections. And at some point, very likely shortly after his death when his writings were collected by students of his school, the revised text was published to become our *First Apology*, followed by the fairly amorphous assemblage of 'out-takes' that became our *Second Apology*.

Which theory we adopt does make some difference, for the *Second Apology* is more 'philosophical' than the *First*: it engages directly with philosophical objections, uses some key terms (such as *logos spermatikos* = λόγος σπερματικός) not found in the longer apology, refers to Justin's public debates with a Cynic named Crescens (8(3).1–6),[18] and contains not a single quotation from scripture. But on either the Boll theory or the cutting-room floor theory there is no need to take that as being in any sense a more mature or more 'authentic' Justin than the assiduous collector of proof texts we see at work in the *First Apology*.

A petition, in any event, had to be submitted in person and to bear the name of the petitioner. So in 153 or so Justin would have gone along to the office of the imperial secretary known as the *a libellis* and handed in his swollen petition. He may actually have hoped that the Emperor and his sons

---

[16] The main problem with the two-apology theory is that *2 Apol.* is too short and flimsy a document to stand alone. The main problem with the one-apology, continuous-text theory is that the flavour of the *Second*, with its philosophical terminology and philosophical concerns, is so different from that of the *First*. The main problem with the appendix theory is that it is hard to see what it actually represents in terms of ancient book production. It is also hard to see what is the point of a supplement that does little more than chivvy the Emperor along to produce an answer to the original petition. The problem is discussed in my 'Justin, Philosopher and Martyr: The Posthumous Creation of the *Second Apology*', in *Justin Martyr and His Worlds*, 22–37.

[17] In the introduction to our edition.

[18] *2 Apol.* 3–8 have a double numbering because of a shuffling of paragraphs in most editions after J. C. T. Otto, *Iustini Philosophi et Martyris Opera quae feruntur Omnia* (= Corpus Apologetarum Christianorum Saeculi Secundi i), vol I, part I, *Opera Iustini Indubitata* (Jena: 1st edn 1842; 2nd edn 1847; 3rd edn 1876).

would read it and be persuaded. But whether they were or not, the Christian Gospel had been, symbolically at least, proclaimed at the heart of the Empire.

It is both difficult for us and important for us to take on board the size of the task Justin faced. Antonine Rome was, as its art, its literature, and its political propaganda suggest, a smug and self-satisfied society, at least at the top. And the language Christians used, the thought-world they lived in, were still in many ways locked in to a framework inherited from Judaism. What Justin did was to unlock doors. It would be wrong to resort to an image like 'breaking out of the ghetto'. He was not trying to leave anything behind. He was trying to explain the Gospel he had received in terms that would be comprehensible to the world around him; he was simply trying to talk.

The tactical ploy that allowed him to do so was the petition; the theological tool that allowed him to do so was the Word, the Logos, of God. Logos of course had been a part of Christian theology since the Johannine prologue, and as Justin uses it it has an even older pedigree as well. For Justin's Logos is above all an agent of revelation. In the background is the Word of the Lord that came to the prophets of the Old Dispensation.

This Logos was 'another God and Lord, under the Maker of all things' (*Dial.* 56.3). Later developments of Logos theology, as with Origen in the next century, would think primarily in cosmic terms, of the one through whom God orders the world. Justin is distinctly uninterested in all that; his Logos is the one through whom God speaks and acts in the world he has made. And so he is the one who appeared in all the theophanies of the Old Testament – coming to Abraham at the oaks of Mamre, wrestling with Jacob, calling Moses from the burning bush.

But – and this is the decisive move Justin makes – precisely as Logos he is also accessible to all humankind. For the basic meaning of Logos in Greek is meaningful discourse, significant utterance, and so the structure, pattern, rationality that lies behind that meaning. In this Logos all men and women have a share, but their vision is obscured, above all by the unremitting activity of the demons, who are all around us, conducting a systematic campaign of disinformation to keep humankind enslaved to them. Some individuals, above all philosophers and, among them, pre-eminently Socrates, are able to penetrate the fog, but their task is hard and filled with peril. We, on the other hand, have access to the teaching – and the power – of the Logos himself, who became a human being 'a hundred and fifty years ago' (*1 Apol.* 46.1) and was born of Mary the Virgin.

Thus, 'those who lived with logos are Christians, though they were reckoned atheists, as, among the Greeks, Socrates and Heraclitus and those like them, and, among the barbarians, Azarias and Mizael and Elijah and many others' (*1 Apol.* 46.3). Yet this does not mean that 'Socrates and Heraclitus and those like them' had some sort of independent access to the truth. What they are able to see is *Christian* truth, in which they have some, albeit restricted, share.

So whatever was well said by any of them belongs to us Christians. For we worship and love the Word from the ingenerate and ineffable God, worshipping him and loving him *after* God ... For all the (pagan) writers were able dimly to see the truth through the sowing of the implanted logos that is in them. For a seed and imitation of something, given according to ability, is one thing, but another matter is the very thing itself, participation and imitation of which comes according to the grace flowing from it. (*2 Apol.* 13.4–6)

Through this concept of the Logos Justin was building bridges. It was a key term in contemporary philosophy, above all in Stoic thought – so influential in Rome and in the imperial household he was addressing. For Stoics, 'Logos' and 'God' were interchangeable terms, though by it they meant an impersonal force, diffused throughout the material world and giving it structure and order. They could, specifically, use the term 'spermatic logos' to refer to the structural principle within things that makes them what they are – that makes puppies grow into dogs and kittens into cats. Justin picks up that term too, but for him it means the personal Logos who sows seeds of truth in the world, so that what the philosophers said rightly was spoken 'from a portion of the divine seed-sowing (*spermatikos*) Logos' (*2 Apol.* 13.3).[19]

Just as Justin has hijacked a normal administrative procedure and turned it into a vehicle for the Gospel, so has he hijacked a widely used philosophical term and turned it into a way of trying to explain to an uncomprehending world who Jesus is. In doing so, he effectively invented a new genre – the apology.[20]

How would Justin's *Apology* have been received? Presumably with indifference or contempt if it was ever read at all. Whatever view we take of his philosophical education, there is a great gulf fixed between his world and that of the cultural and philosophical elite of Antonine Rome. A revealing sign of that is the enthusiasm with which he recounts the fable of Herakles meeting two women on the road, who are Virtue and Vice (*2 Apol.* 11.2–5). The fable comes from the sophist Prodicus, via Xenophon, and became enormously popular in the Graeco-Roman world. Indeed, that is precisely the problem. By Justin's day it had become so hackneyed that it could be parodied in comedy, but was hardly ever told straight except in schoolboy handbooks. We are reading the work of someone who, for all his enthusiasm, remains an outsider.

In a world of intermittent and capricious persecution, even to present such a petition could be a move fraught with peril. But that is also what made the task so urgent, for Justin

---

[19] See also *2 Apol.* 7(8).3.

[20] There are of course apologetic motifs in earlier Jewish and Christian literature, including the New Testament itself, but Justin has produced a new type of work specifically designed to break through to the outside world. On the uniqueness of his achievement, see Sara Parvis, 'Justin Martyr and the Apologetic Tradition', in *Justin Martyr and His Worlds*, 115–27.

believed that it must be worth attempting to persuade people who called themselves Pius and philosophers that Christianity was neither impious nor philosophically bankrupt. It was he who first risked his life, lifted his head above the
parapet, to try to do so. It is no accident that Christianity comes out of the
shadows with Justin ... Because it was he who worked out that if you try hard
enough to understand them, it must be at least theoretically possible to persuade
other human beings to understand you – and that if you could do that, maybe
you could even make the killing stop.[21]

Justin Martyr

Justin in fact lived for another decade or more. They were productive years,
presumably spent, mainly at least, in Rome; at some point after the *Apology*
he produced the *Dialogue with Trypho*.[22] Not far from the year 165 Justin
was arrested with six others and brought before the Urban Prefect, Q. Junius
Rusticus, an austere Stoic and a formative influence on Marcus Aurelius, who
was by then Emperor.[23] What led to the arrest we do not know. As usual in
the second and early third centuries, it could have been something quite
trivial, like personal enmity or an incidental quarrel. The little group are
briefly interviewed by Rusticus, whose main concern is to confirm that they
do indeed profess to be Christians. He shows a desultory interest in where
they meet and how they became Christian, but virtually none in what they
believe.

On the first of those points, Justin is evasive and probably lying in an
attempt to protect his fellow-Christians. He says that he is staying 'above the
baths of one Martinus, son of Timiotinus;[24] this is my second spell in Rome,
and in the whole of that time I have known no other place of assembly than
that one' (*Acta* 3). Rusticus is not concerned enough to press the point. 'And
if anyone wanted to come to me', Justin adds, 'I would share with him the
words of life.' The six, all otherwise unknown, must have been pupils of his
school, and all were presumably arrested in the same raid (4). They make an
interesting list. There is Chariton (a man's name) and Charito (a woman's);
Euelpistus, who is described as an imperial slave; Paion from Cappadocia;
Hierax, who was 'dragged', presumably as a slave, from Iconium (modern
Konya) in Phrygia; and Liberian, the only one with a Latin name. At one
point Rusticus asks, 'Who made you [in the plural] Christians?' Hierax answers

---

[21] Sara Parvis, 'Justin Martyr and the Apologetic Tradition', 127.

[22] *Dial.* 120.6 contains a back-reference to what he had said about Simon Magus 'when addressing
Caesar in writing'. (Simon is discussed at *1 Apol.* 26.2–3 and 56.1–2.)

[23] The date has to be inferred from the years of Rusticus' Prefecture, between 163 and 168. The
acts of the martyrdom are transmitted in three recensions, of which the so-called B recension is
normally regarded as being the closest to the actual court proceedings. There is an edition of the
Greek text of all three versions with English translation in Herbert Musurillo, *The Acts of the
Christian Martyrs*, Oxford Early Christian Texts (Oxford: Clarendon Press, 1972), 42–61. Section
references here are to Musurillo's edition of the B recension.

[24] The text here appears to be corrupt. For a suggested identification, see H. G. Snyder, '"Above
the Bath of Myrtinus": Justin Martyr's "School" in the City of Rome', *Harvard Theological Review*
100 (2007), 335–62.

for himself and says simply, 'I was and will be a Christian.' Paion then jumps in and, without being asked, says, 'I too am a Christian.' Rusticus turns to him and asks, 'Who taught you [in the singular]?' Paion says, '*We* received this good confession from our parents', and Euelpistus, unasked, adds, 'I listened with pleasure to Justin's words, but I too received being a Christian from my parents.'

What is interesting in all of this is that the six are clearly playing a game, and Rusticus cannot be bothered to try to get to the bottom of it all. Just as Justin protects his fellow teachers, so the six are protecting him. All of them would have known that they were about to be sentenced to death, but the six must think they can spare their teacher some suffering if they can downplay his role in spreading the insidious poison of Christianity. And they are indeed all led away to be beheaded, not the cruellest of deaths within the fearsome panoply of Roman punishments.

Justin's influence

'Justin, philosopher and martyr' – the two labels reflect at least a part of what he accomplished. By presenting himself as a philosopher, he found a way of engaging with the outside world, driven by his deep conviction that there was a common universe of discourse accessible to all human beings. All truth was Christian truth, and human beings could be brought to see that – if only they would listen. His death as a martyr reflects and may have been a consequence of his determination to make the Christian Gospel publicly and openly available to those who had ears to hear.

And yet those two labels can be misleading. To pigeonhole Justin as a philosopher can make us lose sight of his real achievement. Modern scholars often conclude that his philosophical culture is shallow, or at best derived from popular handbooks. What, however, is important is not the acuity of his arguments, but the fact that he was willing and able to make them in the first place, that he thought it was possible for all men and women to meet on the common ground of truth. And that in turn points to a second and more fundamental problem with a focus on Justin the philosopher, for the truth was not something reserved for an intellectual or philosophical elite. That which Socrates had struggled to gain a glimpse of was, in the church, available to all. 'Among us it is possible to hear these things and to learn them from those who do not even know the shapes of the letters, uneducated folk and barbarians in speech, but wise and trustworthy in their understanding' (*1 Apol.* 60.11).

> For no one was persuaded by Socrates to die for this teaching of his. But they were persuaded by Christ, who was known in part by Socrates too . . . not only philosophers and the eloquent, but also day-labourers and the absolutely uneducated, scorning mere opinion and fear and death, since he is the power of the ineffable Father and not the contrivance of human reason.
>
> (*2 Apol.* 10.8)

That is why 'Justin the Martyr' can be misleading as well. A willingness to face the prospect of death was for him not primarily a sign of individual sanctity, but rather a public seal on the publicly accessible truth of Christianity. It was simply a consequence of knowing what mattered.

What did Justin leave behind? His works, paradoxically, had enormous influence and yet very soon disappeared from sight. There is, as we have seen, only one manuscript of independent standing, a fourteenth-century omnibus edition of what we recognize as the genuine works of Justin together with a number of later productions sheltering under his name. Yet that manuscript seems to have been copied from a corrupt and badly damaged exemplar.[25] Apart from that we have only a number of excerpts pasted by Eusebius of Caesarea into his *Historia Ecclesiastica* and a few fragments in the eighth-century *Sacra Parallela*.

Nonetheless, Justin's idea caught fire in the second-century church. His pioneering effort was picked up and developed by a succession of apologists. Within fifteen years or so of Justin's death Athenagoras published an apology that mirrors Justin's in many ways and elaborates a number of his arguments, but is written in much better Greek and supported by far more learned allusions. The church was moving up-market and learning to negotiate its way through Graeco-Roman culture. Even Justin's use of the petition was transcended. The *libellus* was a procedure to be used by ordinary folk. The elite would approach the Emperor by letter; public bodies like cities or guilds would send a delegation in person. Athenagoras' work is called the *Embassy* (*Presbeia*), for he presents the church as a public body, able to address the Emperor face to face.

Another twenty years on, at the very end of the second century, Tertullian produced an *Apologeticus*, in Latin, in Roman North Africa. Again, a number of Justin's ideas and arguments are recycled, but the tone is quite different. The work is aimed especially at provincial governors and those of their class, and it preys brilliantly on their anxieties. Where once, less than half a century before, there had been smug complacency, there were now the seeds of fear. The world was changing, and there was the beginning of a nagging doubt that perhaps these troublesome people would be found right after all.

Justin's work was quickly superseded precisely because it was so influential.[26] The writings themselves almost disappeared from view, and their very survival came to hang on the slender thread of a single manuscript. What was left was an almost iconic image of 'Justin, philosopher and martyr', which threatened to swallow up the man himself. He would not have minded.

---

[25] The reliability of the text transmitted by Paris. gr. 450 has been much debated. The conclusion asserted here is argued at length in the edition of the *Apologies* by Denis Minns and myself.

[26] On this point and on Justin's formative influence on later apologists, see Sara Parvis, 'Justin Martyr and the Apologetic Tradition'.

Bibliography

Editions and translations

Among numerous editions of the *Apologies* may be mentioned:

A. W. F. Blunt (ed.), *The Apologies of Justin Martyr* (Cambridge: Cambridge University Press, 1911): Greek text with lucid notes.

M. Marcovich (ed.), *Iustini Martyris Apologiae pro Christianis*, Patristische Texte und Studien 38 (Berlin: Walter de Gruyter, 1997): critical edition of the Greek text with good references to parallels in classical and early Christian literature.

C. Munier (ed.), *Justin, Apologie pour les Chrétiens*, Sources chrétiennes 507 (Paris: du Cerf, 2006): Greek text, French translation, extensive notes.

D. Minns and P. Parvis (eds), *Justin, Philosopher and Martyr: Apologies*, Oxford Early Christian Texts (Oxford: Oxford University Press, 2009): critical edition with introduction, translation, and commentary.

A reliable translation is:

L. W. Barnard, *St. Justin Martyr, The First and Second Apologies*, Ancient Christian Writers 56 (New York: Paulist Press, 1997).

There are two recent critical editions of the *Dialogue with Trypho*:

M. Marcovich (ed.), *Iustini Martyris Dialogus cum Tryphone*, Patristische Texte und Studien 47 (Berlin: Walter de Gruyter, 1997): companion volume to Marcovich's edition of the *Apologies*, in the same format.

P. Bobichon (ed.), *Justin Martyr, Dialogue avec Tryphon*, 2 vols., Paradosis 47/1–2 (Fribourg: Academic Press, 2003): excellent edition of the Greek text with French translation and extensive commentary.

For a good, recent translation see:

T. B. Falls, *St. Justin Martyr, Dialogue with Trypho*, rev. Thomas P. Halton, Michael Slusser (ed.), Selections from the Fathers of the Church 3 (Washington: Catholic University of America Press, 2003).

Secondary literature

For an excellent survey of the extensive scholarly literature on Justin see:

M. Slusser, 'Justin Scholarship, Trends and Trajectories', in *Justin Martyr and His Worlds*, ed. Sara Parvis and Paul Foster (Minneapolis, MN: Fortress, 2007), 13–21.

For one-volume introductions to the man and his work, see:

L. W. Barnard, *Justin Martyr: His Life and Thought* (Cambridge: Cambridge University Press, 1967).

E. F. Osborn, *Justin Martyr* (Tübingen: Mohr Siebeck, 1973).

S. Parvis and P. Foster (eds), *Justin Martyr and His Worlds* (Minneapolis, MN: Fortress, 2007).

2

Tatian

PAUL FOSTER

Introduction

Tatian, Christian apologist and author of the most famous gospel harmony, was a disciple of Justin Martyr. His single complete surviving work, *Oratio ad Graecos*, is an example of the apologetic genre, which sought to offer a robust defence of the Christian faith. By contrast, his gospel harmony, the *Diatessaron*, survives only in fragmentary form, or embedded in later gospel harmonies, as well as being partially recoverable via Ephrem's *Commentary* on the text. What can be reconstructed of this work is potentially important for more fully understanding the textual form of the gospels in the second century. Later writers charge Tatian with heresy due to his association with Encratite Christianity. Such a perspective reflects the concerns of subsequent generations, and for this reason there appears to be no clear 'error' attributed to Tatian.

Biography

According to his own testimony, Tatian was born in Assyria (*Or.* 42). Petersen draws attention to the contemporary geographer Claudius Ptolemaeus who 'describes Assyria as extending from the Tigris River in the west to Media in the East, from the Armenian mountains in the North to Ctesiphon in the South'.[1] Thus the designation 'Assyria' covers a large tract of land largely bounded by the Euphrates and Tigris rivers. Beyond this generalized reference little is known of Tatian's birthplace. If there is little precision in ancient texts about the place of birth, then it must be acknowledged that there is no explicit indication of the date of his birth. However, it is perhaps possible to infer from other events in his life when this is likely to have taken place. The ancient sources refer to Tatian's contact with Justin in Rome. Presumably this occurred during some period between the fifties and the mid-sixties of the second century.[2] Assuming that Tatian was neither a precocious talent nor a

---

[1] W. L. Petersen, *Tatian's Diatessaron: Its Creation, Dissemination, Significance and History in Scholarship* (VC Supp. XXV; Leiden: Brill, 1994), 68.

[2] The exact dates for Justin's period in Rome are difficult to fix. He lived in the city on at least two separate occasions. It appears likely that his martyrdom took place around 165 under the Urban Prefect Q. Junias Rusticus. See the timeline in S. Parvis and P. Foster (eds), *Justin Martyr and His Worlds* (Minneapolis, MN: Fortress, 2007), xiii.

particularly mature student when he attached himself to Justin, it is probable that he was born during the twenties or thirties of the second century, during the reign of Hadrian. After cementing his hold on the imperial office, the majority of Hadrian's term was characterized by relative stability, a commitment to cultural pursuits and a dedication to Stoic and Epicurean philosophy.[3] More widely, a renaissance was taking place among the educated classes that sought a return to the philosophical pinnacle attained by the fourth- and fifth-century BC Attic writers. This period of renewed interest in oratory and philosophy, known as the Second Sophistic, created the cultural backdrop for the young Tatian.[4]

Later in life, Tatian could disdainfully state, 'if a free man, I do not boast of my good birth' (*Or.* 23). Although able to eschew his social status, both his educational opportunities and the financial resources at his disposal reveal that Tatian was a member of the upper echelons of society. Addressing Greek society in his apology he states that he was 'educated first in your learning' (*Or.* 42), thus revealing himself to be the product of Hellenistic philosophical learning. Yet he was not content to satisfy himself with school-room bookish learning. He adopted the peripatetic pursuit of learning which was popular as a type of philosophical 'grand-tour' with young pupils (*Or.* 35). His journey culminated in the imperial capital, yet this did not increase his commitment to the learning he had been pursuing – in fact it appears to have had the opposite effect. His exposure to the prestigious seats of contemporary learning resulted in him issuing the following rebuttal coupled with a declaration of a new-found allegiance: 'having taken my leave of Roman arrogance and Athenian cold cleverness – incoherent bases of doctrine – I sought out the philosophy which you consider barbarous' (*Or.* 35).

Tatian's time in Rome is shrouded from the view of modern scholars apart from a few significant facts. The most formative influence on Tatian during this period was his mentor, teacher and fellow apologist, Justin. Tatian mentions Justin only twice in his *Oratio ad Graecos*. The first occasion provides only a fleeting reference which provides little insight into their relationship (*Or.* 18), the second, following closely after, mentions the role of Crescens in seeking the death of Justin. Here Tatian describes that this embittered opponent sought the death of Tatian along with that of Justin (*Or.* 19). It would appear that by the mid-sixties, at least according to Tatian's own portrayal, both he and Justin were considered to be similar threats by Crescens. The earliest external witness to the link between Justin and Tatian is to be found in the writings of Irenaeus. Describing what he considers to be Tatian's later heretical views, Irenaeus states that 'he was a hearer of Justin's, and as long as he

---

[3] Hadrian's exposure to philosophical ideas was enriched during his time in Athens, and in particular through the friendship he formed with Epictetus in about the year 110 or 111. See, A. R. Birley, *Hadrian: The Restless Emperor* (London: Routledge, 1997), 60.

[4] T. Whitmarsh, *The Second Sophistic* (Oxford: Oxford University Press, 2005).

continued with him he expressed no such views' (*Ad. Haer.* 1.28).[5] Obviously the perspective that sees the 'orthodox' Justin functioning as a restraint on the later 'heretical' views of Tatian is heavily shaped by later evaluations of the two figures, although it is interesting to note that such an outlook had emerged maybe only a decade after Tatian had left Rome. Notwithstanding the motivation behind such a statement, the fact that Irenaeus has to explain the perceived deviation of Tatian from his teacher strongly attests to the authenticity of such a relationship existing between these two figures.

It is impossible to determine for how long Tatian remained under the direct pupillage of his teacher. The two men had much in common. Their ethnicity was similar. Both were born in the Levant: Justin from Neapolis in Samaria, Tatian born somewhere in Assyria. They both had exposure to and ability in philosophical traditions. Yet, both had turned their backs on such learning and instead embraced Christianity, becoming teachers of this new 'philosophy' in Rome.[6] However, at some stage having received instruction in Christianity from Justin, Tatian became a teacher of this religion in his own right. Eusebius records the name of one of his students: 'at that time too Rhodo, of Asiatic race, was, as he narrates himself, the pupil at Rome of Tatian' (*HE* 5.13). It is no longer possible to determine whether Tatian's teaching occurred under the auspices of Justin's school, or if this was a more independent move with a split, albeit amicable, from Justin. Another possibility is that Tatian remained under the influence of Justin as a trusted lieutenant until his martyrdom, and only then did Tatian take control of the Christian philosophical school in Rome. This last alternative may be partially supported by Eusebius' comment that 'after the martyrdom of Justin he left the church, being exalted by the idea of becoming a teacher and puffed up as superior to others' (*HE* 4.29). The polemical edge to these comments is again apparent and their inclusion may be more for the benefit of distancing Tatian and Justin, rather than based on historical accuracy. The fact that Crescens appears to have considered Tatian and Justin as opponents of the same type suggests that at least to informed outsiders there was little to differentiate between the two.

After Justin's death, Tatian appears to have remained in Rome for a number of years. There is a problem with the sole source for events in Tatian's life at this point, which for the period after the death of Justin is the *Panarion* of Epiphanius.[7] As Petersen observes,

> He [Epiphanius] reports that after Justin's death, Tatian left Rome and founded a school in Mesopotamia around the twelfth year of Antoninus Pius' reign (138–61), or about 150. This date contradicts Irenaeus' claim that Tatian

---

[5] Eusebius replicates this tradition (*HE* 4.28).
[6] See Petersen, *Tatian's Diatesseron*, 69; and E. J. Hunt, *Christianity in the Second Century: The Case of Tatian* (London: Routledge, 2003), 52.
[7] See Petersen, *Tatian's Diatesseron*, 71, although some other sources refer to his later heretical period without supplying detailed information of a biographical nature.

lapsed into heresy after Justin's death. If, however, one substitutes the name Marcus Aurelius Antoninus (reigned 161–80) for Antoninus Pius, then one arrives at a date of 172/73 – virtually identical with the date given by Eusebius: 172.[8]

Therefore, probably prior to leaving Rome, Tatian appears to have written his most complete surviving work, *Oratio ad Graecos*. This work was the writing for which Tatian was best known in ancient sources and it was the most respected of his writings among the Church Fathers.

Upon quitting Rome, Tatian returned to the east. His motivation for leaving the imperial capital is unknown. It is easy to speculate that it was to avoid a fate similar to that experienced by Justin, or perhaps his teachings had already moved in a direction that marginalized his own position and following within the Roman churches. Like the location of his birth, his specific place of habitation on returning to the east is unknown. In his *Historia Ecclesiastica* following on immediately from the description of Tatian, his works and perceived heresies, Eusebius states, 'In the same region heresies increased in Mesopotamia . . .' (*HE* 4.30). This would lend weight to the perhaps natural suggestion that Tatian returned to his native Assyria. Furthermore, a Syrian location is supported by Epiphanius' report that during this period Tatian's sphere of influence encompassed the regions of Antioch of Daphne (Syria, on the Orontes), Cilicia, and Pisidia (*Pan.* 46.1.8).[9] It was during this latter phase of Tatian's life that he is reported to have established a philosophical school in Mesopotamia which propagated his Christian teachings. It may be that during this phase of his life he compiled his other famous work, the gospel harmony known as the *Diatessaron*, although it is not impossible that this work was composed or at least commenced in Rome, perhaps expanding a pre-existing although not as extensive gospel harmony. This compilation of the four gospel accounts into a continuous narrative was an important innovation (although there were precedents of harmonizing gospel accounts) and it had a strong impact on Syrian Christianity and beyond for several centuries. It is during this period that Tatian is viewed as espousing and in fact originating Encratite Christianity. Eusebius states that around this period the 'heresy of the Encratites . . . was at that time beginning to sprout' (*HE* 4.28) and moreover, apparently drawing on Irenaeus (*Ad. Haer.* 1.28), Eusebius continues, 'the story goes that Tatian was the author of this error' (*HE* 4.29). The accuracy of this attribution to Tatian as being the originator of Encratite teaching is difficult to assess and in large part depends upon where early Church Fathers draw the boundary between legitimate asceticism and fanatical encratism. In many ways the argument is circular with those viewed as 'orthodox' falling into the first category, while opponents are conveniently labelled as Encratite heretics.

---

[8] Petersen, *Tatian's Diatesseron*, 71.
[9] Petersen, *Tatian's Diatesseron*, 71.

It is not known for how long Tatian continued his teaching in 'Mesopotamia', nor is it known when or where he died. Again one must speculate based on clues and life-expectancy factors. If Tatian was born, as has been suggested, either in the twenties or thirties of the second century, and assuming he died of natural causes, perhaps a death no later than the first decade of the third century is probable. Writing around 180, Irenaeus does describe the heretical innovations of Tatian by writing in the past tense. However, this offers little clue as to whether Tatian himself was already dead by this stage. Here the sources simply run out, and nothing definitive can be said about the end of Tatian's life.

Oratio ad Graecos

Almost certainly the earlier of Tatian's two surviving works, his *Oratio ad Graecos* is a work which goes on the offensive against perceived claims of Greek superiority over other ethnic groups in the areas of culture, philosophical learning and understandings of God, among other things. In this respect the genre of this writing aligns with a number of apologetic texts that became prominent from the second century onwards. Perhaps the first examples of such writings that survive are the single fragment of the *Apology of Quadratus* and the text of the *Apology of Aristides*.[10] Yet it is likely that the principal influence on Tatian in adopting this genre and considering the contents of his treatise is to be attributed to Justin, his mentor and predecessor among the apologists.

The date of Tatian's *Oratio ad Graecos* is not entirely secure. The majority of scholars see this work as being posterior to Justin's apologetic writings, and many would also view its composition as later than the date of Justin's death. For Marcovich, Tatian's description of his mentor as 'the most admirable Justin' (*Or.* 18.6), and also the portrayal of Crescens' pursuit of Justin, leads Marcovich to 'assume that Crescens was successful in his endeavour to bring the death penalty on Justin'.[11] While the evidence is not entirely clear, this does seem the most plausible interpretation.[12] If AD 165 is the lower limit for the date of composition, fixing the upper limit is even more speculative.

---

[10] It is generally agreed that Quadratus and Aristides were the first two recorded Christian apologists: see P. Foster, *The Writings of the Apostolic Fathers* (London: T&T Clark, 2007), 54–57, 59–61; and R. M. Grant, 'Quadratus', in D. N. Freedman (ed.), *Anchor Bible Dictionary*, vol. 5 (New York: Doubleday, 1992), 583. However, this consensus has recently been challenged by Sara Parvis, 'Justin Martyr and the Apologetic Tradition', in S. Parvis and P. Foster (eds), *Justin Martyr and His Worlds* (Minneapolis, MN: Fortress, 2007), 117–22.

[11] M. Marcovich, *Tatiani Oratio ad Graecos/Theophili Antiocheni ad Autolycum* (PTS 43/44; Berlin: de Gruyter, 1995), 2.

[12] Barnard felt that the discrepancy between Tatian's comments about Crescens and the revised form in which Eusebius cites the tradition suggested that the latter knew of the death of Justin but the former did not. On this basis Barnard dates the composition of the *Oratio* to the 160s, but prior to the death of Justin, L. W. Barnard, 'The Heresy of Tatian – Once Again', *JEH* 19 (1968), 1–10. This position for a composition prior to the death of Justin is adopted by Emily J. Hunt, *Christianity in the Second Century: The Case of Tatian* (London: Routledge, 2003), 3.

Here only a much more general sense of the situation reflected by the contents of this text is the only basis for dating, and such a datum is particularly subjective. The main distinction surrounds the date when Tatian left Rome for his return to Syria, which is probably around AD 172. On the one hand Marcovich suggests, 'since Tatian's *Oratio* reflects both the presence of Justin's teaching and the environment of Rome, I think it is highly likely that it was written in Rome between *c.* AD 165–72'.[13] Others have seen it composed outside Rome, but presumably before Tatian settled back in Syria,[14] or alternatively after the return to Syria in AD 172.[15] While the data is inconclusive, the suggestion put forward by Marcovich remains the most persuasive in arguing for a Roman provenance and a dating after the death of Justin. If, however, Barnard is correct that Justin's death had not occurred at the time of writing, it must be noted that this does not materially affect the meaning or interpretation of Tatian's *Oratio ad Graecos.*

The surviving manuscript evidence can be determined with much greater certainty, even to the point of describing the degree of interrelatedness of the extant texts. The Arethas codex (Parisinus 451) dating to AD 913–14, does not contain Tatian's *Oratio ad Graecos.* However, it is lacking four quires (or thirty-two leaves). Two later codices M (Mutinensis Misc. gr. 126) and P (Parisinus gr. 174) copy their contents from Arethas and include the following works missing from the now extant portion of that tenth-century codex: the end of Ps.-Justin's *Cohortio* (cc. 36–38), the complete text of Tatian's *Oratio,* and the beginning of Eusebius' *Praep. ev.* (up to 1.3.5).[16] Codex M contains two separate fragments of the *Oratio* written in different hands, the larger fragment covering fol. 205r–226v (*Or.* 1.1–41.21), and the shorter fragment which comprises the end of the text (*Or.* 41.21–42.6). The third major manuscript of the text V (codex Marianus 343) also appears to be based on codex Arethas, and V may well be a genealogical ancestor of the text (now lost) which was used by Frisius at Zurich and his colleague Gesner to publish the *editio princeps* of *Oratio ad Graecos* in 1546. In terms of the respective qualities of these manuscripts Marcovich notes that, 'Among *M V* and *P,* *M* seems to be the most reliable one. Also *M* and *P* seem to stand together against *V.* In its turn, *P* may become treacherous due to the habits of its scribe to change the original word-order of Tatian.'[17] In addition to these principal witnesses to the text, there exist a number of later manuscripts of the text that appear to be dependent upon either the Arethas codex or the earliest copies (M, V or P),[18] as well as important citations in Patristic writings.

---

13 Marcovich, *Tatiani Oratio ad Graecos,* 3.

14 A. Puech, *Recherches sur le Discours aux Grecs de Tatien* (Paris: Félix Alcan, 1903), 10.

15 R. C. Kukula, *Tatiana Sogenannte Apologie* (Leipzig: Bruck und Verlag von B. G. Teubner, 1900), 52.

16 These details are discussed at length in M. Whittaker (ed.), *Tatian* Oratio ad Graecos *and Fragments* (Oxford: Clarendon Press, 1982), xx–xxii; and Marcovich, *Tatiani Oratio ad Graecos,* 3–5.

17 Marcovich, *Tatiani Oratio ad Graecos,* 4.

18 Among these later copies are codex Etonensis (1534 AD), Parisinus gr. 2376 (1539 AD).

These citations include from Eusebius 'almost one fifth of the *Oratio*: from c. 19 in his *HE* 4.16.8, and cc. 31 and 36–42 in his *Praep. ev.* 10.11.1–5 and 10.11.6–35, respectively'.[19] Also in his *Stromateis* Clement of Alexandria has copied a few passages from the *Oratio*. In particular the large blocks of text preserved by Eusebius are significant for showing the degree of corruption the *Oratio* had suffered prior to the witness of the earliest extant manuscripts, and for allowing for the restoration of the text in those passages where Eusebius preserves the text. The first printed edition of the text was published in 1546 in Zurich, prepared by Conrad Gesner based on a manuscript acquired by Johann Fries from the library of Diego Hurtado in Vienna. This text known as codex Frisianus eventually became lost, but it has been suggested that it is identical with codex Vaticanus Ottobonianus gr. 112. For the textual history of *Oratio ad Graecos*, see Figure 2.1 overleaf.

The contents of this apologetic writing are, to say the least, quite wide ranging. After his opening attack on Greek culture in general and then more specifically on philosophers, Tatian turns to an exposition of theological themes although there is a polemical edge throughout much of this section. In Chapters 22–28 Tatian returns to more direct polemic, attacking a number of Greek practices. After a biographical note describing his conversion, Tatian develops one of his main arguments for the superiority of Christian tradition over Greek tradition based on the antiquity of Moses and the charge that the Greeks borrowed ideas from Moses. Yet even here, Tatian engages in a major digression showing how Christian teachers are more ethical than Hellenistic philosophers since the former teach without discrimination. In summary the contents may be represented as in Table 2.1.

Table 2.1 *Oratio ad Graecos,* **chapter contents**

1	Attack on Greek xenophobia and claims of cultural originality
2–3	Conduct of Greek philosophers does not align with their teachings
4–7	Doctrine of creation and God
8–11	Attack on mythology and astrology
12–15	The two kinds of spirit
16–18	Attack on sorcery and medicine
19	Attack on philosophers
20	Divine spirit as wings of human soul
21	Superiority of Incarnation over mythology of Greek deities
22–28	Attacks on various pagan practices
29–30	Tatian's own conversion
31	Temporal priority and superior antiquity of Moses over Homer
32–35	Christians teach without discrimination and other topics
36–41	Return to the chronological argument (cf. 31)
42	Conclusion

[19] Marcovich, *Tatiani Oratio ad Graecos*, 4.

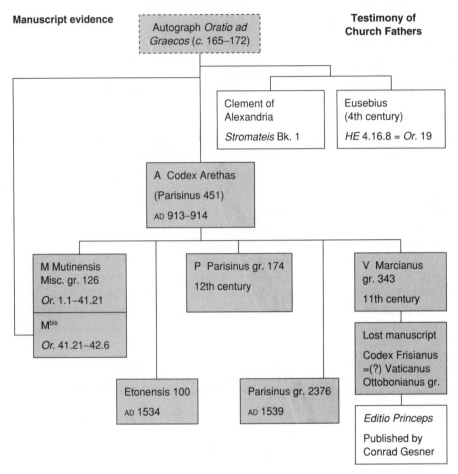

Figure 2.1 The textual history of *Oratio ad Graecos*

This figure is based upon the description of textual witnesses found in the works of Whittaker (ed.), *Tatian* Oratio ad Graecos *and Fragments*, and Marcovich, *Tatiani Oratio ad Graecos*.

The contents of this work not only demonstrate an intimate knowledge of Greek philosophy, but reveal an even deeper radical rejection of its tenets. The structure of the work is a mixture of theological reflection, combined with strong polemical attacks against Tatian's perceived opponents and their practices. However, there is apparently no strict organizing principle to the arrangement of material. The impression is that the work is spontaneous rather than planned. Moreover, as Whittaker has noted, 'Tatian's apologetic is essentially hortatory rather than didactic.'[20] Therefore one may assume that although it is written *against* Greek philosophers, it is actually written for Tatian's Christian audience to read. Therefore its purpose may be to supply

---

[20] Whittaker (ed.), *Tatian* Oratio ad Graecos *and Fragments*, xv.

arguments that could be used by believers to exhort philosophical opponents to convert to the Christian faith.

The *Diatessaron*

Tatian's other famous work was a harmony of the four gospels which resolved discrepancies, deleted duplicate stories and filled those gaps found in individual canonical gospels. The name *Diatessaron*, derived from the Greek διὰ τεσσάρων meaning 'through [the] four', is first attested in the writings of Eusebius, who states that this was the name Tatian used for his own work: 'their [the Encratites] former leader Tatian composed in some way a combination and collection of the gospels, and gave this the name of *The Diatessaron*, and this is still extant in some places' (*HE* 4.29.6). However, in the Syriac-speaking regions the work became known by the title *Da-Meḥalleṭē*, 'the Gospel of the Mixed'. No continuous manuscript, either in the original language or translation, of the *Diatessaron* survives. However, a number of important secondary witnesses survive which allow a partial reconstruction of the text. These witnesses include: 'Ephrem's *Commentary* (extant in both the Syriac original and an Armenian translation, both originating in the fourth century); an Arabic Harmony (twelfth–thirteenth century); a Persian Harmony (1547 CE, a copy of a thirteenth-century ms); Isho'dad of Merv's *Commentary* (Syriac, ninth century).'[21] Furthermore, the influence of the *Diatessaron* may be detected in a number of other texts such as Diatessaronic readings contained in individual Syriac gospels, which were translated into Syriac after the formation of the *Diatessaron*, and also perhaps in later Western gospel harmonies, as well as in other religious and poetic texts.[22]

The original language?

The question of the original language of the *Diatessaron* is contested in modern scholarship. In favour of a Greek original, the only extant fragment of what was claimed to be a portion of the *Diatessaron* is written in Greek.[23] The text preserves an account of the female disciples who were present at Jesus' crucifixion as well as the beginning of the story about Joseph of Arimathea. This fragment was discovered at Dura Europas, and its composition can confidently be dated before the fall of the fortress outpost in AD 256–57. The claim that this fifteen-line scrap of text provides decisive evidence for the *Diatessaron* having been originally written in Greek has been attacked on

---

[21] W. L. Petersen, 'Diatessaron', in D. N. Freedman (ed.), *Anchor Bible Dictionary*, vol. II (New York: Doubleday, 1992), 189.

[22] For a list of possible sources in each category see Petersen, 'Diatessaron', 189.

[23] C. McCarthy, *Saint Ephrem's Commentary on Tatian's Diatessaron: An English Translation of Chester Beatty Syriac MS 709 with Introduction and Notes* (JSS supp 2; Oxford: Oxford University Press, 1993), 5.

two fronts. As early as 1935, Plooij argued that this Greek actually attested an underlying Syriac text.[24] His detailed reasoning was based upon affinities in textual 'corruption' that he saw in both Syriac and Old Latin versions of the *Diatessaron*. In order to sustain the case for an original Greek text, this suggested to Plooij that at least by 180 (less than a decade after the composition of the *Diatessaron*) a problematic reading would have had to come into the Latin version via a non-original Syriac text. He argues the chronological period is too short to allow the required sequence of events which would have seen the composition of the *Diatessaron* in Greek around 173, then a corrupt reading to have occurred in a single copy of a Greek manuscript for the parallel to Luke 23:49, then this corruption to become the predominant reading in the Syriac tradition, which in turn less than seven years later became the basis of the Old Latin text.[25] Yet a number of problems remain with this supposed sequence. First, it is impossible to tell whether this corruption occurred only in a single Greek copy, in fact the Dura fragment shows that it was likely present not only in this manuscript but also in its exemplar. Secondly, the dating of the translation of the *Diatessaron* into an Old Latin form by 180 remains highly speculative, being based on suppositions concerning the dating of Old Latin manuscripts.

More recently, however, another line of attack has been mounted against the Dura Europas text as providing evidence for a Greek original of the *Diatessaron*. In a collaborative article Parker, Taylor, and Goodacre affirm that the Dura text preserves a base-text composed in Greek.[26] What they dispute is the identification of this text with the *Diatessaron*. In their discussion it is argued, on palaeographical grounds, that the manuscript is to be dated to the second half of the second century and that 'none of the analogous manuscripts encourages us to argue for a third century date'.[27] Furthermore, the discussion outlines a number of methodological steps to be taken. After a fresh reconstruction, Parker, Taylor, and Goodacre look for signs that the text has been translated from the Syriac – either Syriacisms or gospel readings derived from a Greek *vorlage*. Moreover, since further *Diatessaronic* texts have been discovered after the discovery of the Dura text, the fragment must be compared against this evidential base. Parker, Taylor, and Goodacre state, '[i]f the text is Tatianic, and the text proves to be a translation out of Syriac, then we will also have evidence concerning the original language of the Diatessaron'.[28] Without rehearsing the detailed discussions, it is argued that no obvious Syriacisms are present in the text. The next stage in the argument involves looking at

---

[24] D. Plooij, 'A Fragment of Tatian's Diatessaron in Greek', *ExpTimes* 46 (1935), 471–76.

[25] Plooij, 'A Fragment of Tatian's Diatessaron in Greek', 476.

[26] D. C. Parker, D. G. K. Taylor, and M. S. Goodacre, 'The Dura-Europas Gospel Harmony', in D. G. K. Taylor (ed.), *Studies in the Early Text of the Gospels and Acts: The Papers of the First Birmingham Colloquium on the Textual Criticism of the New Testament* (Birmingham: University of Birmingham Press, 1999), 198–228.

[27] Parker, Taylor, and Goodacre, 'The Dura-Europas Gospel Harmony', 198–99.

[28] Parker, Taylor, and Goodacre, 'The Dura-Europas Gospel Harmony', 199.

Diatessaronic witnesses. Such witnesses occur in multiple languages such as Arabic, Persian, Latin, Middle Dutch, Middle German, Middle Italian and Middle English, but no Greek comparator text. This means that when phrases in the Dura fragment are determined to be non-Tatianic either on the basis of terminology or syntax, it is necessary to have first determined the hypothetical text that stands behind many of these translations.

The article takes a phrase-by-phrase approach to the Dura fragment, and one is struck by the careful analysis and balanced conclusions such as 'the wording agrees with the Arabic (and Syriac Passion Harmony) ... so it may be Diatessaronic' or 'while the wording of the Dura fragment may be Diatessaronic, the *structure* is not' or again, 'the Dura text agrees with Tatian in order'.[29] Given these extremely balanced observations, coupled with the difficulty of recovering the base-text of a translational version, it is surprising that the conclusion reached is that 'five out of the eight items on which a conclusion is reached proved to be non-Tatianic'.[30] In light of the ambiguous nature of the evidence, and the changes that can occur to syntax structure when moving from one language group to another, it seems strange to classify a reading as non-Tatianic because of slightly different choices of terminology, or because of altered syntax structure. On this last criterion, many modern English translations of the New Testament might be supposed not to be based on the Greek text, because they alter the order of clauses in a given sentence. The presence or otherwise of Syriacisms in this fragment remains contested, although to their credit Goodacre, Taylor, and Parker have severely weakened the claim for such features. However, the decision to label the fragment as non-Tatianic and hence not part of the *Diatessaron* is ultimately not as convincing. In response to Goodacre, Taylor, and Parker, Joosten has written a thoroughgoing reply which questions the type of methodological approach they adopted, in effect judging it as failing to recognize the mixture of local features and Diatessaronic readings which are characteristic of all surviving witnesses.[31] One must, however, remain open to the possibility that the fragment witnesses to another early Greek gospel harmony, circulating in Syria soon after Tatian's own harmony was used in the same geographical region with such large-scale impact. Yet, this may be the less likely possibility.

Others, however, see the case for a Syriac original, rather than Greek, being stronger. In particular the underlying text form of the Old Testament citations used in the *Diatessaron* has been viewed by certain scholars as providing evidence for the text being originally composed in Syriac.[32]

---

[29] Parker, Taylor, and Goodacre, 'The Dura-Europas Gospel Harmony', 218–25.

[30] Parker, Taylor, and Goodacre, 'The Dura-Europas Gospel Harmony', 225.

[31] J. Joosten, 'The Dura Parchment and the Diatessaron', *VC* 57 (2003), 159–75, esp. 163.

[32] W. L. Petersen, 'New Evidence for the Question of the Original Language of the Diatessaron', in W. Schrage (ed.), *Studien zum Text und zur Ethik des Neuen Testaments* (BZNW 47; Berlin: de Gruyter, 1986), 325–43.

While Petersen presents five interesting pieces of textual evidence that may show the *Diatessaron* could reflect direct knowledge of a Semitic text of the Old Testament rather than LXX readings or those preserved in the New Testament, as he himself acknowledges there are in most cases other explanations which would not exclude an underlying Greek *vorlage*.[33] Petersen has proposed three criteria for determining whether a reading is Diatessaronic. These are:

1 The reading should appear in both Eastern and Western Diatessaronic witnesses.
2 The reading should not appear in any non-Diatessaronic sources, which might have contaminated Diatessaronic witnesses.
3 The genre of the sources with the reading should all be identical. All should represent harmonized Lives of Jesus or (as in the case of the Syriac Versions) sources which have a distinct possibility of having been influenced by Diatessaronic tradition.[34]

The first criterion is sensible in that it seeks to exclude regional or individual manuscript variations as being attributed to Tatian. The desire to introduce the second criterion is obvious – the preservation of Diatessaronic purity – but it perhaps excludes too much data and fails to take into account 'cross-contamination' of non-Diatessaronic texts with Diatessaronic readings and *vice versa*. The final criterion allows a common-sense recognition that Syriac sources other than harmonized Lives of Jesus may have Diatessaronic influences, but by excluding this possibility from non-Syriac texts. Petersen in effect privileges the link between Syriac texts and the *Diatessaron*, thereby increasing the chances of supporting the case for the original language being Syriac. The case for seeing Tatian systematically drawing upon the Syriac Old Testament for his biblical citations has been undermined by Shedinger. He argues that even in places where the text of the Syriac Old Testament and the *Diatessaron* align the direction of influence may be from the *Diatessaron* to the Peshitta.[35]

The question of the original language of the *Diatessaron* remains elusive. A number of arguments in favour of a Syriac composition can be marshalled. These include positively the case for semiticisms in the Old Testament citation preserved in the Diatessaronic witnesses. Moreover, the obvious link Tatian has with Syria coupled with the influence of the *Diatessaron* in that context are seen as suggestive of an original composition in Syriac. The major negative arguments include the two different and somewhat competing cases against seeing the Dura Europas fragments as offering strong evidence for a

---

[33] Petersen, 'New Evidence for the Question of the Original Language of the Diatessaron', 333–42.
[34] These three criteria are conveniently listed in a more expansive form in Petersen, 'New Evidence for the Question of the Original Language of the Diatessaron', 327.
[35] See Petersen, 'Diatessaron', 189.

Greek original text. However, in favour of an original composition in Greek a number of arguments can also be offered. Tatian's only surviving work is composed in Greek, showing that he definitely possessed the literary ability required in that language. Secondly, his relationship with Justin is important since Justin is likely to have made use of some harmonizing form of the gospels.[36] It may well be that Tatian expanded a partial already existing gospel harmony, although this may have harmonized fewer than four gospel accounts. Finally, the Dura Europas fragment remains significant. It at least attests that a brief text, which has many affinities with what one might expect to be contained in Tatian's harmony, was circulating in Syria written in Greek about fifty years after Tatian's work. None of these arguments for either Syriac or Greek original composition is decisive, and perhaps ultimately the best position is to state that unless further textual evidence comes to light the question remains irresolvable.

Contents and reconstruction of the text

At a general level the question of the contents of the *Diatessaron* is unnecessary, since the whole agenda of the work is to harmonize material drawn from the four canonical gospel accounts. It is when one turns to the specific questions of ordering, possible omissions, the possible preference of one gospel for the central narrative, and the degree of interweaving of accounts that the enterprise of determining the exact contents and reconstructing the text becomes problematic. Further problems multiply as one begins to consider the textual landscape of early Christianity. The texts of the three synoptic gospels are not themselves literarily independent, but are heavily interdependent. Harmonization is a feature of some early extant gospel manuscripts, so it is difficult to know whether individual cases of harmonization are entirely due to Tatian. To complicate matters further, one cannot tell if Tatian was reliant on a single manuscript of each gospel text or if he was aware of variant readings and consulted multiple copies of one or more of the gospels. Finally, he may have drawn upon existing harmonies of one or more gospel texts. Such uncertainty means that much caution is required and that a degree of hesitancy must attend any statements concerning the specific content of Tatian's *Diatessaron*.

Notwithstanding these difficulties, some indications can be gained from the various Diatessaronic witnesses on the text. Despite being lacunose in places, because of its antiquity the surviving Syriac manuscript of Ephrem's

---

[36] The important work of Bellinzoni demonstrates that at a number of points Justin made use of harmonistic texts as his source for the sayings of Jesus. Specifically in relation to Tatian's work, Bellinzoni states, '[i]t is now apparent that the concept of a gospel harmony did not originate with Tatian; indeed he was a pupil in a school in which gospel harmonies were apparently commonplace. What is new in Tatian's *Diatessaron* and what is not found in Justin's writings is a full gospel harmony rather than one of limited scope and the incorporation into a gospel harmony of the Gospel of John'. A. J. Bellinzoni, *The Sayings of Jesus in the Writings of Justin Martyr* (NovT supp XVII; Leiden: Brill, 1967), 142.

Commentary on the Diatessaron, Chester Beatty MS 709, dating to the late fifth or early sixth century, may be free from the expansionistic tendency of later harmonies both because of its age and more importantly because its main aim is not to transmit a harmonized text, but to comment upon an existing text. By contrast, other early texts, such as the sixth-century Latin Codex Fuldensis, are susceptible to contamination, in this case the vulgarization of readings.[37] The opening sections are easily traceable to specific gospel sources.[38] The *Diatessaron* opens with the Johannine prologue. It then appears to have dropped the Lukan prologue (Luke 1:1–4), but continues by recounting the narrative contained in the rest of Luke 1:5–80. As far as one can tell, Tatian did not preserve the Matthean genealogy, but instead drew upon the first gospel for the story of the conception and birth of Jesus (Matt 1:18–25) and then oscillated between Lukan and Matthean material (combined with the discussion of the identity of the Baptist, John 1:19–28). After this 'oscillation' between sources for the infancy narratives, Tatian begins the proper process of actually harmonizing parallel accounts by weaving together parallel versions of the same story. This does not mean that the technique of 'oscillation' between texts is forgotten, in fact it remains essential – especially where an incident only occurs in one gospel narrative. This is the primary way that the text of the fourth gospel is conjoined to the harmonized synoptic accounts to form the continuous narrative.

Rather than work through the entire sequence of gospel pericopae as preserved in Ephrem's *Commentary* it is illustrative to consider the section of text involving Sections XV and XVI. The encounter with the rich man (Matt 19:16–30; Mark 10:17–31; Luke 18:18–30) is the opening story. According to the order of the *Diatessaron* preserved by Ephrem this is followed by two single-tradition stories, the rich man and Lazarus (which may be attracted to the preceding story by thematic similarity) then the parable of the labourers in the vineyard. Next these are followed by a harmonized version of the request of James and John. Much non-Matthean material is then inserted, some harmonized, some single tradition. Interestingly Tatian places the story of the cleansing of the Temple in this sequence which occurs prior to Jesus' entry into Jerusalem as in the synoptic tradition, but also apparently much later in the narrative sequence than its placement in John 2 (although the encounter with Nicodemus will soon follow). Next the harmonized story of the fig tree occurs, with Tatian skipping over the triumphal entry, although Jesus has already been into Jerusalem to cleanse the Temple. The sequence can be tabulated as in Table 2.2.

---

[37] See Petersen, 'Diatessaron', 189.
[38] Here the edition used is that of McCarthy, *Saint Ephrem's Commentary on Tatian's Diatessaron*, since it incorporates folios rediscovered after the initial publication of the text by Leloir, with the division of the text based on that introduced by Leloir (L. Leloir, *Saint Éphrem Commentaire de l'Évangile concordant texte syriaque (manuscrit Chester Beatty 709)* (CBM 8; Dublin, 1963), but revised by McCarthy to accommodate the additional folios.

Table 2.2 Sections XV and XVI of Ephrem's *Commentary*

XV, §§1–11	Rich Man (Matt 19:16–30; Mark 10:17–31; Luke 18:18–30)
XV, §§12–13	Rich Man and Lazarus (Luke 16:19–31)
XV, §§14–17	Labourers in the Vineyard (Matt 20:1–16)
XV, §§18–19	Request of James and John (Matt 20:20–28; Mark 10:35–45)
XV, §§20–21	Zacchaeus (Luke 19:1–9)
XV, §22	Blind Man of Jericho (Mark 10:46–52; Luke 18:35–43)
XV, §23	Cleansing of the Temple (John 2:13–22)
XV, §24	Pharisee and the Publican (Luke 18:10–14)
XVI, §§1–10	Fig Tree (Matt 21:18–22; Mark 11:12–14, 20–26)
XVI, §§11–15	Jesus and Nicodemus (John 3:1–15)
XVI, §16	Unjust Judge (Luke 18:1–18)
XVI, §17	Authority of Jesus (Matt 21:23–27; Mark 11:27–33; Luke 20:1–8)
XVI, §18	Two Sons (Matt 21:28–32)
XVI, §§19–20	Wicked Vinedressers (Matt 21:33–42; Mark 12:1–12; Luke 20:9–19)
XVI, §21	Tax Due to Caesar (Matt 22:15–22; Mark 12:13–17; Luke 20:20–26)
XVI, §22	Resurrection of the Dead (Matt 22:23–33; Mark 12:18–27; Luke 20:27–40)
XVI, §23	Greatest and First Commandment (Matt 22:34–40; Mark 12:28–34)
XVI, §24	Good Samaritan (Luke 10:25–37)
XVI, §25	'If Anyone Thirsts' (John 7:37)
XVI, §§26–27	Discussions with Jews (John 8:39–56)
XVI, §§28–32	Man Born Blind (John 9:1–41)
XVI, §33	False Shepherds (John 10:8)

This table has been excerpted and slightly modified from the larger continuous table of contents presented by McCarthy, *Saint Ephrem's Commentary on Tatian's Diatessaron*, 378–79.

A number of features immediately become apparent. First the Matthean/ Markan sequence tends to form the bulk of the narrative framework for the *Diatessaron*. This may be due to the prominence of Matthew among the early Church Fathers. Although Tatian is not rigid in maintaining this sequence, he exhibits far greater flexibility in his placement of the Lukan and Johannine pericopae. Secondly, if the commentary treats all sections of the text of the *Diatessaron* it appears that Tatian omitted certain portions of the text of the gospels, for instance the parable of the wedding banquet (Matthew 22:1–14// Luke 14:16–24) is not present. Thirdly, while treating John 7–8 in this section, Tatian seems to have had no knowledge of the *Pericopae Adulterae* as part of the Johannine text. Similarly, Ephrem's *Commentary* betrays no knowledge of the longer ending of Mark's gospel, and surprisingly shows little interest in synoptic resurrection traditions, apparently preferring the Johannine version.

The *Diatessaron* was undoubtedly highly influential among Syrian Christians, but also made an impact further afield. In particular it shaped the text of later gospel harmonies composed both in Semitic and European languages. Since no continuous text of Tatian's own work is preserved, his compositional techniques cannot be known with certainty. It is impossible to tell whether he commenced his work afresh, or modified a gospel harmony of the kind that appears to have been known by his mentor Justin. It does appear that the sequence of events preserved in the Matthean and Markan gospels formed the framework for much of the work, and the material from Luke and John was inserted into this work. Tatian alternates his method, either 'oscillating' between sources to insert single-tradition material into the overall narrative, or harmonizing parallel accounts of the same story. It is virtually impossible to recover the exact wording of any of the pericopae in the form Tatian may have written them, especially as one cannot even be certain of the original language. Study of the *Diatessaron*, although often problematic, is richly illustrative of the dynamic and creative way in which some early Christian figures handled the text of the gospels.

Tatian, the *Gospel of Thomas* and the *Diatessaron*

Parallels between Diatessaronic readings and the *Gospel of Thomas* have been noted primarily after the longer form of the text of *Thomas*, written in Coptic, was discovered among the Nag Hammadi writings. One of the first major studies to discuss this relationship identified how certain readings in gospel harmonies that appear to have been influenced by the *Diatessaron* preserved traditions more closely paralleled sayings in the *Thomasine* form, than the parallel form of the saying contained in the canonical tradition.[39] In discussing the relationship between these two texts Quispel notes that the *Gospel of Thomas* probably should not be classified as Gnostic, but rather be seen as having links with Encratic forms of Christianity.[40] This observation allows for contextual links between Tatian (who is described as the founder of the Encratite movement by Eusebius) and the community behind the *Gospel of Thomas*. This then facilitates the desire to look for textual links between Tatian's *Diatessaron* and the *Gospel of Thomas*. Quispel makes no claims of direct literary dependence. Instead he notes a number of similarities that are present in various shared traditions. Since he sees the two texts inhabiting the same linguistic and textual world, he notes that they may be drawing on common Jewish-Christian gospel traditions.[41]

In contrast to this cautious and tentative set of observations, Nicholas Perrin has advanced a more definitive thesis which advocates a case for direct literary dependence between the two texts. If one were to make an argument for literary dependence it may be expected that the most natural case would be that of seeing the *Diatessaron* as drawing upon the *Gospel of Thomas* regardless of whether one supported a first-century dating for *Thomas* or alternatively

[39] G. Quispel, *Tatian and the Gospel of Thomas: Studies in the History of the Western Diatessaron* (Leiden: Brill, 1975).

[40] Quispel, *Tatian and the Gospel of Thomas*, 84.

[41] Quispel, *Tatian and the Gospel of Thomas*, 106.

composition in the second century, but prior to the middle of that century.[42] However, in a bold and provocative thesis, Perrin argues that the *Diatessaron* is in fact the source upon which the *Gospel of Thomas* draws. He states,

> It appears that the author of GT relied on a text whose sequence of pericopes, though sometimes following the biblical order, more closely followed the order of the *Diatessaron*. The affinities between Thomas's theology and Tatian's encratistic beliefs are significant, as are the textual peculiarities shared by their compositions. But it is in the shared sequence of sayings that I find strong confirmation that GT is dependent on the *Diatessaron*. Thomas had written sources, and among these was the *Diatessaron*.[43]

The problem with this thesis does not arise at a general level for, since the dating of the *Gospel of Thomas* is uncertain, it is not theoretically impossible that it might be a later composition than the *Diatessaron*. Rather, it is when the details of the argument are considered that its plausibility breaks down. There are various stages to the overall argument which Perrin himself outlines in the following manner.

Step 1 *Thomas* was first composed in Syriac.
Step 2 As a Syriac text, GT displays literary unity and reflects the work of one author.
Step 3 It is likely that *Thomas* relied on written Syriac sources.
Step 4 Tatian's *Diatessaron* is the only Syriac text of the synoptic tradition that could have been available to *Thomas*.[44]

Undoubtedly the weakest and most heavily criticized aspect of Perrin's work has been the whole endeavour of reconstructing the underlying Syriac text behind *Thomas*, and then using this reconstructed text (based on linking 'catchwords' between sayings) to justify the claim that the text must have been composed in Syriac. Various reviewers have highlighted the circularity in thinking involved in this theory, and the flaw of basing arguments for a Syriac original on features in a text that one has reconstructed. Furthermore, Poirier has highlighted an extremely important problem, namely, that there

---

[42] The tendency to read the *Gospel of Thomas* as a first-century composition perhaps written prior to the synoptic gospels is exemplified by Helmut Koester who states 'the *Gospel of Thomas* pre-dates the canonical Gospels and rules out the possibility of a dependence upon any of these Gospels' (H. Koester, *Ancient Christian Gospels: Their History and Development* [London/Philadelphia: SCM/TPI, 1990], 85–86). By contrast, other scholars see the *Gospel of Thomas* as drawing upon sayings from the canonical gospels and hence probably composed at some stage in the first half of the second century. See for instance R. M. Grant, 'Notes on the Gospel of Thomas', *VC* 13 (1959), 170–80. More recently April DeConick has articulated a more nuanced theory that sees the formation of the *Gospel of Thomas* as an ongoing process generated by successive oral performance producing a rolling and developing corpus of material. See A. D. DeConick, *Recovering the Original Gospel of Thomas: A History of the Gospel and Its Growth* (LNTS 286; London: T&T Clark, 2005); A. D. DeConick, 'The Gospel of Thomas', *ExpTimes* 118 (2007), 469–79.

[43] N. Perrin, *Thomas and Tatian: The Relationship between the Gospel of Thomas and the Diatessaron* (Academia Biblica 5; Atlanta, GA: SBL, 2002), 189.

[44] These steps are outlined in a slightly fuller form in Perrin, *Thomas and Tatian*, 193.

is no extant evidence for any Syriac literary texts prior to the very end of the second century or the beginning of the third century.[45] Therefore, reconstructed *Thomas* or the putative Syriac *Diatessaron* would also be the two earliest literary texts known in that language. While this is not impossible, it does somewhat stretch the bounds of probability. Another major flaw in Perrin's discussion is that it is predicated on the assumption that the *Diatessaron* was indeed written in Syriac. While this may perhaps even be the majority supposition, he fails to note the highly contested nature of this claim. In fact in his later work he simply makes the terse claim that '[w]e have a Syriac *Thomas* with synoptic-like material that bears uncanny resemblances to Tatian's *Diatessaron*, also written in Syriac'.[46] It is this lack of discussion about the original language of the *Diatessaron* which creates a sense of suspicion about a theory which depends on shared Syriac terms. Since neither the *Gospel of Thomas* nor the *Diatessaron* can confidently be determined to have been composed in Syriac (in fact for *Thomas* there is no evidence that it ever existed in a Syriac form) this whole theory is perhaps best considered as a curiosity in the scholarship of early Christianity and consequently the *Gospel of Thomas* cannot be seen as providing any evidence for the reception of the *Diatessaron*.

Tatian the 'Heretic'?

Over the last few decades there has been a growing recognition that Christianity did not emerge as a pristine stream of orthodoxy which was polluted in the post-apostolic period by the deviant teachings of a handful of heretics. While the corrective to this position should have been recognized ever since the work of Walter Bauer in the 1930s, it is now being accepted that 'orthodoxy' is a later construct imposed on early Christianity by that faction which came to prominence in the fourth-century post-Constantinian church.[47] Without passing judgements on the relative merits of the theological claims of the various groups in the early church one can recognize a series of emergent, developing and sometimes contradictory viewpoints. It is amid the creative and formative period of the late second century that Tatian wrote his various literary outputs. One may postulate that if he had experienced the same fate as his martyred teacher Justin, then the 'crown of martyrdom' would have ensured that he was lauded as an orthodox hero.

Instead later church writers for ideological reasons present Tatian's life in two phases. The first phase occurred when he was under the tutelage of the orthodox Justin in Rome, and the later Syrian phase when he was characterized as the

---

[45] Paul-Hubert Poirier, 'Review of Perrin, Nicholas, *Thomas and Tatian: The Relationship between the Gospel of Thomas and Diatessaron*', *Hugoye: Journal of Syriac Studies* 6 (2003) – article accessed 14 June 2008 from: <http://syrcom.cua.edu/Hugoye/Vol6No2/HV6N2PRPoirier.html>.

[46] N. Perrin, *Thomas, the Other Gospel* (London: SPCK, 2007), 95.

[47] See Walter Bauer, *Orthodoxy and Heresy in Earliest Christianity* (Eng. trans., London: SCM, 1972), German orig., 1934.

founder of the Encratite movement and turned away from the 'orthodoxy'. The exact nature of his behaviour or teaching that led to him being so stigmatized may be much debated, and in the absence of strong evidence it is possible to make only partially informed speculations. Eusebius notes a general tendency of the Encratites to 'blaspheme the Apostle Paul, and reject his epistles' (*HE* 4.29.5). Their use of the 'law and the prophets' may lead to the supposition that these Syrian Encratites had views that aligned with groups commonly thought to be representative of Jewish-Christianity. Another possibility, although the criticism is much more muted, concerns the composition of the *Diatessaron*. Again Eusebius notes that Tatian 'ventured to correct some words of the apostles, as though correcting their style' (*HE* 4.29.5). A number of scholars have contended that Tatian intended his *Diatessaron* to replace the individual gospels with their contradictions.[48] This programme could be seen as standing in tension with the orthodox affirmation of a four-fold gospel canon. Another related possibility links to the heightened ascetic demands of Encratite practice. Hurtado states, 'the only charge that might have a basis is that he [Tatian] taught an ultrastrict renunciation of sex, treating sexual relations between marriage partners as no less evil than fornication. This negative attitude towards sex is exhibited in a number of readings in the *Diatessaron*.'[49] The potential problem with this thesis is that at the very time when writers such as Eusebius stigmatize Tatian with the charge of heresy, there is a rise in support of the practice of sexual continence in the early church. It is also possible that one of Tatian's no longer extant works was the cause of disquiet. For instance, once again Eusebius supplies a tantalizingly incomplete detail stating that 'Tatian prepared a book on Problems, in which he undertook to set out what was unclear and hidden in the divine Scriptures' (*HE* 5.13.8). Bauer sees this work as having a more polemical edge, understanding Tatian to outline in it the 'contradictions in the sacred scriptures'.[50]

In truth, based on the sources which have survived, certainty is impossible and only possibilities remain. Tatian's relationship with Encratite Christians seems to be the basis of the later concern about his 'orthodox' pedigree. Yet, recognition of this simply pushes the problem one step further back, since it is no more transparent as to why this movement was considered to be beyond the pale of 'orthodoxy'. During Tatian's own lifetime there was perhaps nothing particularly 'unorthodox' in his beliefs, teachings or practices. It may be that this link with a group that was later rejected by the dominant emergent Christian mainstream led to his 'guilt by association'. However, his link with Justin (whose orthodoxy was guaranteed through

---

[48] T. Baarda, 'ΔΙΑΦΩΝΙΑ–ΣΥΜΦΩΝΙΑ: Factors in the Harmonization of the Gospels, Especially in the *Diatessaron* of Tatian', in W. L. Petersen (ed.), *Gospel Traditions in the Second Century: Origins, Recensions, Text, and Transmission* (Notre Dame, IN, and London: University of Notre Dame Press, 1989), 133–54.

[49] L. W. Hurtado, *Lord Jesus Christ: Devotion to Jesus in Earliest Christianity* (Grand Rapids, MI: Eerdmans, 2003), 583.

[50] Bauer, *Orthodoxy and Heresy in Earliest Christianity*, 157.

martyrdom) made problematic the simple description of Tatian as being 'heretical' throughout his life. Thus a two-stage portrayal of Tatian emerged. Thus his works and beliefs while in Rome under Justin's influence are affirmed, but his later foundational association with Encratite Christianity in Syria is rejected. The attitude towards the *Diatessaron* by fourth-century and later writers is ambiguous, and it may be an overly bold step to claim that composition of this work was directly related to the charge of heresy.

Conclusions

Tatian is one of the most interesting, but also one of the most elusive, figures of early Christianity in the second half of the second century. His attraction to the philosophical schools of Rome and his subsequent attachment to Justin reflect a wealthy foreigner drawn to the imperial capital in the pursuit of learning and understanding. His writings, of which only two survive, demonstrate a creative mind employing rhetorical and literary skills in defence of new-found faith. Like many converts, Tatian's defence of Christianity may function both as a self-justification of an individual's own adherence to a new faith and serve as a general *apologia* for Christianity. The *Diatessaron*, which itself may represent an expansion of earlier gospel harmonies, had a huge impact on certain sections of the church for several generations. Apart from its dominance in Syrian Christianity for several centuries, Diatessaronic readings have been preserved in gospel harmonies both in the East and West at least down to the late Middle Ages. Yet apart from a few fleeting glimpses of some of the key moments in Tatian's career (and a number of these are provided from hostile sources) relatively little is known about him. His apologetic work *Oratio ad Graecos* represents an important trend in second-century Christianity, as an attempt to provide a robust defence of the faith. Tatian's tractate is certainly not the best example of this genre, but neither is it the worst.[51] His unique aspect in this work is to focus on a rebuttal of Greek cultural pursuits and learning, whereas many of his fellow apologists directed their writings to individuals or representatives of Roman imperial policy.

Tatian, apology writer and gospel scholar, is an intriguing figure although perhaps ultimately elusive. His contribution to modern understanding of early Christianity is to make one aware of the fluidity and creativity that existed in that movement during the second half of the second century. Furthermore, he also demonstrates the ongoing mobility of certain Christians, who spread their faith and teachings as they moved in relative freedom throughout the Roman Empire. Tatian was certainly a Christian of his own

---

[51] On the role of the apologists see R. M. Grant, *Greek Apologists of the Second Century* (Philadelphia, PA: Westminster, 1988). The origins of the writing of Christian apologies may be traced to the shadowy figure of Quadratus. See P. Foster, '*The Apology of Quadratus*', in *The Writings of the Apostolic Fathers* (London: T&T Clark, 2007), 52–62.

time, but he was a highly influential figure among his contemporaries and his legacy was felt for several centuries especially in the Syrian church.

Bibliography

T. Baarda, *Essays on the Diatessaron* (CBET 11; Kampen: Kok Pharos, 1994).

W. Bauer, *Orthodoxy and Heresy in Earliest Christianity* (Eng. trans., London: SCM, 1972).

E. J. Hunt, *Christianity in the Second Century: The Case of Tatian* (London: Routledge, 2003).

J. Joosten, 'The Dura Parchment and the Diatessaron', *VC* 57 (2003), 159–75.

C. McCarthy, *Saint Ephrem's Commentary on Tatian's Diatessaron: An English Translation of Chester Beatty Syriac MS 709 with Introduction and Notes* (JSS supp 2; Oxford: Oxford University Press, 1993).

M. Marcovich, *Tatiani Oratio ad Graecos/Theophili Antiocheni ad Autolycum* (PTS 43/44; Berlin: de Gruyter, 1995).

D. C. Parker, D. G. K. Taylor, and M. S. Goodacre, 'The Dura-Europas Gospel Harmony', in D. G. K. Taylor (ed.), *Studies in the Early Text of the Gospels and Acts: The Papers of the First Birmingham Colloquium on the Textual Criticism of the New Testament* (Birmingham: University of Birmingham Press, 1999), 198–228.

N. Perrin, *Thomas and Tatian: The Relationship between the Gospel of Thomas and the Diatessaron* (Academia Biblica 5; Atlanta, GA: SBL, 2002).

N. Perrin, *Thomas, the Other Gospel* (London: SPCK, 2007).

W. L. Petersen, 'Diatessaron', in D. N. Freedman (ed.), *Anchor Bible Dictionary*, vol. II (New York: Doubleday, 1992).

W. L. Petersen, *Tatian's Diatesseron: Its Creation, Dissemination, Significance and History in Scholarship* (VC Supp. XXV; Leiden: Brill, 1994).

D. Plooij, 'A Fragment of Tatian's Diatessaron in Greek', *ExpTimes* 46 (1935), 471–76.

G. Quispel, *Tatian and the Gospel of Thomas: Studies in the History of the Western Diatessaron* (Leiden: Brill, 1975).

R. F. Shedinger, *Tatian and the Jewish Scriptures: A Textual and Philological Analysis of the Old Testament Citations in Tatian's Diatessaron* (CSCO 591; Leuven: Peeters, 2001).

M. Whittaker (ed.), *Tatian Oratio ad Graecos and Fragments* (Oxford: Clarendon Press, 1982).

3

Irenaeus

DENIS MINNS

Introduction

Irenaeus was a (presumably) younger contemporary of Justin, some of whose writings were known to him,[1] and whom he may also have met personally.[2] Yet the picture of Christianity we get from his works is markedly different from what we see in Justin. This may be partly due to differences in the contexts in which they wrote, and in the objectives they were aiming at. But it seems undeniable that mainstream Christianity had undergone a remarkable development between the early 150s, when Justin composed his *Apology*, and the time when Irenaeus was writing *Adversus Haereses*, during the period when Eleutherus was bishop of Rome (*c.* 175–189). This development is all the more remarkable because of Irenaeus' confident insistence that it is a mark of the authentic church that it does not change.[3]

He was a leader of the Christian community at Lyons in the last quarter of the second century. Motivated by a deep pastoral concern, he set himself to refute what he considered to be distortions of the authentic Gospel, and, in the process, he became one of the earliest Christian writers to attempt a synthesis of the major themes of theology. Largely forgotten during much of the subsequent theological tradition, he has come to be seen as a crucial figure in the early history of the development of Christian doctrine, and has much to say that modern readers will find fresh and stimulating.

Life

From the time of his childhood, Irenaeus had known Polycarp, who was martyred at Smyrna in the late 150s.[4] The latest event in his life that we

---

[1] He quotes from Justin's work against Marcion at *Adversus Haereses* (*AH*) 4.6.2.
[2] Cf. M. Slusser, 'How much did Irenaeus learn from Justin?' *Studia Patristica*, edited by F. Young, M. Edwards and P. Parvis (Leuven: Peeters, 2006), vol. XL, 515–20. Slusser proposes (520) that Irenaeus learnt from Justin 'all that he could, and probably all that Justin had to teach him'.
[3] *AH* 1.10.2–3.
[4] Eusebius, *Ecclesiastical History* (*HE*) 5.20.5–8, quoting Irenaeus' letter to Florinus. On the date of Polycarp's death see S. Parvis, 'The Martyrdom of Polycarp', in *The Writings of the Apostolic Fathers*, edited by P. Foster (London: T&T Clark, 2007), 127–32.

know of is the letter he wrote to Victor, bishop of Rome from *c.* 189 to 199, reprimanding him for the way he had dealt with those Christians who celebrated Easter on the day of the Jewish Passover, rather than on the following Sunday, as was customary in Victor's church (and also in Irenaeus').[5] Though Irenaeus wrote in Greek, and presumably came originally from Asia Minor, where he had encountered Polycarp, Eusebius says that at the time of his letter to Victor he was 'leading the brothers in Gaul',[6] and that he succeeded Pothinus in the episcopacy of Lyons.[7] The Letter of the Churches of Vienne and Lyons from which Eusebius quotes describes Pothinus as 'having been entrusted with the service of episcopacy in Lyons'.[8] Irenaeus does not use the title 'bishop' of himself, and it is possible that monarchical episcopacy had not yet been fully established at Lyons. It has been argued that Victor was the first such bishop to be clearly discernible at Rome,[9] and the letter which Irenaeus carried from the church in Gaul to Victor's predecessor, Eleutherus, while acknowledging that Irenaeus is a 'presbyter of the church', remarks rather pointedly that it is as a 'brother and companion' that he is being commended, since status does not confer righteousness on anyone.[10]

The Christians of Gaul took a lively interest in the affairs of their co-religionists in the East, from where many of them probably came, and wrote to them and to others, particularly about the disturbance caused by the emergence of Montanism.[11] Eusebius quotes at length from a letter from the Christians of Vienne and Lyons to their brethren in Asia and Phrygia describing a recent persecution of Christians by the Roman authorities.[12] This letter, one of the most moving monuments of early Christianity, may have been drafted by Irenaeus.[13] From it we are able to gain a strong sense of the intensity of religious conviction of many of these Christians in the face of appalling tortures, and of the love they had for one another, a love not withdrawn even from those of their number who, succumbing to pain or fear, denied their faith. It was precisely the contrast between this compassion for their fallen brethren and the harsh attitude of some later Christians towards the lapsed that led Eusebius to include the letter in his *Ecclesiastical History*.[14]

---

[5] Eusebius, *HE* 5.24.11–18.
[6] Eusebius, *HE* 5.24.11.
[7] Eusebius, *HE* 5.5.8.
[8] Eusebius, *HE* 5.1.29.
[9] P. Lampe, *From Paul to Valentinus: Christians at Rome in the First Two Centuries* (London: Continuum, 2003), 397.
[10] Eusebius, *HE* 5.4.2.
[11] Eusebius, *HE* 5.1.2; 3.4; 4.1.
[12] Eusebius, *HE* 5.1.3–2.7.
[13] So, at least, P. Nautin proposed, *Lettres et écrivains chrétiens des IIe et IIIe siècles* (Paris: Editions du Cerf, 1961), 54–61.
[14] Eusebius, *HE* 5.2.8.

Writings

Eusebius records that Irenaeus wrote various letters 'in opposition to those at Rome who were degrading the sound constitution of the Church', either by factionalism or by false teaching, and quotes a couple of passages from one of them.[15]

Although *Adversus Haereses* survived in Greek until at least the time of Photius in the ninth century,[16] quotations in Hippolytus, Eusebius and other early Christian authors are all that we have of Irenaeus' writings in their original language, apart from two papyri fragments.[17] Fortunately, however, some of Irenaeus' works were translated into Latin and Armenian. *Against Haereses* survives fully in the Latin translation, and partially in the Armenian, while the much smaller *Demonstration of the Apostolic Preaching* survives only in Armenian.

The *Demonstration* was written after *Adversus Haereses*, and although it warns against the danger of heresy,[18] its concern is principally with catechesis in the Christian faith. In style and content it is reminiscent of what we know of Justin.[19] Justin himself had written a work against heresies, with which Irenaeus was acquainted,[20] but as it has not survived it is impossible to say how much it influenced Irenaeus. But if we cannot be sure to whom the credit for it is primarily due, it can certainly be said that Irenaeus' *Adversus Haereses* presents us with a major development in both the style and content of Christian theology.

The title Irenaeus himself gave to this work was *Refutation and Overturning of the Knowledge falsely so called,*[21] and amongst the various groups of heretics he names there are some who call themselves 'Gnostics'.[22] But Irenaeus himself uses this word to encompass most of the other groups he has in his sights: 'those we call falsely named Gnostics'.[23] It was not until the seventeenth century that the term 'Gnosticism' was used to refer to the views held by 'Gnostics', but even though there was early recognition that it was 'merely a generic term . . . and included many sects that differed considerably from each other',[24] it became commonplace to use the term as though it referred to a historical reality – 'some kind of ancient religious entity with a single origin

---

[15] Eusebius, *HE* 5.20.1–8.

[16] Photius, *Bibliotheca*, 120.

[17] P. Oxy. 405, dated to the end of the second century or the beginning of the third, contains part of *AH* 3.9.3, and Papyrus Jena, dated to the second half of the third century or the first half of the fourth, contains parts of *AH* 5.4.1–13.1.

[18] *Demonstration*, 99–100.

[19] Cf. M. Slusser, 'How much did Irenaeus learn from Justin?', 516.

[20] *AH* 4.6.2.

[21] Eusebius, *HE* 5.7.1; cf. *Demonstration*, 99, and *AH* 2.praef.2; 4.praef.1.

[22] *AH* 1.25.6.

[23] *AH* 1.11.1; cf. 2.praef.1; 13.8; 31.1; 35.2.

[24] *Penny Cyclopedia of the Society for the Diffusion of Useful Knowledge*, vol. XI (London, 1838).

and a distinct set of characteristics'.[25] This has led to a good deal of hand-wringing about the propriety or utility of using the term 'Gnosticism' at all, but if one's concern is to understand Irenaeus it is legitimate to take his account of his opponents at face value, without becoming embroiled in the contemporary debate about terminology.[26] Irenaeus was himself well aware of the multiplicity of what he would call heresies, which he described as springing up like mushrooms from the ground.[27] Nevertheless, he thought they all shared a single error that sufficiently corralled them for the purpose of his attack upon them, and that error was the denial that the Creator is the God and Father of all.[28]

Even at its most elastic, the term 'Gnostic' will not stretch so far as to include Marcion in its embrace. Nevertheless, Marcion's denial that the Creator God of the Old Testament was identical with the God whom Jesus called 'Father' enabled Irenaeus to include him in his taxonomy of heresy.[29] It will be convenient for our purposes here first to sketch the features that Irenaeus found offensive in Marcion's doctrine, and then to adumbrate the wider circle of Irenaeus' targets.

Originally from Pontus, in Asia Minor, Marcion was excommunicated from the Christian community in Rome in the 140s. To understand the origin and novelty of the views which caused such offence to that community we need to recall that, before the fourth century, there did not exist anywhere a physical object answering to what we mean when we speak of 'the Bible'. When Christians in the second century spoke of 'Scriptures' ('writings') they usually meant the books of what we call the Old Testament, though even this they did not possess as a physical unity, bound in a single volume. Justin Martyr, for example, took his scriptural arguments sometimes from thematic collections of quotations from the books of the Old Testament, and sometimes from a scroll containing a single book, such as the prophet Isaiah.[30] He was familiar with the words of Jesus and the narrative of his life and death recorded in the 'memoirs' of his disciples,[31] but the meat of his theological argument in both the *Apology* and the *Dialogue with Trypho* is found in the exegesis of passages from the Pentateuch, the Prophets, and the Psalms.[32] The truth of Christian claims was proved, he thought, by the correspondence between what was foretold in those sources and what came to pass in the teaching of Jesus and the history of his life, death, resurrection, and ascension. Irenaeus' *Demonstration of the Apostolic Teaching* follows the same traditional path.

---

[25] K. L. King, *What Is Gnosticism?* (Cambridge, MA: Belknap, 2003), 2.

[26] E. Osborn, *Irenaeus of Lyons* (Cambridge: Cambridge University Press, 2001), xiv.

[27] *AH* 1.29.1.

[28] *AH* 2.31.1.

[29] *AH* 1.27.2.

[30] Cf. O. Skarsaune, 'Justin and His Bible', in *Justin Martyr and His Worlds*, edited by S. Parvis and P. Foster (Philadelphia, PA: Fortress, 2007), 54–61, 64–68.

[31] That is, the Gospels; cf. Justin, *1 Apol.* 66.3.

[32] Cf. Alain le Boulluec, *La notion d'hérésie dans la littérature grecque (II IIIe siècles)* (Paris: Études augustiniennes, 1985), I, 194.

Marcion proposed a complete break with this tradition. He denied that there was any continuity at all between Old Testament prophecy and the life and teaching of Jesus. He maintained, instead, that Jesus had been sent to give us knowledge of a hitherto completely unknown God, who had no connection whatever with the creator whose rages, jealousies, blood-lusts, and huffs featured so prominently in the sacred writings of the Jews, and to free us from enslavement to that God and from the physical world he had created – including our own bodies. This revelation of Jesus had been completely misunderstood by his disciples, who in their transmission of it contaminated it with references to the creator. Only Paul really understood the message of Jesus, so Marcion's radically new religion was able to equip itself with a radically new and compact Bible: a corpus of Pauline letters, expurgated of letters falsely attributed to Paul, and of interpolations in the genuine letters, and a similarly expurgated edition of the Gospel of Luke.

The other heretical systems described by Irenaeus were not so thoroughly dualistic as Marcion's. They often did distinguish between a supreme and transcendent God and a self-important but lowly creator of the world we inhabit, but this 'demiurge' was presented as having come into existence through some mischance in the divine realm which had the transcendent God as its source. In consequence, disgust at, or disdain for, the material creation was often a feature of these systems also. An important difference between Marcion's system and the others described by Irenaeus is that the latter had a much more generous attitude to 'Scriptures': sometimes admitting all the writings utilized by mainstream Christians, though interpreting them in accordance with their own views, but also making use of other works, allegedly written by Old Testament figures or by disciples of Jesus, but not acknowledged in mainstream Christian communities. They also frequently employed myth and allegory in the elaboration of their ideas.

Theology

In his writings Irenaeus develops a number of theological themes. He does not treat these systematically, but weaves them in various ways into the structure of his argument. The investigation of these central themes will yield a deeper insight into his thought and his contribution to the development of Christian doctrine.

The nature of 'heresies'

From Irenaeus' point of view all of the 'heresies' he confronted were newly minted religions, and to a sophisticated observer quite simply ridiculous – the sort of thing that might appeal to such as had 'spat out their brains'.[33] As such, there was no reason why they should have bothered him any more than

---

[33] *AH* 1.praef.2.

any of the other, older options available in the Roman world's over-supplied market place of religions and philosophies. The word 'heresy' originally belonged in that market place. It meant 'choice', and could be used either positively or pejoratively to indicate the school of thought to which one had chosen to belong. What troubled Irenaeus about the systems he attacked was that, although they were newly minted, they claimed to be the authentic form of the religion to which he himself adhered. It was the falsity of this claim that needed to be exposed and overthrown if these teachers were to be prevented from seducing simple and unsuspecting Christians.[34] While this was being done, the word 'heresy' quite rapidly came to acquire the meaning it still retains: the falsification or distortion of the Christian message.

Where did Irenaeus find the authentic Christian message which the heretics had distorted? A simple answer would be to say that he found it in the Scriptures of both the Old and the New Testaments. But that would also be simplistic. For when his opponents were refuted by means of the Scriptures, Irenaeus says, they called the Scriptures themselves into contention, arguing that these are incorrect, or non-authoritative, or that the truth cannot be found in them by those who do not know the tradition, and specifically the unwritten tradition, passed on by word of mouth, to which Paul is alleged to have referred when he wrote: 'we speak wisdom amongst the perfect, but a wisdom not of this age'.[35] For some of Irenaeus' opponents this appeal to an unwritten tradition, handed down as one teacher took over from his predecessor,[36] was a chief stay of their claim that they held the true teaching of Jesus. It provided them both with an alternative source of religious revelation, and a tool for the interpretation of the Scriptures themselves. It gave the veneer of apostolic authority to what they claimed to be the truth, while permitting them to pass off as that truth whatever fantasies they had themselves invented.

The role of 'tradition'

The idea of teaching *handed on* by a *succession* of teachers was commonplace in the philosophical schools of antiquity, and the heretics whom Irenaeus opposed were not the first Christians to make use of it. Paul commends the Corinthians for maintaining the traditions, just as he had handed them down to them.[37] Among these traditions were the institution of the Eucharist, which, Paul says, he 'received from the Lord, and *handed on*' to them,[38] and the teachings about the death and resurrection of Jesus, which, again, he says he *handed on* to them as he had received them.[39] Irenaeus cannot, then, simply dismiss the idea of tradition itself as a heretical invention. But it is clearly

---

[34] *AH* 1.praef.1.
[35] *AH* 3.2.1, citing 1 Corinthians 2:6.
[36] Cf. the *Letter of Ptolemy to Flora*, in Epiphanius, *Panarion*, 33.7.9.
[37] 1 Corinthians 11:2.
[38] 1 Corinthians 11:23.
[39] 1 Corinthians 15:3.

essential to his own case that the concept be rescued from the heretics and made safe. Tradition ought to guarantee access to the teaching of Jesus himself, for as Jesus said to his disciples: 'he who hears you hears me and whoever spurns you spurns me and him who sent me'.[40] Although what Jesus taught to his disciples was eventually *handed on* in the form of the written Gospels,[41] the possession of such documents is neither necessary nor sufficient for access to the authentic tradition. It is not necessary because that tradition can still be handed down by word of mouth – as it must be to those who are illiterate[42] – and it is not sufficient because written documents do not carry their own tools of interpretation with them.[43] Although some of his opponents had mocked 'the tradition from the Apostles, preserved in the church by the successions of the elders',[44] Irenaeus maintains that only by holding to that tradition can one avoid the charge of claiming as the truth what is in fact one's own invention. After the resurrection of Jesus the Apostles were filled with the Holy Spirit and were given perfect knowledge of the truth. They then went out to the ends of the earth to proclaim the good news.[45] The tradition of the Apostles, therefore, has been made known to the whole world. If any of the Apostles had been made privy to any secret tradition it would have been preserved in the churches founded by those Apostles, passed on to and by those who governed those churches after them. As we have said, monarchical episcopacy may have been only beginning to emerge clearly at Rome at the time Irenaeus was writing, and it has been proposed that the list he provides of twelve persons who had held the episcopacy there in succession had been recently constructed, using names 'borrowed from the tradition of the city of Rome'.[46] Having ready to hand such a list for a church Irenaeus believed had been founded by 'two most glorious Apostles' absolved him of the need to supply similar lists for other churches of apostolic foundation, since the apostolic tradition in any such church would necessarily be the same as the tradition preserved in this 'greatest and most ancient and universally known church'.[47]

The 'measuring rod of truth'

The prefaces to the five books of *Adversus Haereses* suggest that Irenaeus' project grew with the writing. The first book sets out the doctrines of the heretics, with only occasional critical comments. Irenaeus believed that this exposure was an important part of his refutation: the foolishness of the

---

[40] *AH* 3.praef, citing Luke 10:16.
[41] *AH* 3.1.1.
[42] *AH* 3.4.2.
[43] *AH* 2.10.1; 27.3; 3.7.1; 4.26.1.
[44] *AH* 3.2.2.
[45] *AH* 3.1.1.
[46] Lampe, *From Paul to Valentinus*, 404–406.
[47] *AH* 3.3.2; cf. L. Abramowski, 'Irenaeus Adv. Haer. III.3.2: Ecclesia Romana and omnis ecclesia and *ibid.*, 3.3. Anacletus of Rome', *JTS* 28 (1977), 101–104.

heretics' inventions could be left to speak for itself.[48] In the second book Irenaeus attempts to engage with these doctrines on their own terms, and prove them false, and he suggests that this completes the 'unmasking and overthrowing' of the heretics' doctrine envisaged by the title he had given the work.[49] But by the end of this book he has decided to add another, which will provide scriptural proofs of the positions he has been defending, and in the preface of this book he suggests that the three together will provide a 'most complete refutation of all the heretics'.[50] The third book expounds detailed proofs, drawn principally from the four Evangelists, St Paul, and the Acts of the Apostles, for there being one Creator God, and one Christ, the Son of that God, who became incarnate as the new Adam to reverse the apostasy of the first Adam. At the end of the third book Irenaeus says he has held over to a fourth a demonstration drawn from the words of Christ himself.[51] In effect, this book is largely concerned with demonstrating the cohesion of Old Testament and New from the parables of Christ. Irenaeus therefore finds that he has to add a fifth book which will deal with the non-parabolic utterances of Jesus, and engage with the use made by the heretics of the letters of Paul.[52]

This plan of the literary construction of the *Adversus Haereses* should not be confused with the actual strategy Irenaeus brought to bear in his engagement with his opponents. The most important element of that strategy is what Irenaeus called the κανὼν τῆς ἀληθείας.[53] This is still usually, and confusingly, translated into English as 'the rule of truth'. What Irenaeus has in mind is a measuring stick, for which 'ruler' is now more common in English than 'rule'. It is called a measuring rod of *truth* not only because it is used to gauge the truth, but also because to do so accurately it must itself be true. The heretics end up 'proclaiming themselves' rather than the truth because they have twisted the measuring rod out of shape.[54]

Confronted with a claim that something being presented was Christian truth one needed only to hold up to it one's 'measuring rod of truth' to determine whether what was being alleged as the truth actually measured up. Just as a 'cento' made up of verses of Homer taken out of their context and strung together to produce a new story will not fool anyone who actually knows Homer, so someone who has received at baptism the 'measuring rod of truth' will be able to recognize as scriptural the names, phrases, and parables usurped by the heretics, but will not accept as true the blasphemous tales they have woven from them.[55] As the reference to baptism suggests, the

---

[48] *AH* 1.9.1; 31.4; 4.praef.2.
[49] *AH* 2.praef.2.
[50] *AH* 2.35.4; 3.praef.
[51] *AH* 3.25.7.
[52] *AH* 4.41.4; 5.praef.
[53] Cf. *AH* 1.22.1; 2.28.1; 3.11.1; 4.35.4.
[54] *AH* 3.2.1, citing 2 Corinthians 4:5.
[55] *AH* 1.9.5.

'measuring rod of truth' is related to a creed, but the relationship is to the content of the creed, rather than a particular credal formula. In the *Demonstration* Irenaeus speaks of a κανών (the Greek word is transliterated in the Armenian) of *faith* rather than of truth,[56] and tells us that this faith is arranged under three headings by which baptism is completed – faith in the Father, the Son, and the Holy Spirit. The first part of the *Demonstration* (chs 3–42) unpacks this content, and the latter part (42–97) demonstrates it from scriptural proof-texts. The force of the demonstration is the same as with Justin Martyr – the fulfilment of things foretold long before by the Spirit of God through the prophets proves that it was God who foretold them and brought them to fulfilment.[57] The proof is even more compelling when what was foretold is something impossible to our own nature, like resurrection from the dead.

Irenaeus had said that just as someone familiar with Homer would be able to recognize as fraudulent a poem put together from gathered lines of Homer so a Christian could recognize misused elements of Christian teaching, and, 'by taking each of them and putting it back in its proper place and by suiting it to the structure of the truth' would be able to strip bare the heretical invention and demonstrate its lack of substance.[58] Recognizing the truth is not, then, just a matter of knowing the proper context of a scriptural snippet, but also of knowing how it fits in to the whole elaborated framework of the Christian faith. But whereas every educated Greek speaker would have been familiar with Homer from school days, Christians, as we have seen, would not have had such easy access to their Scriptures. And the difficulty was even greater with respect to the whole structure or framework of the Christian faith, for this as yet existed only in inchoate form. It was Irenaeus' great achievement to begin giving solid definition to this framework. Irenaeus may not have been aware of the degree to which his own initial grasp of it was intuitive, and, of course, he did not start from scratch. Because, in the process, he drew upon the work of predecessors who differed in their theological outlook and emphasis, there are some mismatches and loose ends in his synthesis. But these are hardly more glaring than the diversities to be discovered in the New Testament itself, and do not merit the censure they have sometimes attracted. Irenaeus deserves his reputation as the first theologian to try to pull Christian teaching together into a cohesive whole.

The plan of salvation

The central stay of Irenaeus' synthesis is the belief that the God revealed in the Old Testament is the Father of Jesus, and that Old Testament and New Testament both reveal that one God unfolding a single plan for the salvation of the creature he fashioned from the earth to come to be in his own image and likeness. Differences between the Old Testament and the New are to be

---

[56] *Demonstration*, 3.
[57] *Demonstration*, 42; cf. Justin, *1 Apol.*, 30; 42; 52.
[58] *AH* 1.9.4.

explained by the fact that this single plan, or economy, as Irenaeus calls it, necessarily has several stages, adapted to the necessarily gradual development of humankind.[59] Irenaeus explains the need for this necessity by applying to God and his creation the Platonic distinction between being and becoming. Whatever *is*, in the strict sense of the word, *is* necessarily and unchangingly. But in this strict sense of the word only God *is*. Strictly speaking, creation *is* not. That is to say, whatever is created cannot have the same manner of being that God has, it does not exist in the way that God exists; rather it *comes into being*; and since *coming into being* is the only mode of existence available to it, the only possibilities for it are either that it passes out of being, and ceases to have any kind of existence at all, or that it continues to *come into being*. In the ordinary course, things that have come into being will eventually pass out of being, but they can continue to come into being for as long as God wills this,[60] and that is the condition God intends for the creature which God places at the centre of his whole creative work – the creature he formed from mud.[61] So long as the earth-creature remains in the creative hands of God it will continue to develop, to come to be more and more in the image and likeness of God, forever drawing nearer to the condition of the uncreated, but never actually attaining it.[62]

Placing the Genesis account of the creation of humankind at the centre of his theology enabled Irenaeus to rebut the claims of both Marcion and the Gnostics about the inherent evil of the material creation. Human beings, in Irenaeus' view, are not minds or spirits temporarily encased in flesh. Because God fashioned humankind from earth it is essentially corporeal. It is in the image of God because the *incarnate* Son of God serves as the pattern according to which Adam and Eve were fashioned.[63] Human beings will only come to be truly in the *likeness* of God when the risen bodies of the just live not simply by the breath God breathed into his earth-creature in the beginning, but by the Holy Spirit itself, so that their bodies, patterned after Christ, are suffused with the Father's glory.[64]

Because of the importance of the body in the divine plan of salvation Irenaeus holds on firmly to a traditional belief, largely derived from the Book of Revelation, that after the second coming of Christ there will be an earthly kingdom – to endure for a thousand years, before Christ surrenders his kingdom to the Father.[65]

Since God is the Creator of everything that comes into being everything has a goodness, orderliness, and beauty which derives directly from the trinitarian nature of the Creator.

---

[59] *AH* 4.11.1–2; 38.1.
[60] *AH* 2.34.2.
[61] *AH* 5.14.2; 29.1.
[62] *AH* 4.11.1–2; 39.2–3.
[63] *AH* 3.22.3.
[64] *AH* 4.20.2; 5.6.1; 12.2.
[65] *AH* 5.32.1–36.3.

For it is necessary that things that have come into being have received the origin of their being (ἀρχὴ γενέσεως) from some great cause; and the origin of all is God, for He Himself was not made by anyone, but everything was made by him ... And as God is verbal (λογικός), therefore He made created things by the Word; and God is Spirit, so that He adorned all things by the Spirit ... Thus, since the Word 'establishes', that is, works bodily and confers existence (ὕπαρξις), while the Spirit arranges and forms the various 'powers', so rightly is the Son called Word and the Spirit the Wisdom of God.[66]

What is true of creation in general is obviously also true of the creation of humankind:

God, by himself, established, created, and adorned all things, and among all things are ourselves and our world ... Angels did not make or fashion us ... For God had no need of such for making what he had, in himself, predetermined to make, as though he did not have his own hands. For there is always present to him Word and Wisdom, the Son and the Spirit, by whom and in whom he made everything freely and of his own accord ... taking from himself the substance of the things he created and the pattern of the things he made and the comeliness of the things he adorned.[67]

Just as one can glimpse the Creator in the order and beauty of the created world, so one must expect to find beauty or 'fittingness' in the economy of salvation: 'Where there is dovetailing', Irenaeus says, 'there also there is harmoniousness, and where there is harmoniousness, there also there is appropriateness, and where there is appropriateness there also there is suitability'.[68]

This notion that what God has created reflects the beauty of God himself also provides Irenaeus with what has been called his 'aesthetic criterion'.[69] One is able to recognize error because it does not cohere with the whole body of the truth. But, as beauty is so much in the eye of the beholder this can be rather a slippery criterion, and Irenaeus' use of it sometimes leads him to make statements that might strike the modern reader as either fatuous or strange. Irenaeus was the first theologian to argue that there should be neither more nor fewer Gospels than those of Matthew, Mark, Luke, and John. But he does so on the ground that this is 'appropriate' – εἰκός – since there are also four regions of the world and four principal winds.[70] And in his working out of the parallelism between the fall and redemption he seems to place Mary's obedience on a level with Christ's.[71] However, the most important application of this aesthetic criterion is the concept of recapitulation, which Irenaeus deploys to give coherence to his whole theological structure.

---

[66] *Demonstration*, 4–5 (trans. Behr).
[67] *AH* 4.20.1.
[68] *AH* 4.20.7.
[69] Osborn, *Irenaeus*, 18–24.
[70] *AH* 3.11.8.
[71] *AH* 5.19.1.

The idea of 'recapitulation'

In its original, rhetorical, setting, recapitulation has the same meaning as it does in modern usage. It means to sum up an argument or a narrative by highlighting the principal points or 'heads', and Irenaeus uses the word in this sense.[72] But he also adapts it in various ways to explain the cohesion of the divine plan of salvation. The divine Word is from all eternity 'head of things in heaven'. In the Incarnation he attains a headship over things on earth, and in his resurrection a headship over things under the earth.[73] As the new 'head' of redeemed humanity Christ recapitulates its first head, Adam. But Christ also recapitulates Adam by retracing and reversing the principal heads of his history. Thus while Adam was formed from untilled soil, Christ was fashioned from the flesh of the Virgin;[74] while Adam sinned by intemperate eating in the garden, Christ overcame temptation when he fasted in a wilderness;[75] while Satan defeated Adam through disobedience by means of a tree, Christ defeated Satan by his obedience unto death on the tree of the cross.[76] One can even make claims about Adam from what one knows about Christ, such as that since Christ died on a tree on a Friday it will have been on a Friday that Adam sinned at the tree of the knowledge of good and evil.[77]

Adam's sin is archetypal because it is a sin of disobedience. Obedience, for Irenaeus, is not simply a matter of doing what one is told. It represents the totality of a creature's proper stance before its Creator.[78] A creature, as we have seen, does not and cannot exist – in the sense that God *is*; it can only *come into being*. But this coming into being is in fact the effect of God's creative act. So, to be obedient to God is to allow God to be the Creator, to allow oneself to be created, as and when the Creator wills. To be disobedient to God is either to want to be one's own creator, or to want to be brought to perfection sooner than the Creator wills. Irenaeus sees the sin of Adam and Eve as typically adolescent. What they wanted was good – indeed it had been promised to them by God. But they wanted to have it before they had grown strong enough to bear it. Hence they were easily led into disobedience by Satan's false promise that they would become gods themselves.[79]

Because Christ is the pattern after which Adam was fashioned the Incarnation was, from the beginning, the central pivot of the divine plan for the creation of the earth-creature in the image and likeness of God. Because of sin this creative purpose has also had to become a saving one. Irenaeus

---

[72] *AH* 4.2.1.
[73] *AH* 3.16.6; 5.18.3; *Demonstration*, 6, 30.
[74] *AH* 3.21.10–22.2.
[75] *AH* 5.21.2.
[76] *AH* 5.19.1.
[77] *AH* 5.23.2.
[78] *AH* 5.23.2.
[79] *Demonstration*, 12–16.

sees the relationship between God and his human creation as a process of growth and education, in which God is patient in the face of humanity's slow progress. Because he is omnipotent, God could have bestowed perfection on humankind at the beginning.[80] But the perfection of humankind is to be in the image and likeness of God and thus to receive the 'glory' or the 'power of the uncreated'.[81] Human beings will never be able to possess this absolutely, for that would be equivalent to a creature becoming uncreated, which is absurd. But, by God's creative grace, it is possible to be led gradually toward that goal, and thus 'to become near neighbour to the uncreated'.[82] In accustoming himself to our capacity to receive him, then, God is like a mother who is *able* to give adult food to her infant, but instead gives it nourishment in a form that it can absorb. Thus, while he who is 'the perfect bread of the Father' could have revealed himself to human beings in his indescribable glory, instead 'he offered himself to us as milk – his coming as a human being – so that nourished, as it were, at the breast of his flesh we might become accustomed to eating and drinking the Word of God, and be able to retain within us the bread of immortality which is the Spirit of the Father'.[83]

Even before the sin of Adam and Eve the Son of God conversed with them in the garden, prefiguring his Incarnation.[84] It is this 'Word' that sounds throughout the Old Testament.[85] All the theophanies recorded there – the burning bush, the oak of Mamre, Mount Sinai, and so on – are in fact epiphanies of the Word, prophecies of the Incarnation, in which the Word accustoms himself to humanity.[86] The ceremonial Law of the Old Testament is a temporary dispensation, adapted to humankind's slavery to sin: the Law drags towards salvation the slave who is reluctant to obey.[87] But with the Incarnation the Creator comes himself in search of his lost sheep, to carry it home on his shoulders,[88] and with the outpouring of the Holy Spirit at Pentecost God's creative and salvific plan draws to its completion.[89] God now deals with his creature as with a son, and it is expected that human beings will realize their filial relationship with him by obeying him freely.[90] For it is by this obedience, this receptiveness to the creative grace of God, that human beings are brought to their goal of being in the image and likeness of God – their bodies rendered incorruptibly alive and made glorious by the indwelling of the Spirit. By the waters of baptism the clay of which we are

---

[80] *AH* 4.38.1.
[81] *AH* 4.38.3.
[82] *AH* 4.38.3.
[83] *AH* 4.38.2.
[84] *Demonstration*, 12.
[85] *AH* 5.15.4; 16.1; 17.2; 22.1.
[86] *Demonstration*, 44–46; *AH* 3.17.1; 20.2; 4.5.2; 7.4; 9.1; 10.1; 12.4.
[87] *AH* 4.13.2.
[88] *AH* 5.15.2.
[89] *AH* 3.17.1–2; cf. 2.22.2.
[90] *AH* 4.13.2.

made coheres, so that we may be shaped by the creative hands of God.[91] In the Eucharist our bodies are nourished by the body and blood of the Lord. Just as the eucharistic elements consist of an earthly and a divine element so in holy communion our earthly bodies begin to shed their corruptibility as they receive the hope of a resurrection into eternity.[92]

Trinitarian and Christological thought

The way in which Irenaeus speaks of the Son and the Spirit being involved in the creation and redemption of humankind makes it plain that he understands both to be divine in the full sense of the term. He does not, however, address the problem that will preoccupy the church in the fourth century about how the persons of the Trinity can be distinct from one another while there is yet one God. While he sometimes suggests an ascending order from Spirit to Son to Father,[93] his understanding of the Trinity is not subordinationist, as Justin's was. The Son and the Spirit are not lower-order divinities but the Father's own hands.[94] The Son is described as that which is visible of the Father, and the Father as that which is invisible of the Son.[95]

In his Christology Irenaeus anticipates the later formulation of the Chalcedonian Definition to the extent that he regards Christ as fully human and fully divine and yet a single reality,[96] but the difficulties with this way of speaking, which will so trouble the church in the fifth century, do not seem to have bothered him.

The re-emergence and reception of the study of Irenaeus

The influence of Irenaeus' outlook has been discerned in the trinitarian theology of some writers of the fourth century,[97] and he was cited by Theodoret of Cyrus in his Christological dialogues – the *Eranistes*.[98] But, although it is in Irenaeus' writings that we first see clearly the emergence of what is called 'early catholicism', further developments in Christian doctrine and practice in the immediately succeeding centuries meant that Irenaeus' writings came to seem too old fashioned, or ill adapted, to serve as useful tools in dealing with the issues then confronting the church, and his name dropped out of theological discussion until Erasmus printed the first edition of the *Adversus Haereses* in 1526. Because Irenaeus' views on the sin of Adam

---

[91] *AH* 3.17.2.
[92] *AH* 4.18.5.
[93] *Demonstration*, 7.
[94] *AH* 3.21.10; 4.praef.4; 20.1; 5.1.3; 6.1; 28.4.
[95] *AH* 4.6.6.
[96] *AH* 3.18.7; 19.2–3.
[97] Cf. K. Anatolios, *Athanasius: The Coherence of His Thought* (London: Routledge, 1998), 4, 23, 25, 205–206; S. Parvis, *Marcellus of Ancyra and the Lost Years of the Arian Controversy 325–345* (Oxford: Oxford University Press, 2006), 2, 31–34, 122.
[98] Theodoret of Cyrus, *Eranistes* (trans. G. H. Ettlinger, Oxford: Clarendon Press, 1975), 1.15–21; 2.3–8; 3.2–4.

and on the economy of salvation are so markedly different from the intellectual heritage bequeathed to the West by Augustine, they were the occasion of some eyebrow-raising amongst the Reformers.[99] From the nineteenth century onwards, however, despite some negative scholarly judgements, Irenaeus' reputation as a major theologian of the early church has grown in both Catholic and Protestant circles. He is crucial to the understanding of the development of doctrine in the early church, but he also has much that is fresh and invigorating to offer to contemporary Christian theology, both in content and in style.

Bibliography

The writings of Irenaeus: editions and translations

Adversus Haereses

The critical edition, with French translation, is provided by:

Irénée de Lyon, *Contre les Hérésies*, édition critique par A. Rousseau, L. Doutreleau (B. Hemmerdinger, C. Mercier), Sources chrétiennes Nos 100 (2 vols), 152, 153, 210, 211, 263, 264, 293, 294 (Paris: Editions du Cerf, 1965–82).

An accurate, modern English translation of *Adversus Haereses* is sorely needed. There are older translations by J. Keble in the *Library of the Fathers* (1872), by A. Roberts and W. H. Rambaut in the *Ante-Nicene Fathers* (Edinburgh, 1868–69, reprint Grand Rapids, MI: Eerdmans, 1979). A translation of book one by D. Unger has appeared in *Ancient Christian Writers* (Mahwah, NJ: Paulist Press, 1992). There is a good translation of some extended extracts in R. M. Grant, *Irenaeus of Lyons* (London: Routledge, 1997).

Demonstration of the Apostolic Preaching

Irénée de Lyon, *Démonstration de la prédication apostolique*, introduction, traduction et notes par A. Rousseau, Sources chrétiennes No. 406 (Paris, 1995), provides a Latin and a French translation of the Armenian, with extensive notes.

The most recent English translation is:

St Irenaeus of Lyons, *On the Apostolic Preaching*, translation and introduction by J. Behr (New York: St Vladimir's Seminary Press, 1997).

Irenaeus' Demonstration of the Apostolic Preaching: A theological commentary and translation, by I. M. MacKenzie (Aldershot: Ashgate, 2002) reprints the translation of J. A. Robinson for SPCK, 1920.

St Irenaeus, *Proof of the Apostolic Preaching*, translated and annotated by J. P. Smith, *Ancient Christian Writers* No. 16 (Westminster, MD: Newman Press, 1952; reprint, Mahwah, NJ: Paulist Press, 1978) remains useful.

Monographs

J. Behr, *Asceticism and Anthropology in Irenaeus and Clement* (Oxford: Oxford University Press, 2000).

---

[99] The Centuriators of Magdeburg, for example objected to Irenaeus' views about Adam's creation in the image and likeness of God (*Ecclesiastica Historia . . . Secunda Centuria* (Basle, 1560), col. 57.

M. A. Donovan, *One Right Reading? A Guide to Irenaeus* (Collegeville, MN: Liturgical Press, 1997).

D. Minns, *Irenaeus* (London: Geoffrey Chapman, 1994).

E. Osborn, *Irenaeus of Lyons* (Cambridge: Cambridge University Press, 2001).

G. Wingren, *Man and the Incarnation: A Study in the Biblical Theology of Irenaeus* (Philadelphia, PA: Muhlenberg Press, 1959).

There is an extensive bibliography on Irenaeus in other languages. The following may provide an introduction:

J. Fantino, *La théologie d'Irénée: Lecture des Écritures en réponse à l'exégèse gnostique. Une approche trinitaire* (Paris: Editions du Cerf, 1994).

R. Noormann, *Irenäus als Paulusinterpret: Zur rezeption und Wirkung der paulinischen und deuteropaulinischen Briefe im Werk des Irenäus von Lyon* (Tübingen: Mohr Siebeck, 1994).

A. Orbe, *Espiritualidad de San Ireneo* (Rome: Editrice Pontificia Università Gregoriana, 1989).

4

Theophilus of Antioch

RICK ROGERS

Introduction

Theophilus, a second-century bishop from Syrian Antioch, was an apologist, a biblical exegete, a historian, an evangelist, a heresiologist, a theologian, and a teacher. In spite of his impressive literary contributions, however, this bishop is one of the most under-appreciated authors in early church history. He is overshadowed by the mystique surrounding the martyrdoms of Ignatius and Justin and the litigious polemics of Athenagoras and Tatian, not to mention the extensive theological endowments of Irenaeus and Tertullian.[1] The likely reason many readers pay less attention to Theophilus than to these other personalities is his lack of a discernible role in the developmental history of an orthodox theology. In fact, one of the foremost students of early church theology and expert on the second-century apologists, Robert M. Grant, has concluded that Theophilus appears to reflect a heretical Jewish-Christian background.[2] Nevertheless, in the last couple of decades, early church historians have shifted their focus from the evolution of the 'one true Christianity' to an appreciation for the 'many different Christianities'.[3] This bishop's story must be considered within that larger narrative of second-century Christian heterodoxy. Before taking an in-depth look at his theology, let us consider what we can actually know about Theophilus and his extant work, *To Autolycus*.

Life and writings

What do we know of Theophilus' life and writings from the ancient church? Only Eusebius (*c.* 260–339) and Jerome (*c.* 347–420) tell us anything regarding

---

[1] R. Rogers, *Theophilus of Antioch: The Life and Thought of a Second-Century Bishop* (Lanham, MD: Lexington Books, 2000) 9(1). While much of the material in this article can be found in an expanded form in my book, some of the ideas and conclusions developed there have been revised here.

[2] R. M. Grant, *Jesus after the Gospels: The Christ of the Second Century* (Louisville, KY: Westminster John Knox Press, 1990) 68–82. We will, of course, return to this issue in some detail in a discussion of Theophilus' theology in 'The theology of *To Autolycus*' below (p. 61).

[3] G. J. Riley, *One Jesus, Many Christs: How Jesus Inspired Not One True Christianity, But Many* (San Francisco, CA: Harper, 1997), is a good example of such a historian.

his career. Let us begin with the later and briefer testimony. According to Jerome (scholar, translator, polemicist, and ascetic), in his *Lives of Illustrious Men*:

> Theophilus, sixth bishop of the church of Antioch, in the reign of the emperor Marcus Antoninus Verus composed a book *Against Marcion*, which is still extant, also three volumes *To Autolycus* and one *Against the Heresy of Hermogenes* and other short and elegant treatises, well fitted for the edification of the church. (*Lives* 25)

Jerome knew Theophilus was the sixth bishop of the church at Antioch and an author of a number of treatises – three of which he mentions by name. While he specifically characterizes some unnamed Theophilian documents as 'short and elegant treatises', he seems to have appreciated the quality of all these documents. The only distinguishing mark about *To Autolycus* is that it was a three-volume work. Far more noteworthy is his claim that all of these books by Theophilus were 'well fitted for the edification of the church'. Out of the 135 early church personalities Jerome discusses in his *Lives*, these are the only documents for which he makes this claim. While one should not read too much into this observation, especially given the higher praise he lavishes on several more famous authors, neither should one underestimate the value he seems to be placing on *To Autolycus*.[4] Here is a collection of texts obviously addressed to a 'pagan' and yet, according to this famous scholar, deemed useful for the instruction and improvement of the church.

Immediately following the above text, Jerome speaks of other works said to belong to Theophilus:

> I have read, under his name, commentaries *On the Gospel* and *On the Proverbs of Solomon*, which do not appear to me to correspond in style and language with the elegance and expressiveness of the above works. (*Lives* 25)

This passage not only reasserts his appreciation for the literary quality of all the earlier works, especially in comparison with a couple of biblical commentaries, but it also conveys concern regarding the authenticity of these poorer works which have come to Jerome 'under [Theophilus'] name'. It is remarkable, given his proclivity for at least a brief theological comment, that Jerome chose to say nothing about the bishop's thought. This would seem to suggest that he found no objectionable content in Theophilus' theology, or in any of the bishop's particular works.

Eusebius, bishop of Caesarea and the first major church historian, is only slightly more informative in his *Ecclesiastical History*. His testimony, confirmed by Jerome, is that Theophilus was the sixth bishop of Antioch 'from the Apostles' (*HE* 4.20.1).[5] Eusebius then turns to Theophilus' writings. He says:

---

[4] Rogers, *Theophilus*, 10(4).

[5] Eusebius outlines two traditions (*HE* 3.22.1; 3.36.2), one list beginning with Peter and a second with Evodius. See G. Downey, *A History of Antioch in Syria from Seleucus to Arab Conquest* (Princeton, NJ: Princeton University Press, 1961) 284ff., for a detailed discussion of this problem.

> Of Theophilus, whom we have mentioned as bishop of the church of the Antiochenes, three elementary treatises are extant, addressed to Autolycus and another with the title, *Against the Heresy of Hermogenes*, in which he has quoted the Apocalypse of John and there are also extant some other books of his on instruction. (*HE* 4.24.1)

Eusebius speaks of Theophilus' 'extant' works, suggesting he is aware of some titles that are no longer available. Of more interest is his use of the ambiguous adjective, 'elementary'. Is Eusebius making a pejorative comment on the Autolycian corpus? According to Grant, Eusebius is indicating that the style of these documents is 'resolutely plain' and perhaps insinuating an unsophisticated theology.[6] Grant is right, in part. While Eusebius' term, 'elementary', could have been his assessment of their relative size when compared to other documents of Theophilus, it is more likely he is commenting on their relative value to the Christian community. Eusebius' additional observations that Theophilus made use of the Apocalypse of John and composed other books 'on instruction' suggests that he is discussing only the content of Theophilus' works and not their size or literary quality. After all, as was pointed out above, the bishop's books to Autolycus are written to a pagan audience and not to those Christians who are better informed in the doctrinal matters of the church. Therefore, their pedagogical value for one such as Eusebius would of course be 'elementary', an important point to which we will return. If this is true, Jerome seems slightly more impressed with the ecclesiastical value of *To Autolycus* than does Eusebius. Nevertheless, contrary to Grant, neither seems to have questioned the bishop's literary style.

Whatever else Theophilus may have written about, the fact that he is a formidable presence who chose to deal with one of the most serious of contemporary issues, namely, heresy, ultimately determined his value for Eusebius. In the historian's words regarding another book:

> It is clear that Theophilus joined with the others in this campaign against [heretics] from a noble treatise, which he made against Marcion, which has been preserved until now with the others that we have mentioned. (*HE* 4.24.1)

A reference to 'the heretics' is mentioned a few sentences earlier in this same paragraph. It is on this crucial issue that Eusebius appears to find Theophilus a soul mate. He colourfully reports:

> The heretics were even then no less defiling the pure seed of apostolic teaching like tares and the shepherds of the churches in every place, as though driving off wild beasts from Christ's sheep, excluded them at one time by rebukes and exhortations to the brethren, at another by their more complete exposure, by unwritten and personal inquiry and conversation and ultimately correcting their opinions by accurate arguments in written treatises. (*HE* 4.24.1)

---

[6] R. M. Grant, *Greek Apologists of the Second Century* (Philadelphia, PA: Westminster Press, 1988) 144.

It is entirely possible that this tradition of Theophilus as heresiologist, along with the approval of Eusebius, preserved the bishop's name from the fate of those whom some scholars have claimed he anticipated, namely, Paul of Samosata (fl. *c.* 260–68) and Marcellus of Ancyra (*c.* 280–374) – both of whom were declared heretics by the later church.[7] Eusebius appears to be claiming Theophilus as a 'shepherd' of the primitive church who, along with others, made a 'campaign' against Marcion, Hermogenes and other such heretics of his day. With this important testimonial, despite an undeveloped 'orthodox' theology, it would seem that Theophilus' reputation as an acceptable bishop was firmly established in the eyes of the Catholic Church.

In addition to Eusebius' and Jerome's contributions, information about Theophilus and his career can be inferred from his own words in his only extant works, the three books of the collection called *To Autolycus*. Sometime between Eusebius and Jerome, these independent works were recognized as a trilogy. The title of Theophilus' trilogy was probably derived from an opening comment in the second book, where he acknowledges the name of his dialogical partner. It seems that Theophilus was having an ongoing conversation with someone he called a 'friend'. Theophilus treats his interlocutor as an inquiring pagan gentleman, eventually addressing him as 'O excellent Autolycus' (2.1, 3.1).[8]

Given the nondescript character of these references to Autolycus and the fact that these documents appear to be treatises, one could make a reasonable case for Autolycus being nothing more than an imagined opponent, that is, a fictional character posing the theological questions Theophilus is prepared to discuss. Such a practice is not unusual in the ancient and classical world.[9] However, on a closer inspection of these writings, one discovers a real relationship unfolding between Theophilus and Autolycus. In their initial conversation, Theophilus accuses Autolycus of having personally 'attacked' and 'ridiculed' him (1.1, 12). Before they began their second conversation, however, Theophilus' mood seems to have changed and he reminds Autolycus, 'we parted from each other with great friendliness when each went to his own house' (2.1). Occasionally the reader of *To Autolycus* will sense Theophilus' affection for his conversational partner, although it is usually tied to a respect for his learning and eagerness to know more, as is apparent in the following passage:

> As far as the other writers whose works you [Autolycus] have read ... you have [an] accurate knowledge ... He who loves learning must really love it ... Meet with us more often, so that by hearing a living voice you may accurately learn what is true. (2.38)

---

[7] On Theophilus anticipating Paul and Marcellus, see R. L. Sample, '*The Messiah as Prophet: The Christology of Paul of Samosata*' (PhD diss., Northwestern University, 1977) 159, 193.

[8] All Theophilian texts are from R. M. Grant, *Theophilus of Antioch: Ad Autolycum* (Oxford: Oxford University Press, 1970).

[9] Cf. *The Epistle to Diognetus* and Justin's *Dialogue with Trypho*.

Later in their third discussion, Theophilus implies that Autolycus is a hard-working historian who is deservedly called 'a lover of learning' (3.15). This language throughout *To Autolycus* of specific encounters, of familiarity with intellectual development and of commitment to personal growth, not to mention the conversational tone of all three books, seems an excessive contrivance if Autolycus were no more than a literary fiction.[10]

The bishop appears to invest considerable energy in this relationship, leading me to conclude that this Autolycus was a real person. In the first two books, Theophilus treats Autolycus as though he were an incredulous schoolboy, attempting to win him over with gentle criticism and generous affirmation. In the third book, Theophilus is less effusive and somewhat more businesslike with Autolycus, much as a mentor would be with his protégé or a former teacher with a maturing peer. This suggests that the third book was written a few years after the first two books, when the relationship between the two men had grown. J. Bentivegna is right that there is a 'warmth' in these books shown toward the reader that is not found in any of the other so-called apologetic works of the second century.[11] Nevertheless, Theophilus clearly signals a wider readership. His carefully composed presentations are more like a series of treatises than epistles and thus he would not have intended them to be merely private affairs. Whether he is real or fictional, clearly Autolycus is the perfect nemesis and foil for our educationally minded bishop – this curious and perhaps sympathetic pagan who does not speak back.[12]

What about Theophilus' dates and personal background? Eusebius' *Chronicle* dates Theophilus' episcopate from 169 to 177 even though the death of Marcus Aurelius (17 March 180) is mentioned in the third book (3.27, 28). Actually, this 180 date is the only contextual one we have for Theophilus' career, although there is no reason to doubt Eusebius' 169 reference. Theophilus may well have died around 188 CE, for Maximinus, his immediate successor, is said to have been made bishop of Antioch in that year.[13] Theophilus' extant books do not inform us about his episcopacy or even that he was a resident of Antioch.[14] In one passage where he is discussing the location of Eden in relation to the Tigris and Euphrates rivers, he makes an off-the-cuff remark that these rivers border on 'our own *klimata*' (2.24), that is, 'regions'. Beyond

---

[10] See D. E. Aune, *The New Testament in Its Literary Environment* (Philadelphia, PA: Westminster Press, 1987) 200–201, for a discussion of this art form.

[11] J. Bentivegna, 'A Christianity without Christ by Theophilus of Antioch', *Studia patristica* 13 (1975) 107.

[12] Liddell and Scott, 1064b–1065a. A possible meaning for the name 'Autolycus' could be 'the silent one' or one who is practising the self-imposed (*auto*) silence of a wolf (*lykos*) on the prowl. See the discussion in Rogers, *Theophilus*, 12–13(25).

[13] Downey, *A History of Antioch*, 300f., tries to resolve the problem of Theophilus' dates.

[14] In the second century, Antioch was a pagan city with a large Jewish population and a very small Christian community. See W. A. Meeks and R. L. Wilkens, *Jews and Christians in Antioch in the First Four Centuries of the Common Era* (Society of Biblical Literature Sources for Biblical Study 13; Missoula, MT: Scholars Press, 1978).

concluding that Theophilus was a Greek-educated Syrian, nothing more is known about his life.[15]

Theophilus' most personal revelation comes in a carefully crafted account of his adult conversion:

> Do not disbelieve, then, but believe. I too did not believe that resurrection would take place, but now that I have considered these matters I believe. At that time I encountered the sacred writings of the holy prophets, who through the spirit of God foretold past events in the way that they happened, present events in the way they are happening and future events in the order in which they will be accomplished. Because I obtained proof from the events, which took place after being predicted, I do not disbelieve but believe, in obedience to God. If you will, you too must obey him and believe him, so that after disbelieving now you will not be persuaded later, punished with eternal tortures. (1.14)

Theophilus' opening imperative is noteworthy on at least two counts. First, his words are not unlike Jesus' words to Thomas in John 20:27 – 'Do not be faithless, but believing' – which the bishop may be echoing. The 'Doubting Thomas' story is unique to the Gospel of John, which is the only New Testament book Theophilus mentions by name (2.22).[16] Thomas is an important figure in the bishop's Syrian church.[17] Therefore, this story may have been familiar and the phrase idiomatic even to a Syrian pagan like Autolycus. Second, these words are a gentle prod introducing Theophilus' reason for his belief in what he earlier called 'the general resurrection of all men' (1.13). Of course, in John, the phrase is much more of a reprimand of Thomas for not believing in the resurrection of Jesus.

After this opening salvo, Theophilus tells his readers that he became a believer because of his encounter with 'the sacred writings of the holy prophets' and his conviction of their valid predictions. The bishop then turns from this personal revelation to his central point, telling Autolycus that he had better pay attention now, for persuasion from disbelief is inevitable and severe. Theophilus' God demands acknowledgement and obeisance, even if these gestures must be exacted 'with eternal tortures'. Theophilus does not seem to be preoccupied with God's vengeance, but he does occasionally raise the spectre.[18] He is, however, a man highly committed to 'the sacred writings of the holy prophets'. As will be discussed below, his theology features the role of these prophets who were the agents of his own transformation from a doubting Theophilus.

---

[15] Cf. J. Quasten, *Patrology. Volume One: The Beginnings of Patristic Literature* (Utrecht and Brussels: Spectrum, 1950) 236, and Grant, *Theophilus*, ix. Both try to develop a more nuanced personality from hazy references in *To Autolycus* (1.14; 2.1, 25, 28; 3.4).

[16] While Theophilus quotes from eight New Testament books and alludes to some sixty-four NT texts, apart from John, he never mentions a New Testament book, canon or collection. See Rogers, *Theophilus*, 13(33), 23–24.

[17] B. Layton, *The Gnostic Scriptures* (Garden City, NY: Doubleday, 1987) 359–65.

[18] Grant, *Theophilus*, 1.3; 2.8, 14, 25, 26, 36, 37, 38; 3.7, 11.

While his conversion account establishes his debt to Jewish scripture, Theophilus begins this very same document identifying himself in no uncertain terms as a Christian, saying:

> You call me a Christian as if I were bearing an evil name, I acknowledge that I am a Christian. I bear this name beloved by God in the hope of being useful to God. It is not the case, as you suppose, that the name of God is offensive. Perhaps you yourself are of no use to God and therefore think about God in this way. (1.1)

Aware of the negative history surrounding the term 'Christian', Theophilus' objection becomes a rather transparent attempt to educate Autolycus about the elements of his name. Theophilus' name actually means 'beloved by God'. Moreover, 'Theophilus' intimates a phonetic similarity between the Greek root 'Christ' (*christos*) and the term 'useful' (*chrestos*), which is for the bishop an important theological issue.

While his definition of a Christian will be explored more fully below, consider once again that Theophilus was not only a bishop but also an author who composed several books judged by no less an authority than Jerome as 'fitting for the edification of the church'. Given that Theophilus' immediate audience does not appear to be the Christian community, it seems reasonable to assume that the theological substance of these documents is 'elementary', following Eusebius' observation. Nevertheless, while Eusebius' comment is not necessarily contradicted by Jerome's, the later scholar seems more appreciative of the theological content of *To Autolycus*. As an expression of the bishop's religious opinion, it is maintained here that *To Autolycus* represents the essentials of his Christian faith. This is an extremely significant point given the premium Theophilus places on the role of the 'holy prophets'.

The rhetoric of *To Autolycus*

Theophilus' theology is related to the genre of his writings and is based on his rhetoric. As stated above, Theophilus' *To Autolycus* is composed of a series of three independent documents. These collective documents have been widely called, apology, biblical exegesis, and chronology. However, these three descriptive terms are better applied to each of the books respectively, as marks of distinction rather than inclusive characterizations of the collection as a whole. In other words, trying to characterize Theophilus' collection with the above typical nomenclature is not very useful. Since, as I have argued in my book, the theology in these documents is only what the bishop assumed was absolutely necessary to convince someone of his need for conversion, *To Autolycus* is an invitation and exhortation to take up a particular kind of religious life. In this sense then, *To Autolycus* is best called 'protreptic literature'.

A. J. Malherbe and S. K. Stowers tell us that the Greek literary genre, *protrepsis*, which was practised by orators in the political arena and used by Aristotle and the Sophists, was designed to recruit students to join a school or to accept a set of teachings as normative for their lives.[19] Helmut Koester defines this genre as 'an invitation to a philosophical way of life, directed to all those who were willing to engage in the search for the true philosophy and make it the rule for their life and conduct'.[20] *Protrepsis* is the proper category for Theophilus' *To Autolycus*. Furthermore, regarding the discourse of *To Autolycus*, scholars are dealing with a religious literature, which could actually be called a 'protreptic theology'. The bishop's theology is a specific kind of rhetoric designed to recruit converts to a moral life consistent with biblical law.

With this discussion of genre as background, let us take a closer look at Theophilus' rhetoric, that is, how he achieves his theological agenda. It is likely that the bishop made use of several of his own sermons, lectures and other pastoral notes in the construction of *To Autolycus*. In so doing, he produced a set of three documents, which I have titled, using Theophilus' own Greek designations, as: *Homilia*, *Syngramma*, and *Hypomnema*.[21] Over the course of these three books one should notice the author's adjustments in terms of audience, purpose, and theology.

In the *Homilia*, Theophilus is writing to a slightly hostile reader, whom he considers a nemesis. This reader is obviously well educated in Greek literature, but possesses, at least in the bishop's mind, little information regarding the Christian faith. The bishop's purpose is, therefore, to introduce his reader to the philosophical foundations of his religion and in the process to defend its veracity. Theophilus tells Autolycus that in his *Homilia* 'I set forth the nature of my religion for you' (2.1). Why was this necessary? Because Autolycus, claims the bishop, 'supposed that our teaching was mere foolishness'. The primary theological subjects explored in his *Homilia* are God's nature and how one might encounter the divine presence through his works. There is in this first book an initial invitation to the reader to change his religious perspective. But the bishop is willing to use some personal intimidation to make the point that such a change is a necessity. The theological discourse of the *Homilia* is designed to capture Autolycus' attention and perhaps nudge him into accepting the challenge of listening to Theophilus' God and his biblical dictates.

In the *Syngramma*, Theophilus has modulated his polemics and appears to be writing to a more receptive reader whose hostility has subsided into scepticism regarding the bishop's religion. The reader, who now seems to possess basic knowledge regarding the foundational issues of this religion, is presumed by Theophilus to be curious about and ready to engage with

---

[19] A. J. Malherbe, *Moral Exhortation: A Greco-Roman Sourcebook* (Philadelphia, PA: Westminster Press, 1986) 122 and S. K. Stowers, *Letter Writing in Greco-Roman Antiquity* (Philadelphia, PA: Westminster Press, 1986) 112–13.

[20] H. Koester, *Introduction to the New Testament. Volume Two: History and Literature of Early Christianity* (Philadelphia, PA: Fortress Press, 1982) 339–40.

[21] Rogers, *Theophilus*, 15–16. These Greek terms are loosely translated, 'Lecture', 'Treatise', and 'Memorandum', respectively.

controversial biblical materials. In the *Syngramma*, while still attempting to convince Autolycus of the value of Christianity, the bishop takes this opportunity to provide an educational critique of Greek religion. With some sarcasm directed at the mythology of the Greek philosophers, poets, and historians, Theophilus offers a long discussion regarding the 'origin of the world', which is essentially a commentary on the early chapters of Genesis. Theophilus seems to think Autolycus, or the audience he represents, was prepared to digest such material and could benefit from it. In fact, the *Syngramma* seems to possess material that would have been highly beneficial even to Theophilus' church. Such an observation may have led Jerome to exceed Eusebius' characterization of these documents. The bishop's purpose is to educate his audience about the more refined nature of his religion and its literature and in so doing he intensely promotes its ethical demands. However, his focus in the *Syngramma* has shifted from God's nature to man's condition and the role of the logos in human salvation. In other words, there is in this second book an open invitation for the reader to continue his education in a theology designed to convince him of the seriousness of the human condition and to inform him about the nature of divine redemption.

Finally, in the *Hypomnema*, Theophilus has intensified his polemic against pagan thought in general, but it is less personal than in the *Homilia* and oriented more toward morality than in the *Syngramma*. The *Hypomnema* contrasts what Theophilus believes to be the inherent deficiency of Autolycus' values over against a Christian ethic. He argues the uselessness, inconsistency and immorality of Greek authors, juxtaposing the merit, consistency and probity of the law, prophets, and gospels. Add to this the evidence of contemporary Christian conduct which is based on these biblical writings and, the bishop claims, a powerful case has been made for the superiority of his scriptures over Autolycus' Greek literature. Theophilus addresses Autolycus as a reader now more highly informed about the Christian religion and of late deeply involved with the bishop himself, a reader who may be ready to consider conversion – but still needs to resolve some peripheral matters. The reader understands the seriousness of the human condition and is prepared for specifics regarding the nature of divine redemption. The bishop's purpose is, therefore, to facilitate the conversion of his audience by clarifying the essence and necessity of biblical morality while attempting to remove any outstanding issues that might derail acceptance of this new way of life. With less attention on the nature of God and the role of the logos, the bishop's theological focus is now centred on the content of *nomos* and its essential place in the conversion process. In other words, there is in this third book an urgent invitation to convert to the Christian way of life, which is based on biblical morality.

Therefore, I believe we can observe an intended rhetorical development within Theophilus' three books, which naturally corresponds to an intellectual and emotional evolution in the reader. Autolycus is the bishop's naive nemesis in the *Homilia*, a thoughtful sceptic in the *Syngramma* and a protégé, or at least an anticipated convert, in the *Hypomnema*. In other words, this incremental development within the books of *To Autolycus* reflects a growth in Theophilus' readership over a period of time, one which demanded his literary shift in purpose and his willingness to add theological information appropriate for a maturing audience.

The theology of *To Autolycus*

In 1993, W. R. Schoedel challenged the claim of R. M. Grant that Theophilus presents modern readers with an example of a Jewish-Christian thinker.[22] Schoedel criticized Grant's argument that Theophilus' 'Christology' is distinctively Jewish Christian. On my reading of Theophilus' *To Autolycus*, Grant's case would have been more compelling if he had argued in terms of Theophilus' soteriology rather than his Christology. However, the notion of 'soteriology' is not a conventional category in the scholarly analysis of early church theologians or second-century apologists. Nevertheless, much of Theophilus' theology is best understood in the context of soteriology.

Before looking at the specific soteriological ideas developed in *To Autolycus*, consider what is missing in the theological work of Theophilus. While he identifies himself as a Christian, he appears to ignore the historical Jesus. In fact, Theophilus is silent regarding the incarnation and the passion, both of which were important in the development of second-century Christian theories of sacrificial atonement. These unacknowledged theological elements are in a sense the key to unlocking the religious character of *To Autolycus*. It is true that in comparable literature of this period there is an apparent disinterest in the historical Jesus, which may be a matter of apologetic convention and scope.[23] Nevertheless, this lack of apologetic interest in Jesus as a human figure does not mean he was ignored as a divine one. Some early Christian authors, given their anxiety regarding hostile audiences, did not draw specific attention to the story of the historical Jesus nor did they explore the Christological foundations of Christian piety. Many of these authors were preoccupied with self-defence and community preservation, as would be expected. However, *To Autolycus* appears to be written in a context secure enough not only to address publicly the deeper resources for and expressions of early Christian piety, but also to take on the additional task of carefully defining the term 'Christian'.

Grant suspects that this bishop chooses to offer a 'Jesus-less Christianity' in order to promote a heretical type of religion. In fact, he appears to believe Theophilus is substituting Adam for Christ in his reading of selected New Testament passages so as to set the stage for his 'revision' of and likely polemic against Pauline Christology. Grant's pointed demonstration of this matter is presented by his paralleling a passage from Theophilus (2.27) with

---

[22] W. R. Schoedel, 'Theophilus of Antioch: Jewish Christian?', *Illinois Classical Studies* 18 (1993) 279–97.

[23] Rogers, *Theophilus*, 156ff.

a similar text from Paul (Rom 5:15–21).[24] In this Romans text, Paul says: 'Many died through one man's trespass', namely, Adam. The text continues, 'The grace of God and the free gift abound for many.' Notice Theophilus' language: 'What man acquired for himself through his neglect and disobedience, God now freely gives him through love and mercy.' The bishop's context in *To Autolycus* makes it clear that he too is talking about Adam. Now in what follows, Grant wants us to observe that Theophilus, in contradistinction with Paul, is contrasting 'Adam in the past with humanity in the present', without any explicit reference to Jesus.[25] First, Paul writes: 'As by *one man's* disobedience many were made sinners, so by *one man's* obedience many will be made righteous to eternal life.' With the phrase, 'one man's obedience', Paul is referring to the passion of Christ. Now what does Theophilus do with this text? He says: 'For as by disobedience *man* [i.e. Adam] gained death for himself, so by obedience to the will of God *whoever will* can obtain eternal life for himself.' How is this possible? Theophilus continues, 'For God gave us a law and holy commandments; *everyone* who does them can be saved and attaining to the resurrection can inherit imperishability.' So, Grant contends that Theophilus 'rephrased Paul', thus, 'intentionally or not, minimized the saving work of Christ'.[26] To solidify the point, Grant makes one further contrast, saying that Theophilus' insistence on 'our message' (2.1) is intended to replace Paul's 'message of the cross' (1 Cor 1:18).[27]

While Grant should be credited with the persistent observation of a 'missing Jesus' feature in Theophilian theology, the bishop's teachings in *To Autolycus* do not supply enough data to suggest, let alone reconstruct, his Christology *per se*. Thus, with Schoedel, I must agree that Grant's project of discovering Theophilus' Jewish-Christian Christology falls short.

There is, however, considerable language for historians of the evolution of Christology, and even Trinitarian theology, to consider. Theophilus talks at length about the logos (word), though he never explicitly refers to the incarnation of the logos. At one point, Theophilus does quote from John 1:1–3 (2.22), suggesting an understanding of that Gospel's notion of Jesus as the incarnation of the logos. But this reference alone does not constitute a Johannine Christology either.[28] When expounding upon the creation story in Genesis, Theophilus speaks about the agents (the spiritual forces) of creation, logos and sophia (wisdom), as though they were God's two hands (2.18). Earlier in this same scriptural study, the bishop also spoke of a *trias*

---

[24] Grant, *Jesus*, 77–79, and Rogers, *Theophilus*, 161–63.

[25] Grant, *Jesus*, 78.

[26] Grant, *Jesus*, 79.

[27] Grant, *Jesus*, 79. This observation was made over seventy years ago by F. R. M. Hitchcock in his 'Loofs' Theory of Theophilus of Antioch as a Source of Irenaeus', *Journal of Theological Studies* 38 (1937) 265.

[28] While Schoedel, 'Theophilus', 279–97, is right about Grant's putting 'insufficient weight' on Theophilus' citation of John's Gospel, any expectations of a Christology, let alone an orthodox one, are unwarranted.

(threesome) 'of God and his logos and his sophia' (2.15). But as I have shown, Theophilus is not intending or attempting a Trinitarian formula here as he immediately speaks of a *tetras* (foursome) of 'God, logos, sophia [and] man', nor elsewhere, as he regularly speaks of pneuma (spirit) as an agent of God independent of both logos and sophia.[29] Rather, using contemporary Greco-Jewish language and analogy, he speaks of all these spiritual forces to give his biblical exegesis about how God ordained the world *gravitas*.

Having said this, the theological discourse of *To Autolycus* does supply us with an explicit and developed soteriology that is not muted by this 'missing Jesus' feature. While Theophilus may have 'minimized the saving work of Christ' and certainly does not use Trinitarian language, it is important to see that he has clearly emphasized the salvific function of the law to a degree that a saviour figure is not a necessary part of his protreptic theology. Theophilus formulates in *To Autolycus* a theology which promotes the idea that law is an effective means of salvation. Thus, Theophilus sought to promote a religion that is essentially a nomistic Christianity. This adjective 'nomistic' is derived from the Greek word *nomos* (law), a concept emphasized throughout *To Autolycus*, in a way broadly sympathetic with the Epistle of James.[30]

Theophilus intended by this collection of books to provide an attractive invitation to a Christian way of life. The essence of Theophilus' invitation is essentially his doctrine of salvation, or soteriology. How is salvation achieved? The 'why' of salvation is taken for granted by the bishop. He believes man's nature is inclined toward assuming immortal status. In other words, divine immortality is the natural destiny of humanity (2.24, 27).[31] The question of 'how' leads Theophilus and his readers into a complex and engaging discussion of the significance and content of the law, particularly, moral law.

While Theophilus alerts his readers to the biblical meaning of paradise lost and paradise regained, he is far more concerned with the time between what was and what could be, or what he calls 'the fixed period of time' and its limited duration (2.26). The bishop seeks to demonstrate that human transformation from the post-paradise world back to paradise depends on education. Though he does not explain the language of 'recall to paradise' (2.26), he thinks of it as salvation or a matter of hearing and doing *nomos*.[32] Originally, according to Theophilus, the *nomos* of paradise consisted of only a single commandment: 'Of the tree of the knowledge of good and evil you shall not eat' (Gen 2:17). But man failed himself as well as God when he broke that single commandment. Man was then removed from the garden and from

---

[29] See Rogers, *Theophilus*, 73–118, for a full discussion of Theophilus' teachings on the agents of God and 75–77 for specific arguments debunking the bishop's supposed Trinitarian teaching. S. Compton, 'Theophilus of Antioch and the "Two Hands of God"', *Theandros: Online Journal of Orthodox Christian Theology and Philosophy* 4.2 (2006), offers a counter argument.

[30] James 1:25; 2:8, 12. However, for the author of *To Autolycus*, there is no necessity for faith in the unique divine intervention of 'Jesus Christ, the Lord of glory' (James 2:1).

[31] See Rogers, *Theophilus*, 60–1, on Theophilus' use of *Theopoiesis*.

[32] Cf. the Jewish mystical teaching on *Tikkun Olam*.

access to the tree of life, which had prolonged his mortal body. However, outside of the security of paradise, man was given an opportunity to acquire an education in a curriculum the bishop called the 'ten chapters of the great and marvellous law', or simply the *deka kephalaia* (3.9). Then God, as Theophilus outlines this scheme, expanded his law to include the moral teachings of Solomon, the Prophets, the Gospels, and the Pauline epistles, dividing *nomos* into four categories, commandments dealing with repentance, justice, chastity and good will (3.11–14).[33] For Theophilus, this fourfold law became the full curriculum of salvation.

God's logos is linked to *nomos* in the bishop's thought.[34] Theophilus introduced divine agency in order to explain the transcendent God's activity in the world without blurring his vision of monotheism. While the agency of the logos is understood by Theophilus as God's way of working in the creation, he also makes clear that the logos is God's instrument of prophetic witness to salvific *nomos*. For Theophilus, the divine logos informed individuals and communities of the content and meaning of salvific *nomos*. Therefore, after the fall, the logos is the spiritual force behind the publication of an expanded positive law designed to give humanity an opportunity for repentance.

This activity of the logos was especially prolific in the nomistic teachings of Moses and Solomon, the Prophets, and the Sermon on the Mount (2.10, 3.13–14). But the bishop believes such activity is also present in some of the Pauline letters and even in the 'living voice' of the contemporary church, as that particular voice expounds the significance of *nomos* for a righteous life (2.38). Apparently, when it comes to *nomos* there is a chain of prophet-like teachers who are all informed by the logos of God, perhaps even Theophilus himself as he formulates an appropriate invitation to Autolycus.

With this outline of the specifics of his theology, consider once again how Theophilus identifies himself. In the beginning of the *Homilia*, he says to Autolycus: 'I acknowledge that I am a Christian . . . in the hope of being useful to God' (1.1). However, at the end of the *Homilia*, Theophilus defines, with provocative language, exactly what it means to be a Christian. He says, 'what is anointed is sweet and useful' (1.12). At the beginning of the *Homilia*, Theophilus hints at a connection between the meaning of the term Christian and the *sui generis* activity of usefulness, although he does not here explain in so many words how he intends to be 'useful'. But at the conclusion of that same book he has much more to say about the matter. Here the bishop tells his readers that the thing which is anointed – as a boat is 'caulked', a house is 'whitewashed', a baby is 'oiled', an ornament is 'polished' – is thus made useful. After these several analogies he makes an evangelical-like invitation: 'Do you [Autolycus] not want to be anointed with the oil of God?' And then the bishop concludes: 'We are actually called Christians just because we

---

[33] Cf. the fourfold division of Stoic virtues of prudence, temperance, courage, and justice, which is represented in Hellenistic Judaism, in 4 Maccabees 2:2–4 and Wisdom 7:7.

[34] Rogers, *Theophilus*, 143–44.

are anointed with the oil of God.' In this final chapter of his initial discussion with Autolycus, Theophilus is concerned that his reader should understand the precise meaning and significance of the honourable title, 'Christian'.

Listening to his several analogies, the reader is being taught the proper definition of the title Christian. Notice that the bishop is of the opinion that it is not the personal noun, 'Christ', but the verb 'to be anointed' which provides the primary derivative meaning of the term Christian. Thus, Theophilus seems to be inviting Autolycus not to follow a particular person who is a 'Christ' (an anointed one), but simply to 'be anointed with the oil of God' himself. Given the candid and assertive nature of the bishop's explanation and the lack of any hint of the historical Jesus, as the Christ, in these three books, I think it is unlikely that Theophilus' readers would have misunderstood this teaching. Theophilus does not equivocate on what he thinks it means to be a Christian. To be a Christian is to be anointed, to be anointed is to be useful, to be useful is to do good works. Perhaps revising Paul (Rom 2:6), the bishop tells his audience, 'To those who with endurance seek imperishability through good works, [God] will give eternal life' (1.14).

It is reasonable to think on the basis of the teachings of *To Autolycus* that Theophilus, in his other non-extant books or in his teaching to his community, would have portrayed Jesus as a prophet similar to Moses, Solomon, Isaiah, Jeremiah, and perhaps even Paul. Just as the pre-fallen Adam could have been conceived as a 'Christ' figure, a person anointed as useful in promoting the keeping of God's law, so Moses, Solomon, the biblical prophets, Jesus, Paul, and the bishop himself are, in this qualified sense, Christ figures too. They are men whom God has anointed for a largely promotional or prophetic task within his creation.

If one believes the bishop had more to say about Jesus in this regard, as I suspect he did, then it is possible to conclude that Theophilus' profile of this first-century figure was not so much concealed from an immature audience, or reserved for a mature audience, as it was situated in an appropriate ecclesiastical theology or context. Theophilus sought his readers' conversion by presenting them with a protreptic theology in *To Autolycus*. He wanted Autolycus to join his community. So the bishop was careful not to exceed his theoretical needs in formulating an attractive invitation to the Christian faith. He would not have wanted to complicate his presentation or do anything that might have distracted his readers. So, what theological material could he dispense with as unessential for his invitation? On the one hand, he certainly could not leave out any information necessary to effect Autolycus' salvation. On the other hand, he could postpone discussions about the notion of Christ figures whose works were exemplary for human salvation. Once again, without minimizing the work of Jesus, the bishop must emphasize the moral teachings of Moses, Solomon, and the Prophets, along with the teachings of what he understood to be the 'gospel voice', as he calls it. It is the word of the law in those teachings that the protreptic theology of *To Autolycus* must promote. As it stands, I think it is fair to say that Theophilus' books present his readers with a protreptic theology that invites them to become Christians by being anointed into a life of law-abiding service to God.

Conclusions

Where does Theophilus' theology fit in early Christian thought? Considering the orientation toward law in the Epistle of James and the concern with morality based on biblical law in the works of Irenaeus, one might conclude that Theophilus' thought falls within a similar trajectory.[35] Nevertheless, without depreciating this plausible connection, I have argued in my own book that the sanctifying value James places on 'good works' is different from the soteriological value of *nomos* in Theophilus' *To Autolycus*. And furthermore, Irenaeus, who complements James's emphasis on the logos as the Christ and the salvific word of *nomos*, exceeds Theophilus' teaching in *To Autolycus*, where the logos is presented as the provider of salvific *nomos*. In fact, while James and Irenaeus, as well as Paul, Ignatius, Justin, Tatian, and Athenagoras, all important figures in Catholic tradition, can be said to esteem *nomos*, it is the logos in the person of Jesus the Christ who is, in the final analysis, salvific for them.

In *To Autolycus*, however, Theophilus portrays the logos as a literary personification of God, who provides salvific *nomos*. This shift in these books from salvific logos to salvific *nomos* was not acknowledged by Eusebius or Jerome and, therefore, the modern reader should not be too hasty to dislodge the bishop from his traditional place in the stream of Catholic tradition or to dismiss his possible interest in some form of sacrificial atonement. Moreover, while Theophilus appears to be an anomaly within that stream, I believe that this perceived difference is primarily owing to his protreptic agenda in *To Autolycus*.

Nonetheless, it seems reasonable to suggest that this bishop emphasized a monotheistic religion that was, especially in respect to the soteriological value of *nomos*, closer to Hellenistic Judaism than was any New Testament author or other Church Father. Of course, this is not to allege as does Grant that Theophilus was a 'radical' Judaizer, who upheld the 'liberal' Judaism of the Diaspora. While human righteousness and salvation are inseparably bound in the teachings of *To Autolycus*, I think it might be better to say that Theophilus was a heterodox theologian, who upheld the conservative Christianity of Antioch.

---

[35] Rogers, *Theophilus*, 173–86.

Select bibliography

Bardy, G., *Théophile d'Antioche: Trois livres à Autolycus* (Paris: Du Cerf, 1948).

Bentivegna, J., 'A Christianity without Christ by Theophilus of Antioch', *Studia patristica* 13 (1975) 107–30.

Bergamelli, F., 'Il languaggio simbolico delle immagini nella catechesi missionari di Teofilo di Antiochia', *Salesianum* 41 (1979) 273–97.

Compton, S., 'Theophilus of Antioch and the "Two Hands of God"', *Theandros: Online Journal of Orthodox Christian Theology and Philosophy* 4.2 (2006).

Dods, M., 'Theophilus of Antioch to Autolycus', *The Ante-Nicene Fathers* 2 (Grand Rapids, MI: Eerdmans, 1953).

Grant, R. M., *Greek Apologists of the Second Century* (Philadelphia, PA: Westminster Press, 1988).

Grant, R. M., *Jesus After the Gospels: The Christ of the Second Century* (Louisville, KY: Westminster John Knox Press, 1990).

Grant, R. M., *Theophilus of Antioch: Ad Autolycum* (Oxford: Oxford University Press, 1970).

Hitchcock, F. R. M., 'Loofs' Theory of Theophilus of Antioch as a Source of Irenaeus', *Journal of Theological Studies* 38 (1937) 130–39.

McVey, K. E., 'The Use of Stoic Cosmogeny in Theophilus of Antioch's Hexaemeron', *Biblical Hermeneutics in Historical Perspective: Studies in Honor of Karlfried Froehlich on his Sixtieth Birthday*, edited by M. S. Burrows and P. Rorem (Grand Rapids, MI: Eerdmans, 1991).

Martin, J. P., 'La antropología de Filón y la de Teófilo de Antioquia: sus lecturas de Genesis 2–5', *Salmaticensis* 36 (1989) 23–71.

Martin, J. P., 'Filon Hebreo y Teofilo Cristiano: la continuidad de una teologia natural', *Salmaticensis* 37 (1990) 302–17.

Rogers, R., *Theophilus of Antioch: The Life and Thought of a Second-Century Bishop* (Lanham, MD: Lexington Books, 2000).

Schoedel, W. R., 'Theophilus of Antioch: Jewish Christian?', *Illinois Classical Studies* 18 (1993) 279–97.

Zeegers-VanderVorst, N., 'Les Citations du Nouveau Testament dans les livres à Autolycus de Théophile d'Antioche', *Texte und Untersuchungen zur Geschichte der altchristlichen Literatur* 115 (1975) 371–82.

5

Clement of Alexandria

JUDITH L. KOVACS

Introduction

An exuberant and dynamic thinker, Titus Flavius Clemens of Alexandria (c. 150–c. 215) was a biblical exegete, Platonic philosopher, polymath and apologist for Christianity. Clement cites widely from the Bible and Greek poetry, drama and philosophical writings.[1] He calls Plato 'lover of the truth' and Euripides 'the philosopher of the stage' (*Misc.* 5.11.70.2). Classicists value Clement for preserving fragments of works otherwise lost, including writings of pre-Socratic philosophers and ancient plays. As the first to attempt a thoroughgoing synthesis of the Bible and Greek philosophy, Clement began a long tradition of Christian philosophical reflection.

He was one of the leading Christian thinkers and writers of his time. He lived and taught in the North African city of Alexandria – perhaps intellectually the most lively and stimulating city in the Roman Empire. A number of Clement's works survive and they reveal a wide-ranging mind that is able to synthesize perspectives from the Bible, Greek philosophers, the writings of the tragedians, and post-biblical Christian authors. Clement's thought has influenced Christian thinkers down through the centuries, such as John Wesley, and for modern theologians his methods represent the beginning of a long tradition of Christian philosophical reflection.

Clement's life and context

Little is known of Clement's life or his role in the church. The only glimpse he provides of his own biography is found at the beginning of his most important work, the *Miscellanies*, where he describes his travels in search of wisdom:

> Now this book of mine is not a piece of writing artfully crafted for display, but it consists of notes stored up for my old age, as a remedy against forgetfulness. It is a mere reflection and shadow of the vigorous and animated teachings and the blessed and truly remarkable men I was privileged to hear. One of these,

---

[1] According to Eric Osborn, *Clement of Alexandria* (Cambridge: CUP, 2005), 4–5, Clement cites scripture 5,121 times and quotes from 348 different classical authors, including Plato 600 times and Homer 240 times.

an Ionian, I met in Greece, others in the larger Greek world – one was from Syria and another from Egypt – still others in the East, where I met one from Assyria and another who was a Hebrew by birth. Last of all I found the most powerful teacher of all, having tracked him down in Egypt where he was hidden away. And there my search ended. He was the true Sicilian bee, who by plucking the flowers of the prophetic and apostolic meadow engendered pure knowledge in the souls of his hearers.   (*Misc.* 1.1.11.1–2)[2]

Because of this passage and the extensive use Clement makes of Greek litera-ture it is often assumed that he was born in Athens to pagan parents and later converted to Christianity, but neither point is certain. Epiphanius, the only ancient witness who mentions Clement's origins, reports that some say he was born in Athens and others in Alexandria (*Heresies* 32.6.1).

The last teacher Clement mentions, the 'Sicilian bee', must be 'our blessed Pantainos' whose exegesis of Psalm 18:6 Clement quotes with approval (*Proph. Sel.* 56.2). Eusebius, the fourth-century church historian, reports in his *Historia Ecclesiastica* (*HE*) that Pantainos was head of the Christian 'school of sacred learning' in Alexandria (5.10.1–4), and that Clement succeeded him as director of this school and counted Origen among his pupils (6.6.1). Many scholars think, however, that an official catechetical school was not instituted in Alexandria until the time of Origen (*c.* 202) and that Pantainos and Clement gave their lessons as private teachers.

It is frequently said that Clement arrived in Alexandria around the year 180 and left there during the persecution of Christians under the emperor Severus in 202, but the only clear evidence we have for the chronology of Clement's life is contained in two letters of Alexander, bishop of Jerusalem, quoted by Eusebius. In the first, written in 211 to the church in Antioch, probably while Alexander was in Cappadocia (central Turkey), he writes: 'I am sending you these lines, my dear brothers, by Clement the blessed presbyter, a man virtuous and approved, of whom you have already heard and will now come to know' (*HE* 6.11.6). The second, written to Origen in 215, presupposes Clement's death. Alexander writes of Pantainos together with 'the holy Clement, who was my master and benefited me, and all others like them. Through these I came to know you, who are the best in all things, and my master and brother' (*HE* 6.14.9). Taken together, these letters suggest that Clement left Alexandria no later than the year 211 and died some time between 211 and 215.

At the time Alexander writes, the word 'presbyter' could mean either priest or bishop. Alexander's use of the title suggests that Clement had an official position in the church. In addition, it has been argued that Clement's use of such a large number of Jewish and Christian writings implies he had access

---

[2] All quotations from Clement's works are my own translations, from the edition of O. Stählin et al., GCS vols 12, 15 and 17. For editions and English translations of Clement's works, and abbreviated titles of them, see the Bibliography. Biblical texts are from the New Revised Standard Version of the Bible, copyright © 1989 by the Division of Christian Education of the National Council of the Churches of Christ in the USA. Used by permission. All rights reserved.

to a Christian library, which in turn suggests that there was in his time an institution of Christian education in Alexandria.[3] If this is correct, the picture Eusebius gives of Clement's role in a 'catechetical school' may not be so far off the mark. Whatever Clement's ecclesiastical status may have been – layman or priest, private teacher or official head of catechetical instruction – his writings are the earliest surviving works whose connection with Alexandrian Christianity is certain. Our picture of the origins of the church in Alexandria before his time is shadowy indeed.

While we know little about Clement's biography, we are better informed about his intellectual context. Alexandria was a large, cosmopolitan city, which was home to many diverse ethnic groups: Egyptians and other native Africans, Greeks, Romans and Jews. The city was prominent in trade and known for its culture and its educational institutions, the museum and library.[4] In addition to his wide knowledge of Greek literature and philosophy, Clement knew the Bible well. He quotes or alludes to most biblical books, as well as early Christian works such as *Barnabas*, the *Didache*, the *Shepherd of Hermas*, *1 Clement*, and works no longer extant such as the *Gospel of the Egyptians*. He gives considerable attention to Old Testament books and also knew post-biblical Jewish works such as the Wisdom of Solomon, the Wisdom of Ben Sira, and the *Antiquities* of Josephus.[5] He learned much from the Jewish allegorical exegete, Philo of Alexandria (*c.* 20 BCE–*c.* 50 CE), whose writings use philosophical categories to interpret the Old Testament.[6]

Among the Greek philosophers, Clement's favourites are Plato and Heraclitus. Like Albinus, Eudorus and other Middle Platonists, he combines Platonic, Aristotelian and Stoic ideas. Opinion is divided about the extent to which Clement's synthesis was dependent on that of earlier Middle Platonists.[7] Among the ideas he shares with the Platonic tradition are the sharp contrast between physical (or sensible) reality (*to aistheton*) and intelligible reality (*to noeton*) and an emphasis on the need for purification from sensible things in order to achieve 'likeness to God' and a life of contemplation. The influence of Stoic ideas is particularly evident in Clement's ethics, for example, in the importance he attaches to healing the passions (i.e. emotions and desires) and his description of the final goal of the moral life as *apatheia*, which means 'imperturbability' or the total eradication of the passions.

---

[3] A. van den Hoek, 'The Catechetical School of Early Christian Alexandria and Its Philonic Heritage', *HTR* 90 (1997), 59–87.

[4] For a recent overview of social, cultural and religious milieux in Alexandria at the time of Clement, see H. Hägg, *Clement of Alexandria and the Beginnings of Christian Apophaticism* (Oxford: OUP, 2006), 15–70.

[5] On the importance of Hellenistic Judaism for Clement's project, see P. Ashwin-Siejkowski, *Clement of Alexandria: A Project of Christian Perfection* (London/New York: T&T Clark International, 2008), 39–78.

[6] A. van den Hoek, *Clement of Alexandria and His Use of Philo in the* Stromateis (Leiden: Brill, 1988).

[7] S. R. C. Lilla, *Clement of Alexandria: A Study in Christian Platonism and Gnosticism* (Oxford: OUP, 1971); D. Wyrwa, *Die christliche Platonaneignung in den Stromateis des Clemens von Alexandrien* (Berlin: De Gruyter, 1983).

Alexandria was home to some of the earliest Christian gnostic teachers.[8] Walter Bauer argued that Christianity first reached Egypt in a gnostic form[9] – a hypothesis that is less popular today than when it was first proposed. In any case we know that in the latter half of the second century Basilides and Valentinus both taught there. Clement quotes brief passages from these teachers, sometimes with approval and sometimes to refute their ideas, and he is the primary source for the little we know about their teachings. That he has a particular interest in the teachings of the followers of Valentinus is further attested by his *Excerpts from Theodotus*, which appears to be a personal notebook in which he copied portions of a number of their writings and added a few of his own comments.

Clement is known as a particularly irenic thinker, who affirms seeds of truth wherever he finds them. Nonetheless, his writings contain many polemical passages. His theology was formulated in critical conversation with several groups: (1) Greeks who cling to the old religion; (2) simple believers who oppose the use of Greek philosophy to interpret Christian teaching; (3) Marcion and Christian gnostics such as Basilides and Valentinus and their followers. Following Justin and other apologists, and anticipating Origen's *Against Celsus*, Clement provides a spirited defence of Christianity addressed to its pagan critics. Disputing the charge that Christians were 'atheists', he argues that the true 'Gnostic' – that is the ecclesiastical Christian who has achieved maturity in his practice and his understanding – is in fact the only truly pious one. He expresses the hope that 'when the philosophers learn what the true Christian is like, they will condemn their own stupidity in rashly and indiscriminately persecuting the name of Christian' (*Misc.* 7.1.1.1).

Clement's translation of the teachings of the Bible into philosophical terms was challenged by simple believers who insisted on 'bare faith' (*Misc.* 1.9.43.1) and claimed that philosophy was from the devil (*Misc.* 1.16.80.5). In their turn, the followers of Valentinus depreciated the faith of the Christian majority – the group with which Clement allies himself – for its lack of *gnosis*, that is, superior knowledge (*Misc.* 2.3.10.2). Clement worked hard to counter this charge, and he also responded to Valentinian views on the god of the Old Testament, the law, the role of fear in the religious life and martyrdom. He disputes the claim that Valentinus and Basilides were the true heirs of the apostles Peter and Paul (*Misc.* 7.17.106.3–107.2). Book 3 of his *Miscellanies* is devoted to refuting the ideas of Marcion and various gnostic teachers about marriage and sex. Here Clement takes issue with both libertines and radical ascetics. The nineteenth-century translators of Clement's works for the *Ante-Nicene Library* regarded this book as too sensational for the average

---

[8] To avoid confusion, I used the word 'gnostics' (with lower-case 'g') to speak of groups such as the followers of Valentinus and 'Gnostic' (with upper-case 'G') to refer to Clement's ideal Christian, who comes from the majority church.

[9] Bauer, *Orthodoxy and Heresy in Earliest Christianity*, tr. by Philadelphia Seminar on Christian Origins, R. A. Kraft and G. Krodel (eds) (Philadelphia, PA: Fortress, 1971; German original, 1934; 1964), 44–60.

reader – apparently because of Clement's description of libertine views on sexuality – so they translated the Greek text into Latin instead of English!

Clement's own position *vis-à-vis* these diverse fronts is complex. Despite his admiration for Greek culture and philosophy, he sharply attacks Graeco-Roman religion, especially the mystery religions, accusing them of error and immorality (see especially his *Exhortation*). Although he identifies with the Christian majority and defends the great church against the criticisms of Valentinian gnostics (see, e.g. *Instr.* 1.6.25–52; *Misc.* 4.13.89–93), he is at times quite critical of simple believers. His stance toward many gnostic teachers is unreservedly critical, but he affirms Valentinian teaching on marriage (*Misc.* 3.1.1), and he has clearly learned much from Valentinian teachers, especially in his exegesis of scripture and his portrayal of the path to perfection.[10] One obvious indication of this indebtedness is his use of the term 'Gnostic' to designate the ideal Christian who has achieved moral and spiritual perfection – a usage that is clearly polemical.

Clement's writings

Clement is known primarily for a trilogy: the *Exhortation* (*Protreptikos*), an invitation to the Christian faith modelled on Greek invitations to the philosophical life and intended for educated pagans; the *Instructor* (*Paidagogos*), a treatise on the Christian way of life addressed to new believers; and the seven books of his *Miscellanies* (*Stromateis*), his most advanced surviving work of theological reflection. This last work, whose Greek title means something like 'Patchwork Quilts', is made up of individual chapters on a wide variety of topics, woven together like different-coloured threads in a tapestry. Among the many subjects it takes up are: that philosophy is a divine gift to the Greeks (*Misc.* 1, chap. 2); that faith is the way to wisdom (2, chap. 2); those who say intercourse and birth are evil blaspheme Christ, who shared in human birth (3, chap. 17); that women should lead a philosophical life, just like men (4, chap. 8); why scripture conceals the truth in figurative language (5, chap. 4); that the true Gnostic who becomes free from the passions is equal to the angels (6, chap. 13); that Christians are not atheists, as pagan critics assert (7, chap. 1).

Clement, like Plato, worried that to commit his most advanced teaching to writing might mean that it would reach people who were not ready for it and consequently would be harmed by it. It is for this reason, he says, that he writes the *Miscellanies* in a deliberately obscure style which both conceals the truth from the unprepared and reveals it obliquely to those who are sufficiently advanced.

---

[10] J. L. Kovacs, 'Echoes of Valentinian Exegesis in Clement of Alexandria and Origen: The Interpretation of 1 Cor 3.1–3', in L. Perrone (ed.), *Origeniana Octava* (Leuven: Peeters, 2004), 317–29; Kovacs, 'Clement of Alexandria and Valentinian Exegesis in the *Excerpts from Theodotus*', *Studia Patristica* 41, F. Young, M. Edwards, P. Parvis (eds) (Leuven: Peeters, 2006), 187–200; Ashwin-Siejkowski, *Clement of Alexandria*, 109–46.

In the most important manuscript of the *Miscellanies*, the eleventh-century codex *Laurentianus V 3*, books 1–7 are followed by an eighth *Miscellany*, which appears to be a collection of notes rather than a book intended for publication, then the *Excerpts from Theodotus*, and a fragmentary work called *Selections from the Prophets* (*Eklogai Prophetikai*). Another writing, a homily on the story of the rich young ruler in Mark 10:17–31 entitled *Who is the Rich Man Who Shall be Saved?* (*Quis Dives Salvetur*), is preserved in a twelfth-century manuscript. Like the *Instructor*, which deals with such matters as proper behaviour in the baths and at dinner parties and instructs Christian women not to wear gold, elaborate hair-dos, or fancy make-up, this sermon reveals that the intended audience of Clement's works included wealthy Christians. Clement argues that Jesus' command to the rich young ruler to sell all his possessions is not to be taken literally but understood as a counsel to detach the soul from unworthy thoughts. His command to 'give to the poor', however, is to be carried out through generous giving of alms.

Eusebius lists several other writings of Clement: *Sketches* (*Hypotyposes*), *On the Pascha*, *On Fasting*, *On Slander*, *To the Newly Baptized* and the *Ecclesiastical Canon* or *Against the Judaizers*, adding that the last-named work was dedicated to Alexander, the bishop whose letters he had quoted earlier (*HE* 6.13.1–14.7). Maximus the Confessor quotes a few sentences from Clement's *On Providence*. These works are either entirely lost or extant only in small fragments. According to Eusebius, Clement's *Sketches* contained brief explanations of selected texts from all of the Christian scriptures. The surviving fragments include comments on the Psalms, the Catholic letters and 1 John.

Clement's writings reflect the seriousness with which he takes his vocation as a Christian teacher. Interpreting the Gospel in the light of Greek ideas of education (*paideia*), he presents Christ as the consummate teacher who seeks to train all humanity up to perfection. The Christian teacher, Clement writes, is 'the image of the Lord', who shares in the execution of the divine plan for salvation (*Misc.* 7.9.52.1–3). Education, which involves a one-to-one relationship of master and disciple, is moral and spiritual as well as intellectual. It aims to reform the attitudes and habits of the disciple and bring him to intellectual understanding of what was first accepted by faith.[11] The sequence of Clement's three main works – the *Exhortation*, the *Instructor* and the *Miscellanies* – mirrors what Clement says about the pedagogy of the Logos, the divine plan of progressive education:

> Just as those who have a bodily illness need a doctor, in the same way those who are ill in their soul need an instructor (*paidagogos*) so that he might heal our passions, and then lead us to the house of a teacher (*didaskalos*), making the soul pure, ready for knowledge, and able to receive the revelation of the Word

---

[11] J. L. Kovacs, 'Divine Pedagogy and the Gnostic Teacher according to Clement of Alexandria', *JECS* 9 (2001), 3–25. For similar ideas of education as 'psychagogy' among Greek philosophers, see P. Rabbow, *Seelenführung: Methodik der Exerzitien in der Antike* (Munich: Kösel, 1954), and P. Hadot, *Philosophy as a Way of Life*, tr. M. Chase, ed. A. I. Davidson (Oxford: Blackwell, 1995).

(*Logos*). The Logos, who is supremely benevolent, being eager to perfect us by the progressive stages of salvation, makes use of an excellent plan, well-suited for effective education: first he exhorts us [to convert], then he trains us, and, finally, he teaches. (*Instr.* 1.1.3.3)

The correspondence between the educational programme outlined here and two of Clement's writings is clear. The *Exhortation*, which calls on the Greeks to abandon their vain idols for the one true Teacher, prepares for the *Instructor*, in which Clement provides elementary moral instruction for new Christians. Less clear is how the *Miscellanies* fits into this scheme. Some argue that it corresponds to the third level of teaching described in the passage just quoted; others suggest that Clement originally intended to write a more systematic work called the *Teacher* (*Didaskalos*) but then altered his plan and wrote the more diffuse and enigmatic *Miscellanies* instead. Still others hold that the summit of Clement's programme of teaching – corresponding to the third stage of Christ's activity as teacher (*didaskalos*) – was written down in a series of exegetical works that included the *Sketches* (*Hypotyposes*), now sadly almost entirely lost.[12]

Clement's theology

Eric Osborn captures well both the spirit of Clement's theological thinking and the difficulty it presents for interpreters who seek to summarize his most significant ideas: 'No one enjoyed theology more than Clement, yet his skilful synthesis of Athens and Jerusalem has furrowed many brows.'[13] The sense of joyful discovery of truth, evident in *Misc.* 1.1.11.1–2 (quoted above), permeates his works. Steeped in ancient learning and culture, Clement discovered Jesus Christ, the divine Logos, as a 'new song'. In his *Exhortation*, he contrasts Christ with the singers of ancient Greece:

See what great power the new song has! It has made men out of stones, men out of wild beasts. Those who were as good as dead, who had no share in the true life, came to life again merely from hearing this song.... And he, the Wisdom from on high, the celestial Word, is also the perfectly-pitched, harmonious, and holy instrument of God. And what does this instrument – the Word of God, the Lord, the New Song – desire? To open the eyes of the blind, to unstop the ears of the deaf, to lead to righteousness those who are limping or going astray, to reveal God to the foolish, to put an end to decay, to conquer death, to reconcile disobedient children to their Father. This instrument of God loves mankind. The Lord pities, instructs, exhorts, admonishes, saves, protects, and – what is more – promises us the kingdom of heaven as a reward for learning, receiving only this as his benefit: that we are saved. (*Exhort.* 1.4.5–6.2)

---

[12] Osborn, *Clement of Alexandria*, 77–78; Kovacs, 'Divine Pedagogy and the Gnostic Teacher', 23–25; P. Nautin, 'La fin des *Stromates* et les *Hypotyposes* de Clément d'Alexandrie', *VC* 30 (1976), 268–302; B. Bucur, 'The Other Clement of Alexandria: cosmic hierarchy and interiorized apocalypticism', *VC* 60 (2006), 252–54.

[13] Osborn, *Clement of Alexandria*, xii.

Clement's *Instructor* ends with an exuberant hymn to Christ, the divine Teacher and Word (Logos), who oversees all things, which reads in part:

> Bridle of untrained colts, Wing of birds that fly on course,
> Steady rudder of ships, Shepherd of the royal flock ...
> All-conquering Word of the supreme Father,
> Lord of wisdom, Ever-joyful support in woe,
> Jesus, Saviour of the mortal race,
> Shepherd, Husbandman, Rudder, Bridle ...
> Fisher of men whom you rescue from the sea of wickedness,
> Drawing them out of the hostile waters,
> With the sweet bait of Life ...
> Eternal Word, Boundless time, Light everlasting,
> Fount of mercy, Fashioner of goodness,
> Adored Life of those who praise God, Jesus Christ!
> Milk from heaven, Expressed from the tender breasts
> Of the Bride[14] who from your wisdom bestows gracious gifts ...
> With simple praises, And well-tuned hymns,
> Let us celebrate Christ the King,
> As holy payment for his life-giving teaching.
>
> (*Instr.* 3.12; Stählin 1.291.17–292.57)

As for the 'furrowed brows' of which Osborn speaks, there are several reasons why interpreters have found Clement's theology difficult to summarize. One is the diffuse and enigmatic character of his *Miscellanies*. Clement says that he is deliberately concealing part of the truth, because he considers it dangerous to entrust the most advanced teachings to a written work (*Misc.* 1.1.14.4). Secondly, the *Miscellanies* is an incomplete work. At the end of book 7 Clement promises a continuation but apparently never accomplished it, nor did he fulfil an earlier promise to discuss advanced topics such as cosmogony after he has initiated his readers into the 'lesser mysteries' (*Misc.* 4.1.1.1–3.3). A more fundamental reason is that Clement is an explorer of uncharted territory, who lays the foundation for a new Christian literature intended for the wider world and is one of the first to address questions that have engaged Christian thinkers through the centuries: what is the relation of faith and reason, of divine revelation and human thinking, of scripture and philosophy? Affirming the 'rule of the Church' (*Misc.* 6.15.124.4–125.3) – that is an early creed that celebrates the acts of salvation described in the Bible – he goes on to ask how the biblical narrative of what God *does* can be translated into metaphysical terms. His theology has the character of a dynamic exploration rather than a well worked-out theological system.

Despite these difficulties, some characteristic ideas are clear. The following sketch of Clement's theology will focus on his answers to the following questions:

---

[14] I.e. 'the church'.

1 What is the purpose of human life?
2 Who is God and how can he be known? The transcendent Father and Christ, the divine Logos.
3 How is the revelation in scripture to be understood?
4 What is God's plan for human salvation? – The pedagogy of the Logos.
5 How are believers to become perfect? From faith to knowledge.

1 What is the purpose of human life?

In book 2 of the *Miscellanies* Clement surveys the answers of Greek philosophers – including Epicureans, Aristotelians, Stoics, pre-Socratics and Platonists – to the question 'What is the purpose of human life, the most perfect good?' (2.21.127.1–22.136.5). The best answer, Clement asserts, was given by Plato, who said that human happiness comes from achieving 'likeness to God, so that as far as possible a man becomes righteous and holy with wisdom' (*Theat.* 176b). For Clement this is a prime example of the concurrence of the best of Greek philosophy with the revelation given in scripture, since according to Genesis 1:26 God creates man 'in his own image and likeness'. Clement suggests that the 'image' and 'likeness' in this text point to two different things: while the 'image' of God is bestowed on human beings at their creation, the term 'likeness' points to what they can become through a long process of purification and perfection, guided by a teacher who forms their actions and habits as well as their understanding. This is what Paul has in mind when he writes: 'be imitators of me, as I am of Christ and Christ is of God' (1 Cor 11:1).

Clement goes on to set these reflections on achieving 'likeness to God' in the context of eschatological promises from the New Testament: 'eternal life' (John 3:16), 'rest' (Heb 4:9) and 'adoption' as God's children (Rom 8:15). He understands all these promises to refer to close communion with the perfect God. Clement speaks of this final end as vision or 'contemplation' and describes it through the biblical language of love.[15] Faith, Clement says, leads to knowledge which finds its end in love, 'giving the loving to the loved' (*Misc.* 7.10.57.4).

2 Who is God and how can he be known? The transcendent Father and Christ, the divine Logos

The knowledge and love of God is the *raison d'être* of human life, the primary source of human happiness. The God of whom Clement speaks is of course the God of the scriptures. He affirms a triune God and insists again and again, in arguments against Marcion and gnostic groups, that the same God is proclaimed in the Old Testament and the New. Despite his emphasis on 'seeing' God, Clement is keenly aware of the gulf that exists between human beings and God. He is an early exponent of apophatic or negative theology, which

---

[15] Osborn, *Clement of Alexandria*, 132–49, 254–68.

emphasizes the inadequacy of all human concepts and images for knowledge of God the Father.[16] This is a central theme of book 5 of the *Miscellanies*, where Clement quotes from Plato, 'For it is a difficult task to discover the Father and Maker of this universe; and having found him, it is impossible to declare him to all' (5.12.78.2; Plato, *Timaeus* 78c). Clement associates this text with the biblical account of Moses' ascent on Mount Sinai, quoting Exodus 20:1: 'Moses entered into the thick darkness where God was.' The phrase 'thick darkness', Clement explains, teaches that God is invisible and incapable of being expressed in words. Paul conveys the same truth when he says that, when he was 'caught up into the third heaven', he heard 'unutterable words' (2 Cor 12:6–7). Thinking about God requires rigorous purification of the mind, an analysis in which the seeker abstracts not only from material, anthropomorphic images, but also from all human concepts in order to come to know 'not what God is, but what he is not' (*Misc.* 5.11.71.3).

Knowing God is not impossible, however, and this is the gracious good news of the 'new song'. Knowledge of God comes through divine grace, through the revelation of Jesus Christ the divine Logos (Word). As the texts from the *Exhortation* and the *Instructor* quoted above illustrate, Clement uses many titles to describe Jesus Christ. He is shepherd, king, creator and saviour, who took on human flesh and died in order to rescue human beings from the power of sin. Above all, however, Clement understands him as the Logos (Word) of John 1:1, the divine revealer and teacher who makes God known and teaches the path to communion with him.

3 How is the revelation in scripture to be understood?

Clement's extensive use of Greek philosophy has led some of his readers to think he is more a Platonist than a Christian, but Clement insists that the primary source of his philosophy is scripture (*Misc.* 7.1.1.4). He knows the Bible well and quotes from it frequently. His quotations and allusions range over most of the books of the Old and New Testaments, most especially from the letters of Paul, the Gospel of John and the wisdom books (Proverbs, Ben Sirach and the Wisdom of Solomon).

Along with fellow Alexandrians Philo and Origen, Clement used allegory to interpret the Old Testament. Although he did not compose commentaries on whole books of scripture, as Origen did, his *Miscellanies* contain many examples of allegorical exegesis, some of which are adapted from Philo's works. In each of the last four books of this work, Clement includes one chapter that he specifically identifies as a model exegesis. Of these, the chapters in books 5 and 6 treat passages from the Old Testament (the high priest's entry into the holy of holies and the decalogue), while those in books 4 and 7 provide early examples of the allegorical or spiritual exegesis of New

---

[16] Hägg, *Clement of Alexandria and the Beginnings of Christian Apophaticism*, 153–268.

Testament texts, one each from the Gospels (the beatitudes) and the letters of Paul (1 Cor 6).[17] His exegetical discussions exemplify features that will become characteristic of patristic exegesis – careful attention to scriptural images and symbols, understanding specific passages in the context of the whole canon and concern for how the study of scripture can foster the spiritual life of the interpreter.

In book 5 of the *Miscellanies* Clement provides a theoretical justification for his view that scripture has a meaning that transcends the literal sense, making two main arguments. The first is a historical one: he surveys passages from Old and New Testaments, Greek poets and philosophers, and Egyptian writings to demonstrate how 'all who have spoken of divine things, barbarians as well as Greeks, have hidden the first principles and conveyed the truth through symbols, allegories and metaphors' (*Misc.* 5.4.21.4). Secondly, Clement's view of scripture and its interpretation is closely related to his apophatic theology, the second main theme of *Miscellanies* 5. The immaterial God cannot be contained within sensible reality, even in the letters of scripture; thus allegorical exegesis is required in order to glimpse the transcendent realities of which the biblical words are symbols.

4 What is God's plan for human salvation? – The pedagogy of the Logos

Salvation comes through revelation from God, most especially in the giving of the scriptures and the incarnation of the divine Logos. The Word who became incarnate was pre-existent before the ages (John 1:1); he is the source of the order of the cosmos and of all wisdom. As the supreme teacher, he has a comprehensive plan for the education and salvation of all humanity; throughout the ages he has deposited seeds of truth in various cultures. The most complete revelation of truth, however, is in the Bible, which speaks of God's perfection and the extravagant love by which God seeks to draw all people to himself (John 6:40).

Clement adapts ancient ideas about education (*paideia*) to describe the pedagogy of the Logos. The divine Word is both Instructor (*paidagogos*) and Teacher (*didaskalos*) who carefully arranges his curriculum, knowing that certain things must be learned before others, just as in secular education the liberal arts (geometry, music, etc.) need to be mastered before the student is ready for rhetoric and philosophy. The word *paidagogos* – used as the title for the second volume of Clement's trilogy – is found in Galatians 3:24, where Paul says, 'The law was our *paidagogos* until Christ came.' For Paul the word means 'disciplinarian' (so NRSV), and it characterizes the law's keeping people under guard until the messiah came. Early Christian theologians, however, understood *paidagogos* in a more positive sense as 'instructor' and took the verse to mean that the Old Testament was a preliminary teaching that prepared

---

[17] *Misc.* 4.6.25–40; 5.6.32–40; 6.17.133–148; 7.14.84–88.

the way for receiving the good news of Jesus Christ. This idea is important for Clement, and to it he adds something new: just as the law was God's preliminary covenant with the Jews, so philosophy was a divine covenant with the Greeks, to prepare them for the more complete revelation in the Gospel: 'Before the coming of the Lord philosophy was necessary for the Greeks, for righteousness, and now it is still useful for the devout life, as preliminary instruction for those who use demonstration to enrich faith' (*Misc.* 1.5.28.1–3). After the incarnation, philosophy 'is still useful'. Clement's works are full of examples of what he means by this, for example, his use of Plato's phrase 'likeness to God' to help express the ultimate goal of the Christian life.

5 How are believers to become perfect? From faith to knowledge

Clement gives much attention to the subject of spiritual progress. He views the Christian life as an exacting but joyful discipline, a pursuit of perfection. Plato wrote, 'like is dear to like' (*Gorgias* 510d, quoted in *Instr.* 1.6.28.2) and Jesus said, 'Be perfect as your heavenly Father is perfect' (Matt 5:48, quoted in *Misc.* 6.12.104.2). Clement takes very seriously biblical references to becoming 'perfect' (or 'mature'),[18] and he urges his readers to a life in which moral discipline, intellectual training and imitation of the works of divine love go hand in hand.

The complex pedagogy of the Logos, evident on a large scale in the arrangement of the universe and the periods of salvation history, is also at work in the life of the individual Christian. The divine Logos has various means of training:

> All people belong to Him – some through knowledge, while others not yet in this way, some as 'friends' (John 15:14–15), others as 'faithful servants' (Heb 3:5), and others as merely 'servants.' The Logos is the teacher who educates the Gnostic by mysteries, the believer by good hopes and the hard of heart by corrective discipline that works through the senses. He is the source of providence, operating for the individual, the community, and the whole universe. (*Misc.* 7.2.5.6–6.1)

Some are taught through 'mysteries', others are led on by hope of heavenly reward, while others – those at the beginning of their spiritual journey – are motivated by fear of punishment. The divine pedagogue uses many methods of care, including persuasive words, threats and punishments (*Misc.* 7.61.1–3). In the Old Testament, for example, he uses punishment and reproof to cure the passions of the soul (*Instr.* 1.8.64.4).

This divine pedagogy leads the individual Christian through two distinct stages, as the simple believer moves to a more complete apprehension and

---

[18] The Greek word *teleios* can have either meaning. Other biblical texts that use this word in reference to human beings are: Matt 19:21; 1 Cor 2:6; 14:10; Eph 4:13; Phil 3:15; Col 1:28; 4:12; Heb 5:14; James 1:4; 3:2.

application of the truth. Clement refers to these stages as 'faith' (*pistis*) and 'knowledge' (*gnosis*):

> Through knowledge 'faith is made perfect' (James 2:22) ... Now faith is an inward good, which, without searching for God, confesses that he exists and glorifies him for existing. Hence beginning with faith and increased in it by the grace of God, we must attain knowledge of God, insofar as this is possible ... Faith we could say is the concise knowledge of those in a hurry, but knowledge is a firm and sure demonstration of the things received through faith, built upon the 'foundation of faith' (1 Cor 3:10) ... And it seems to me that the first saving transformation is the movement from paganism to faith ... and the second one is the movement from faith to knowledge. And when knowledge has terminated in love, at that point it presents what is 'dear' to what is 'dear' (*Gorgias* 510d) – that which knows to what is known.
>
> (*Misc.* 7.10.55.2–3; 57.3–4)

'Faith' refers to accepting the basic teachings of the creed and the literal sense of scripture, while *gnosis* designates a deeper, more integrated theology. Clement defends the church's 'faith' against its critics but insists that the divine Teacher wants Christians to move on to 'knowledge'. He cites 1 Corinthians 3:10–12 to support both of these points (*Misc.* 5.4.26.1–5). The movement from faith to *gnosis* involves mastering the kind of philosophical investigation that accords with piety (*Misc.* 5.1.5.2) and also discovering the deeper meaning of scripture (*Misc.* 5.10.60–61). Clement emphasizes that the student must undergo rigorous moral purification before being entrusted with *gnosis*. Growth in wisdom presupposes control of the passions and progress in righteousness and holiness. While the believer strives to *moderate* the passions, imperturbability (*apatheia*) is the goal of the Gnostic (*Misc.* 6.9.74.1–2).

Clement's use of the word 'Gnostic' to describe the perfected Christian reflects his high evaluation of learning as well as the centrality of the knowledge of God in his theology. It is also polemical: Clement offers his vision of Gnostic perfection as an alternative to the systems of gnostic theologians such as Valentinus and his followers.[19] The 'true Gnostic', he claims, is the 'ecclesiastical' gnostic – the one whose home is in the majority church (*Misc.* 7.16.97.4).

Spiritual progress is not limited to the present life. After death the Gnostic soul ascends through the angelic ranks, becoming ever purer and closer to the godlike perfection commanded in Matthew 5:48. As promised in Matthew 5:8, 'Blessed are the pure in heart, for they shall see God', and 1 Corinthians 13:12, 'Now we see in a mirror dimly but then we will see face to face', the summit of the Christian life is the direct vision of God:

---

[19] Ashwin-Siejkowski, *Clement of Alexandria*, 109–44; Kovacs, 'Echoes of Valentinian Exegesis in Clement of Alexandria and Origen', 328; Kovacs, 'Concealment and Gnostic Exegesis: Clement of Alexandria's Interpretation of the Tabernacle', *Studia Patristica* 31, E. A. Livingstone (ed.) (Leuven: Peeters, 1997), 415–18.

Gnostic souls ... counted as holy among the holy ... continue to ascend to higher and higher spheres until they no longer greet the promised vision of God in or through mirrors (1 Cor 13:12) but feast on a vision [of God] that is never cloying for these intensely loving souls, a vision as clear as can be and utterly pure. Throughout eternity they enjoy perpetual gladness.   (*Misc.* 7.3.13.1)

Clement's legacy[20]

In the first centuries after his death, Clement was held in high esteem by those who took up the task of Christian theological exploration. The letters of Alexander cited above typify his reputation among the Greek Fathers. Eusebius calls him 'a celebrated guardian of the orthodoxy of the Church' (*HE* 3.32.2), and Cyril of Alexandria describes him as 'an eloquent and learned man, who has studied deeply the writings of the Greeks as perhaps few before him did' (*Against Julian* 6–7). Although Clement was less known in the Latin-speaking West, Jerome gives his opinion that Clement was 'the most learned of all. What is there in his books that lacks learning? No, rather, what is there that does not reflect the very heart of philosophy?' (*Epistle* 70.4).

Whatever one thinks about Clement's official role in an Alexandrian cat-echetical school, his writings are the earliest that survive from an Alexandrian 'school' in the more general sense of a particular way of thinking about the Bible and Christian theology. His approach to exegesis and several of his characteristic emphases are carried on and developed further by numerous Greek Fathers, especially by Origen in the third century and Gregory of Nyssa, Gregory of Nazianzus, Evagrius and Didymus the Blind in the fourth. These theologians echo many of the ideas discussed in this article, including the belief that God has an ordered plan for salvation (the divine 'economy'), evident not only in the different periods of salvation history but also in the life of the individual Christian.[21] They also continue Clement's understanding of the Christian life as a pursuit of perfection, with various stages of training and discipline, and his emphasis on the gradual ascent of the soul to the beatific vision.

To a large extent Clement's theological and exegetical legacy has been mediated through Origen, the most gifted theologian among the Greek-speaking Fathers. Origen never mentions Clement but it is very likely that he knew his writings. One of his lost works had the same unusual title as Clement's most important writing, the *Miscellanies*. Origen's exegesis of specific

---

[20] In this sketch of Clement's legacy I draw on the fuller treatments in W. H. Wagner, 'A Father's Fate: Attitudes toward and Interpretations of Clement of Alexandria', *Journal of Religious History* 6 (1971), 209–31, and A. Knauber, 'Die patrologische Schätzung des Clemens von Alexandrien bis zu seinem neuerlichen Bekanntwerden durch den ersten Druckeditionen des Sechzehnten Jahrhunderts', in P. Granfield and J. A. Jungmann (eds), *Kuriakon* (Münster: Aschendorff, 1973), 289–308.

[21] On this point see the articles by J. L. Kovacs, J. W. Trigg and R. D. Young, published together under the general title 'Human Participation in God's Plan: The Legacy of Clement of Alexandria', *JECS* 9 (2001), 1–71.

biblical texts often follows that of Clement,[22] and he takes up many of Clement's ideas and develops them in greater depth. Ironically, this has contributed to the neglect of Clement, for two quite different reasons. On the one hand Origen's sheer brilliance puts Clement's dynamic, ground-breaking explorations in the shade. On the other hand, criticisms of Origen, whose theology was condemned at the Second Council of Constantinople in 553, has caused his Alexandrian forerunner to come under suspicion.

Doubts about Clement's orthodoxy reached a high point with Photius, a scholar of Constantinople in the mid-ninth century. Photius said that Clement's work of biblical interpretation, the *Outlines* (*Hypotyposes*), contained many 'godless and fantastic ideas', including the eternity of matter, a doctrine of transmigration and a heretical view that there were two divine *Logoi* (*Myriobiblion* 109–11). Although we have only a few fragments of Clement's *Outlines* against which to test these assertions, it appears that Photius has misunderstood what Clement wrote. In any case, he judges Clement's theology anachronistically, by the standards of later orthodoxy.

Evidence of the influence of Clement's works during the Middle Ages is scant. Since then Clement has found his champions, especially in Renaissance Florence, where there was a revival of interest in the Greek Fathers, and in England, as well as some critics. Among Clement's English admirers were John Potter, bishop of Oxford and later archbishop of Canterbury, who published an edition of Clement's works in Greek and Latin in 1715, and the early John Wesley.[23] Wesley was initially attracted to Clement's theology, especially his portrait of the perfect Christian and his emphasis on divine love, but in his later years he judged that Clement's theology was insufficiently scriptural. In the early twentieth century an influential scholarly book described Clement as a 'Christian liberal' and claimed him as a forerunner of the modern English: 'in his distrust of extremes, in his love of peace, in his reverent, and sober piety, he anticipates some of the best characteristics of our race'.[24] An echo of English interest in Clement is preserved in the hymnal of the American Episcopal Church, which contains two hymns whose text is based on words of Clement, 'Sunset to sunrise changes now' (Hymn 163) and 'Jesus, our mighty Lord, our strength in sadness, the Father's conquering Word' (Hymn 478), a loose paraphrase of the hymn at the end of Clement's *Instructor* quoted above.[25]

Although not widely acknowledged, Clement's legacy endures. He stands at the beginning of a long tradition of Christian philosophical reflection. He was the first to focus attention on central problems of Christian theology,

---

[22] See, e.g. Kovacs, 'Echoes of Valentinian Exegesis in Clement of Alexandria and Origen', 325–29.

[23] Wagner, 'A Father's Fate', 225–26.

[24] R. B. Tollinton, *Clement of Alexandria: A Study in Christian Liberalism* (London: Williams & Norgate, 1914), 2:283.

[25] *The Hymnal 1982, according to the use of The Episcopal Church* [USA] (New York: Church Publisher, 1982).

such as how to reconcile faith and knowledge and how to use secular learning to elucidate the revelation given in scripture. His exuberant and optimistic spirit stands as encouragement to theologians through the ages, along with a Gospel text that was one of his favourites: 'Seek and you shall find' (Matt 7:7).[26]

Bibliography

Clement's works (with abbreviated titles)

Exhortation	(*Exhort.*)
Instructor	(*Instr.*)
Miscellanies	(*Misc.*)
Who is The Rich Man Who Shall be Saved?	(*Rich Man*)
Excerpts from Theodotus	(*Theodotus*)
Prophetic Selections	(*Proph. Sel.*).

Editions

Stählin, O. (ed.), *Clemens Alexandrinus*, 1. Bd., *Protrepticus und Paedagogus*; 2. Bd., *Stromata*, Buch I–VI; 3. Bd., *Stromata*, Buch VII und VIII; *Excerpta ex Theodoto*; *Eclogae propheticae*; *Quis dives salvetur*; *Fragmente*; 4. Bd., *Register*; GCS, 4 vols. (J. C. Hinrich: Leipzig, 1905–36. Revision by U. Treu: 1, 3 Aufl., 1972; L. Früchtel: 2, 4 Aufl., 1985; 3, 2 Aufl., 1970; 4, 1, 2 Aufl., 1980).

Markovich, M. (ed.), Clementis Alexandrini *Protrepticus* (VC 34; Leiden: Brill, 1995).

Markovich, M. (ed.), Clementis Alexandrini *Pedagogus* (VC 61; Leiden: Brill, 2002).

English translations

Butterworth, G. W., *Clement of Alexandria, Exhortation* (LCL 92; London/Cambridge MA: Harvard University Press, 1919, 1982).

Ferguson, J., *Miscellanies*, books 1–3, FC 85 (Washington: CUA, 1991).

Wilson, W., *Clement of Alexandria* (Ante-Nicene Christian Library, vols. 4 and 12 and parts of vols. 22 and 24; Edinburgh, 1882 and 1884).

Studies

Ashwin-Siejkowski, P., *Clement of Alexandria. A Project of Christian Perfection* (London/New York: T&T Clark International, 2008).

Bucur, B., 'The Other Clement of Alexandria: cosmic hierarchy and interiorized apocalypticism', *VC* 60 (2006), 251–68.

Hägg, H., *Clement of Alexandria and the Beginnings of Christian Apophaticism* (OECS; Oxford: OUP, 2006).

Knauber, A., 'Die patrologische Schätzung des Clemens von Alexandrien bis zu seinem neuerlichen Bekanntwerden durch den ersten Druckeditionen des Sechzehnten Jahrhunderts', in P. Granfield and J. A. Jungmann (eds), *Kuriakon* (Münster: Aschendorff, 1973), 289–308.

---

[26] Clement cites or alludes to Matt 7:7 (or the parallel in Luke 11:9) in *Instr.* 1.10.91.3; 3.7.40.2; *Misc.* 1.10.51.4; 2.20.117.2; 3.7.57.2; 4.2.5.3; 5.1.11.1; 5.3.16.6; 6.9.78.1; 6.12.101.4; 7.12.73.1; 8.1.1.2; *Rich Man* 10.2.

Kovacs, J. L. 'Clement of Alexandria and Valentinian Exegesis in the *Excerpts from Theodotus*', *Studia Patristica* 41, F. Young, M. Edwards, P. Parvis (eds) (Leuven: Peeters, 2006), 187–200.

Kovacs, J. L., 'Divine Pedagogy and the Gnostic Teacher according to Clement of Alexandria', *JECS* 9 (2001), 3–25.

Kovacs, J. L., 'Echoes of Valentinian Exegesis in Clement of Alexandria and Origen: The Interpretation of 1 Cor 3.1–3', in L. Perrone (ed.), *Origeniana Octava* (Leuven: Peeters, 2004), 317–29.

Lilla, S. R. C., *Clement of Alexandria: A Study in Christian Platonism and Gnosticism* (Oxford: OUP, 1971).

Méhat, A., *Étude sur les 'Stromates' de Clément d'Alexandrie* (Paris: Du Seuil, 1966).

Osborn, E., *Clement of Alexandria* (Cambridge: CUP, 2005).

Van den Hoek, A., 'The Catechetical School of Early Christian Alexandria and Its Philonic Heritage', *HTR* 90 (1997), 59–87.

Van den Hoek, A., *Clement of Alexandria and His Use of Philo in the* Stromateis (Leiden: Brill, 1988).

Wagner, W. H., 'A Father's Fate: Attitudes toward and Interpretations of Clement of Alexandria', *Journal of Religious History* 6 (1971), 209–31.

Wyrwa, D., *Die christliche Platonaneignung in den Stromateis des Clemens von Alexandrien* (Berlin: De Gruyter, 1983).

6

Tertullian

EVERETT FERGUSON

Introduction

Quintus Septimus Florens Tertullianus stands at the beginning of Christian Latin theological literature.[1] When he began writing for the public about 197, one or two generations of Latin-speaking Christians preceded him in North Africa. Their contributions combined with his own linguistic genius and creativity produced the technical vocabulary of later Latin theology. Words like trinity, substance, person, sacrament, merit and so on received their later significance from his usage.

Tertullian offers many paradoxes: an African who was a master of Latin and Greek rhetoric and literature; the principal propagator (if not creator) of theological Latin, but sharp critic of the Roman Church; a beneficiary of Roman rule and culture, but defender of the persecuted Christian Church; outspoken opponent of heresy, but suspect of being a schismatic; champion of rational argument, but often quoted as representative of Christian anti-rationalism.

Life

Tertullian's life, whose outer limits were between about 160 and 240, was spent in Carthage.[2] Much of the meagre traditional picture of him, in part derived from Jerome (*Lives* 53), is wrong or doubtful: that his father was a centurion rests on a false reading in a manuscript of his works; that he was the jurist Tertullianus is impossible; that he was a presbyter is possible, if the two passages where he identifies himself with the laity (*Exhortation to Chastity* 7.3; *Monogamy* 12.3) are rhetorical flourishes. He seemingly includes himself among those who preached in church on Sundays (*On the Soul* 9.4), so he may have been one of the lay elders later mentioned in North African churches. Tertullian's identification with the New Prophecy of Montanism is

---

[1] For fuller bibliography see R. D. Sider, "Approaches to Tertullian: A Study of Recent Scholarship," *The Second Century* 2 (1982), 228–260; and idem, "Tertullian," in E. Ferguson et al., eds., Encyclopedia of Early Christianity, 2nd ed. (New York: Garland [Taylor and Francis], 1997), 1107–1109; R. Braun et al., eds., *Chronica tertullianea et cyprianea, 1975–1994: Bibliographie critique de la première littérature latine chrétienne* (Paris: Études Augustiniennes, 1999). An earlier survey on Tertullian by W. H. C. Frend, "Their Word to Our Day IX: Tertullian," *Expository Times* 81 (1970), 136–141.
[2] See especially Barnes in the bibliography.

certain, but recent study casts doubt upon the idea that he went into schism from the main body of the church.[3] Augustine's statement that he converted Tertullianists to the Catholic Church (*Heresies* 86) may not mean that Tertullian separated from the Montanists to establish his own sect but be Augustine's name for the Montanist party in North Africa.

Tertullian tells us that he was brought up a pagan (*Repentance* 1.1) and confesses to adultery at some time in his life (*Resurrection of the Flesh* 59.3). He was married (*To His Wife*). He was knowledgeable of Plato and the Stoics, especially Seneca. Stoicism influenced his metaphysics, logic and ethics. Impressed by the constancy of Christian martyrs, Tertullian was converted as an adult. *Apology* 50.15 may be autobiographical:

> Who that contemplates it [Christians' obstinacy before persecution] is not excited to inquire what is at the bottom of it? Who, after inquiry, does not embrace our doctrines? And when he has embraced them, does not desire to suffer that he may become a partaker of the fullness of God's grace?

To be inferred further from Tertullian's writings are that he came from a family with sufficient means to provide a good education, that he received advanced training in rhetoric (his knowledge of law came from the practice of rhetoric), that he had contacts with Christian theology from the eastern Mediterranean, and that he knew what was occurring in the church at Rome.

Christianity had come to Carthage either from the Greek-speaking east or from Rome (or both). Tertullian himself knew Greek and wrote in Greek as well as Latin, although none of his Greek works survives; the Christians to whom he wrote were mainly Latin speaking. He had access to Latin translations of at least some of the Bible, but he often provided his own translation from the Greek.

His literary activity falls mostly during the reigns of Septimius Severus (193–211) and Caracalla (211–217), when the Roman empire in North Africa was prosperous. There was provincial persecution that produced Christian martyrs (e.g. Perpetua and Felicitas in 203), but whether there was an edict by Severus (202) forbidding conversion is debated. Tertullian's writings indicate that many Christians were well off and that there was keen intellectual debate over the interpretation of Scripture between competing versions of Christian faith (Valentinians, Marcionites, Montanists, Monarchians) as well as within the orthodox Church over the exercise of discipline and practical matters of conduct.

The posture Tertullian takes in his writings is that of a Christian, an African and a non-Roman. He presumably came from the new elite of North Africa, who prospered under Roman rule but were not Roman colonizers nor the

---

[3] J. Berton, *Tertullien: le schismatique. Les problemes de la vie chrétienne et de l'autorité* (Paris: Fischbacher, 1928) – Tertullian was schismatic in attitude if not in fact; D. Powell, "Tertullianists and Cataphrygians," *Vigiliae Christianae* 29 (1975), 33–54 – not a schismatic body but an *ecclesiola in ecclesia*; D. I. Rankin, "Was Tertullian a Schismatic?" *Prudentia* 18 (1986), 73–79 – answers "No."

poorer indigenous population. He addressed those of the same social class, whether Christian or non-Christian.[4]

Writings

Thirty-one works generally accepted as by Tertullian survive.[5] They are all to some extent controversial writings and demonstrate his skills as a forensic orator. They may be grouped topically in three broad categories: (1) apologetical writings – mostly against paganism (*On Idolatry; On the Shows; On the Crown; Testimony of the Soul*) and persecution by the empire (*Apology* – addressing a Roman audience; *To the Nations* – addressing the North African elite class; *Scapula* – proconsul of Africa) but including a work *Against the Jews*; (2) anti-heretical and doctrinal writings – directed against heretics in general (*Prescription against Heretics*), Marcion (*Against Marcion*), Gnostics (*Against Valentinians; Antidote for the Scorpion's Sting*, which sting is that martyrdom is unnecessary), the docetism shared by Marcion and the Gnostics (*On the Flesh of Christ; On the Resurrection of the Flesh*), Monarchians (*Against Praxeas*) and other errors (*Against Hermogenes; On the Soul; On Baptism*); and (3) moral and disciplinary writings – both orthodox (*On Prayer; On Patience; On Repentance; To the Martyrs; To His Wife; On the Dress of Women; On the Pallium*) and those influenced by Montanism (*Exhortation to Chastity; On Monogamy; On the Veiling of Virgins; On Modesty; On Flight; On Fasting*).

The *Apology*, one of his early writings (197), is Tertullian's literary masterpiece. Preserved in two recensions, it was the most copied and widely circulated of his works. Tertullian challenges the legal basis of the persecutions and disproves the charges on which the hatred against Christians ostensibly rested. He called for freedom of religion: to take away religious liberty is the height of irreligion (*Apol.* 24.6–10). He proceeds to refute the notion that Rome ruled the world because of the worship of its gods. Then he shows that Christians are not enemies of the state nor of the human race, demonstrated by their conduct and the character of their assemblies. He concludes with the argument that persecution has actually aided the spread of Christianity, summed up in one of his memorable phrases, 'the blood of Christians is seed' (*Apol.* 50.13).

The *Prescription against Heretics* is a preemptive strike against heretics by appealing to a principle of Roman law that would rule a claimant's case out of court. The apostolic faith is preserved in the churches of apostolic foundation and those who like them adhere to the rule of faith. To those churches the Scriptures belong, and heretics have no right to argue from them.

Tertullian's major polemical work, and his longest, *Against Marcion*, shows by the care and thoroughness of his argument that after two generations the

---

[4] D. E. Wilhite, *Tertullian the African* (Berlin: De Gruyter, 2007), 67, 71, 74, 145, 159.

[5] For an introduction to the writings by Tertullian see J. Quasten, *Patrology*, vol. 2 (Utrecht: Spectrum, 1953), 251–319, supplemented for the principal writings by the entries under their title in J. Neusner and A. J. Avery-Peck, eds., *Encyclopedia of Religious and Philosophical Writings in Late Antiquity* (Leiden: Brill, 2007).

teachings of Marcion were still a threat to the Church. Book 1 argues against Marcion's two gods – the Creator, who was the just God of the Old Testament, and the Father of Jesus Christ, the previously unknown God of grace. Tertullian's contention is that 'God is not, if he is not one' (*Against Marcion* 1.3.1). There cannot be two supreme beings, since the attribute of the Supreme Being is to have no equal. Book 2 responds to Marcion's arguments against the God of the Old Testament; the Creator is the one true God. Book 3 demonstrates from the prophecies of the Old Testament that Jesus Christ is the Son of the God of the Old Testament. Book 4 then argues from Marcion's Gospel (an edited Luke) and Book 5 from Marcion's Apostle (10 letters of Paul) that Marcion's scriptures refute him. The one God is just and good, both Creator and Redeemer.

On the Soul is Tertullian's second longest work and the first major treatment of the subject by a Christian. It accepts the Stoic view, against Platonists, of the materiality of the soul and is much indebted to a Greek work of the same title by the physician Soranus of Ephesus. Body and soul are conceived together and are derived from the parents (traducianism). Thus Tertullian opposes the soul's pre-existence, natural (as opposed to a created) immortality and transmigration. He offers this definition of the soul: 'The soul is sprung from the breath of God, immortal, possessing body, having form, simple in its substance, intelligent in its own nature, developing its power in various ways, free in its determinations, subject to changes of accidents, in its faculties mutable, rational, supreme' (*On the Soul* 22).

On the Flesh of Christ and *On the Resurrection of the Flesh* defend the flesh against heretical disparagements, affirming in the first the real incarnation of Christ and in the second a real resurrection of the flesh. As preliminary to the flesh rising again, *On the Flesh of Christ* examines the flesh of Christ: did it ever exist? from where did it come? and of what kind was it? Tertullian affirmed that it was fitting and possible for Christ to be truly born and that he truly lived and died in genuine human flesh. *On the Resurrection of the Flesh* argues for the dignity of the flesh, the power of God to restore the flesh, and the good reasons for the flesh to be raised for the judgement, and then fills most of the space examining biblical passages. Against the contention from 1 Corinthians 15:50 that 'flesh and blood cannot inherit the kingdom of God', Tertullian responds that the words apply to the sins not the substance of flesh (chap. 50).

Tertullian's *Against Praxeas* comes from his Montanist years and opposes a teaching that in defence of a strict monotheism made Father, Son and Holy Spirit identical as different modes of revelation of the one God. Praxeas ('Busybody') may be Tertullian's nickname for his opponent. Tertullian argues that monarchy is consistent with three persons administering the divine rule. He advances an 'economic trinity', a dispensation and internal disposition of the one divine substance.

On Baptism is the earliest surviving work on this subject. Its point of departure is the rejection of the efficacy of water baptism by a woman of the Cainite sect. Tertullian responds by extensive praise of water as a means of

God's working. He gives much information on the doctrine and ceremony of baptism at Carthage, including his own rejection of infant baptism.

Tertullian's *On Prayer* provides the earliest commentary on the Lord's prayer. The work also provides practical instructions about prayer.

Recent study demonstrates Tertullian's indebtedness to classical rhetoric for the organization of the contents of his works and for his strategies of argumentation. He infuses the rhetorical structure with his own passion, keenness of intellect and wit. Even those repelled by some of his ideas may be fascinated by his vigorous style. His abbreviated, sometimes cryptic, statements are a challenge to his translators and readers. He is known for startling, striking turns of phrase, rugged and memorable expressions.

Two of the statements for which Tertullian is most often quoted have been taken out of context to produce at best a caricature and at worst a falsification of him. 'What has Athens to do with Jerusalem?' (*Prescription against Heretics* 7) is part of an argument that philosophy is the source of the errors of heretics. Philosophy for Tertullian, like Judaism and natural law, was incomplete without the perfection found in Christ. Although he has much criticism of philosophy as based on human opinion, he does not repudiate it wholesale and indeed makes much use of it, especially Stoicism. Tertullian loved such antithetical statements, and they must be balanced by the wholeness of his thought.

'It is credible because it is foolish [*credibile est quia ineptum est*] ... certain because it is impossible [*certum est quia impossibile est*]' (*On the Flesh of Christ* 5.4) is often misquoted as 'I believe because it is absurd' [*credo quia absurdum est*], which Tertullian never said.[6] The statements are made about the death of the Son of God and his burial and resurrection. The words have their significance precisely because there is a paradox. Such things are unworthy of God, and ordinarily the silly and impossible are to be rejected. Tertullian is arguing for the incarnation. If God is joined to a human being in a way that is shameful and seemingly impossible, the person who results is then truly God and truly a human being.[7]

Tertullian was no fideist nor example of Christian anti-rationalism. Indeed his favourite word is reason (*ratio*). In the very tract *On the Flesh of Christ* Tertullian demands of his opponents 'I must have reasons' (10.1).

Theology

Tertullian marked out the rational lines along which much of subsequent Western theology would proceed.[8] His basic religious ideas are items known

---

[6] R. D. Sider, "*Credo quia absurdum*," *Classical World* 73 (1980), 417–419.

[7] E. Osborn, *Tertullian, First Theologian of the West* (Cambridge: Cambridge University Press, 1997), 49, 62.

[8] For the theology of Tertullian see in addition to Osborn in the bibliography R. E. Roberts, *The Theology of Tertullian* (London: Epworth, 1924); G. L. Bray, *Holiness and the Will of God: Perspectives on the Theology of Tertullian* (Atlanta: John Knox, 1979); R. Kearsley, *Tertullian's Theology of Divine Power* (Carlisle: Paternoster, 1998).

by nature: existence of God, demons, immortality of the soul, and judgement (*On the Resurrection of the Flesh* 3.1–2; *Testimony of the Soul* 2; 4; 6). These items may have provided the structure of his religious belief when he was converted to Christianity, which provided a confirmation to him of those beliefs. God's existence is proved by his work and wisdom in creating the world out of nothing, by the testimony of 'the soul by nature "Christian"', and by his revelation in Scripture (*Apology* 17.1–18.1). He is 'everywhere known, everywhere present, everywhere powerful, an object whom all ought to worship' (*To the Nations* 2.8). God is one, 'unbegotten, unmade, eternal' (*Against Marcion* 1.9). The creation demonstrates that God is; redemption in Christ demonstrates what he is.

Making the first use of *trinitas* as a technical term, Tertullian affirms that monotheism is consistent with an internal trinity. The one God within himself is three – one in quality, substance and power, but distinct in sequence, aspect and manifestation (*Against Praxeas* 2.4). This trinity does not destroy the divine unity but administers it. Tertullian introduces the words 'substance' (*substantia* – the Stoic word for the 'stuff' or constitutive material of something) for the divine unity and 'person' (*persona*) for the individual entities of Father, Son and Holy Spirit. In order to explain plural manifestations of one reality Tertullian uses the metaphors of political monarchy (one imperial rule administered by a father and son) and of human reason expressed by the spoken word (the Greek *logos* that had been employed by the Greek apologists before him, for which Tertullian chose *sermo* as the equivalent, but the Latin tradition chose *verbum*). He also presented physical illustrations: root, tree and fruit; fountain, stream and river; sun, ray and apex. It may be noted that unlike some modern analogies that explain how plural entities may be one Tertullian begins with oneness and explains how that can be plural.

In *Against Praxeas* Tertullian starts with the Trinity and comes at his Christology from his trinitarian doctrine, but it seems that in the development of his thought the economy of God's nature was a result of his consideration of the economy or administration of the plan of salvation. This plan involved the Word becoming flesh. In describing this union Tertullian had access to Aristotelian and Stoic analyses of different kinds of union of physical things. He presents the union of the incarnation as 'man mixed with God' (*Apology* 21; *Against Marcion* 2.27), but he clarifies that these two substances formed a composition in which the properties of each were preserved in 'unconfused union', so each was separable from the other (*Against Praxeas* 27). In regard to Christology, as with the Trinity, Tertullian passed on the formula accepted by the West as orthodox: in the one person of Jesus Christ there are two substances.

Tertullian interprets the theophanies of the Old Testament as pre-incarnate appearances of Christ (*Against Praxeas* 14; 16). There are two advents of Christ, the first in humility and the second yet to come in majesty; not understanding this, the Jews failed to recognize Jesus (*Against the Jews* 14; *Against Marcion* 3.7). As part of the claim for Christ's having a fully ordinary human birth at his first coming Tertullian explains that Mary had a virgin conception but not properly a 'virgin birth', for the birth was that of a married woman (*On the Flesh of Christ* 23); and indeed Mary married after his birth (*On Monogamy* 8).

The purpose of the incarnation was the salvation of humanity. The circumstances surrounding the birth, life and death of Christ may have been shameful, but 'nothing is so worthy of God as the salvation of humanity' (*Against Marcion* 2.27.1). He continues that what Marcion considers humiliation

> is the sacrament of human salvation. God entered into converse with man, so that man might be taught how to act like God. God dealt on equal terms with man so that man might be able to deal on equal terms with God. God was found to be small so that man might become very great.

Like Irenaeus, Tertullian portrays Christ's work as recapitulation. Recapitulation includes three sets of motifs: Christ corrects and perfects all; as Victor he is the climax of saving history; and as the perfection of being, goodness and truth he gives life to the dying, righteousness to sinners and truth to those in error.[9] Tertullian's soteriological images are redemption and liberation (*On Idolatry* 5; *Against Marcion* 5.4.9; *On Flight* 2.6; 12.2–3), propitiatory sacrifice (*Against Marcion* 5.7.3; 3.7.7), reconciling mediation (*Against Marcion* 4.20.11; 5.19.5–6), teaching and enlightenment (*Apology* 21.7; *Against Marcion* 4.25.3–5, 11) and healing (*Antidote for the Scorpion's Sting* 5; *On the Flesh of Christ* 4.4).[10]

According to Tertullian heretics, like philosophers, begin with the same set of questions: 'Whence comes evil? Why is it permitted? What is the origin of man? In what way does he come?' (*Prescription against Heretics* 7). Tertullian distinguished two kinds of evil involving human beings: sins instigated by the devil (*mala culpae*) and punishments inflicted by God (*mala poenae*). 'The crowning sin is idolatry' (*On the Shows* 2). The answer to the human problem is the paradox of Christ crucified and risen.

Human beings are made in the image of God. This means possessing spirit, reason and especially freedom (*Against Marcion* 2.5–9). Basic to Tertullian's doctrines of human nature, the origin of sin and reception of salvation is free will (*On the Soul* 21; *Exhortation to Chastity* 2). A corruption of the soul has proceeded from the sin of Adam, so Tertullian shows the origins of the idea of original sin; but he does not have the later doctrine of original sin, for this corruption is not equated with guilt (*On the Soul* 16; 40–41). The soul is in a state of innocence until puberty (age 14) – *On the Soul* 38. Since the soul originates with the body at conception, voluntary abortion is murder: 'it does not matter whether you take away a life that is born or destroy one that is coming to birth' (*Apology* 9.6–7; *Exhortation to Chastity* 12).

The Holy Spirit comes from the Father through the Son (*Against Praxeas* 4). He is now the vicar of Christ (*Prescription against Heretics* 28; *Veiling*

---

[9] Osborn, *Tertullian*, 17.
[10] See Viciano in the bibliography.

of Virgins 1). The Spirit bestowed spiritual gifts (*Against Marcion* 5.8). Tertullian claimed these as manifest again among the Montanists (*On the Soul* 9), but he denied that miracles such as those of the prophets, Christ, and the apostles were present in the Church of his day (*On Modesty* 21). The Spirit was the instrument of revelation (*On the Soul* 1). Righteousness was in its infancy under the Law and the Prophets, reached the fervour of youth through the Gospel, and was settling into maturity as the Paraclete through the Montanist prophets was guiding Christians into a more rigorous discipline (*Veiling of Virgins* 1).

Tertullian offered several images of the Church: ark, ship, camp, body of Christ, Trinity, Spirit, school and sect; especially prominent in him are mother, bride and virgin.[11] Tertullian insisted that the Church was identified by its historical connection with the apostles and adherence to apostolic doctrine. He acknowledged the distinction of clergy and laity and the ecclesiastical order of bishop, presbyters and deacons (*Prescription against Heretics* 41; *On Flight* 11). He referred also to other distinct positions – teachers, readers, widows, virgins, prophets and martyrs. Especially in his Montanist writings Tertullian strongly affirmed that all Christians are priests (*Exhortation to Chastity* 7.3; *On Fasting* 11) by reason of putting on the High Priest Christ in baptism (*On Monogamy* 7).[12]

Tertullian incidentally gives a brief summary of activities in the assembly on the Lord's day: readings from the Scriptures, chanting Psalms, preaching sermons and praying (*On the Soul* 9.4). A fuller, more deliberate account occurs in *Apology* 39.1–5, which describes the prayers, the readings from sacred texts, teaching and exhortation, administering discipline and the contribution (done monthly). Later in the chapter (39.16–18) he describes the love feast. Notable is absence of mention of the eucharist, to which Tertullian makes allusion on other occasions (e.g. *On Idolatry* 7 – hands raised in prayer and handling the body of the Lord; *On the Crown* 3 – the eucharist received before daybreak from those presiding). He understood the bread and wine as symbolic of the body and blood and used them as indicative of the real flesh and blood of the Saviour[13] and along with the water of baptism as arguments for the creation as the product of the good Creator (*On Prayer* 6; *Against Marcion* 1.14; 3.19; 4.40; *On the Resurrection of the Flesh* 8).

As a catholic, Tertullian opposed women exercising liturgical functions (*Prescription against Heretics* 41), and even as a Montanist he reiterated the prohibition against women speaking in church, teaching, baptizing and presiding at the eucharist (*On the Veiling of Virgins* 9; cf. *On the Soul* 9 for a woman receiving visions in the church assembly but reporting them only after the service). Tertullian is infamous for some negative words about women

---

[11] D. Rankin, *Tertullian and the Church* (Cambridge: Cambridge University Press, 1995), 65–90.

[12] M. Bévenot, "Tertullian's Thoughts on the Christian 'Priesthood'," in *Corona Gratiarum: Miscellanea Patristica, historica et liturgica Eligio Dekkers O.S.B. Oblata* (Brugge: Sint Pietersabdij, 1965), 125–137.

[13] Bévenot, "Tertullian's Thoughts on the Christian 'Priesthood'."

('gateway of the devil' – *On the Dress of Women* 1.1), but on this subject as on others there is a duality in Tertullian and the negative words must be balanced by the beautiful encomium on the mutual happiness of a Christian husband and wife (*To His Wife* 2.8), unmatched in early Christian literature. Although he says less about it, Tertullian required modesty also in males' appearance (*On the Dress of Women* 2.8).

Tertullian moved from a position preferring that a spouse remain unmarried after the death of a mate (*To His Wife*) to insisting on remaining unmarried, likening monogamy to monotheism (*On Monogamy* 1). He outlined degrees of chastity: virginity from one's birth, virginity from the second birth of baptism (either in the married state or abstinence by mutual consent) and remaining unmarried after death of the spouse (*Exhortation to Chastity* 1).

Tertullian was embroiled in the controversy that affected the churches of Rome and Carthage (and elsewhere) over the Church's forgiveness of post-baptismal sins. He early described the penitential discipline for receiving sinners back into the Church (*On Repentance* 9–10). Tertullian later took a position severely restricting forgiveness for the major sins of idolatry, murder and adultery (*On Modesty* 5).

Another example of the way Tertullian's writings reflect different situations and so can be used to represent conflicting positions has to do with Christian participation in the military. In defending Christianity to Roman authorities he refers to the presence of Christians in the army (*Apology* 5.6; cf. 37.4–5 and 42.2–3), but in addressing fellow Christians he argues that service in the military is inconsistent with the Christian life (*On the Crown* 11; *On Idolatry* 19).

Discipline was Tertullian's word for practical precepts. He derived his rules for conduct from Scripture, nature or reason, and discipline, that is, ecclesiastical teaching (*On the Veiling of Virgins* 16).

Tertullian's discussions of Christian practice involved considerable debate over biblical interpretation and the relation of Scripture and custom (or tradition).[14] His writings give numerous glimpses into the intramural controversies among Christians about the meaning of Scripture on matters of doctrine and on its application to conduct. The breadth of Tertullian's knowledge of the Bible, both Old and New Testament, is astonishing. His summary statement of its contents is 'law, prophets, and writings of evangelists and apostles' (*Prescription against Heretics* 36). There are readily recognized quotations and allusions to all the Old Testament canonical and deuterocanonical books except Ruth, Obadiah, 1 Chronicles, Esther and 2 Maccabees and all the New Testament books except James, 2 Peter (these are possible), 2 and 3 John. Tertullian thought Barnabas wrote Hebrews (*On Modesty* 20) and the apostle John wrote Revelation. Concerning books now counted as non-canonical he quoted *Enoch*, and among the deuterocanonical books he

---

[14] G. D. Dunn, "Tertullian's Scriptural Exegesis in *de praescriptione haereticorum*," *Journal of Early Christian Studies* 14 (2000), 141–155; J. Quasten, "Tertullian and *Traditio*," *Traditio* 2 (1944), 451–484.

liked the Wisdom of Solomon. He expressly repudiated the *Shepherd of Hermas* as apocryphal (the first Latin writer to use this term for spurious books) and not in the 'divine canon' (*On Modesty* 10.12; cf. 'all our canon' in *On Monogamy* 7) and the *Acts of Paul* (*On Baptism* 17). Although one cannot claim that Tertullian knew a closed collection of New Testament books, his frequent references to a 'New Testament' and use of 'Scripture' for New Testament writings make evident that he had a definite entity in mind (e.g. *Against the Jews* 9; *Against Praxeas* 15; *Prescription against Heretics* 17; 38) and that by his usage it included certainly the Four Gospels, Acts, thirteen letters of Paul, Hebrews, 1 Peter, 1 John, Jude and Revelation.

It is possible to extract from Tertullian several of his principles of exegesis.[15] The meaning of words is a guiding principle (*Prescription against Heretics* 9). Tertullian assembles passages where the same word is used (e.g. *On Prayer*), and he holds that in determining meaning one must take Scripture as a whole. He frequently argues from context. He bases his interpretations on simplicity (unless this gives a superficial meaning) and clearness. He normally stays with the literal meaning of a text, but he gives attention to how one identifies figurative language (*On the Resurrection of the Flesh* 20). Obscure passages are to be interpreted by clear ones (ibid., 21). Meaning may be limited by times and circumstances (*On Flight* 6), but texts may also be applied to other occasions where that is useful (*On the Dress of Women* 2.2). Paul in writing to one church was writing to all (*Against Marcion* 5.17). Tertullian appeals to both commands and examples in Scripture (*On Fasting* 11); the silence of Scripture is prohibitive (*On the Crown* 2; *To His Wife* 1.3).

Scripture, coming from God and inspired by the Holy Spirit, was authoritative for Tertullian. The 'Rule of Faith' is a summary of Scripture, and Scripture is to be interpreted according to the 'Rule of Faith' (statements of its content in *Prescription against Heretics* 13; *Against Praxeas* 2; *On the Veiling of Virgins* 1).[16] The 'Rule' functioned for Tertullian as the first principles did in Platonic and Stoic philosophy – the foundational ideas, undemonstrable themselves but the 'givens' that are the basis of all reasoning. Tertullian took various stands on matters of custom and tradition. In *On Prayer* 15 he rejects those practices lacking 'the authority of any precept of the Lord or of the apostles'. In *On the Crown* 3, however, he cites customs that no passage of Scripture prescribed but that were derived from tradition and were to be observed. Yet, 'what savours of opposition to truth will be heresy, even if it be an ancient custom' (*On the Veiling of Virgins* 1).

---

[15] In addition to O'Malley in the bibliography note R. P. C. Hanson, "Notes on Tertullian's Interpretation of Scripture," *Journal of Theological Studies*, n.s. 12 (1961), 273–279; J. H. Waszink, "Tertullian's Principles and Methods of Exegesis," in W. R. Schoedel and R. L. Wilken, eds., *Early Christian Literature and the Classical Intellectual Tradition: In Honorem Robert M. Grant* (Paris: Beauchesne, 1979), 17–31, repr. in E. Ferguson, ed., *The Bible in the Early Church*, Studies in Early Christianity 3 (New York: Garland [Taylor and Francis], 1993), 271–285.

[16] L. W. Countryman, "Tertullian and the Regula fidei," *The Second Century* 2 (1982), 208–227.

The human being is a union of soul and flesh, dissolved at death (*Resurrection of the Flesh* 19) but joined again in a glorified body at the final resurrection. In the intermediate state souls are in Hades, consisting of two parts – a place of consolation for the good and a place of punishment for the bad (*On the Soul* 7; 56; 58). The souls of martyrs bypass Hades and go to paradise (*On the Soul* 55; *On the Resurrection of the Flesh* 43). There are four main elements involved in the second advent of Christ: Christ's return in glory (described in *On Shows* 30), the resurrection in the same body in which one died (*On the Soul* 56; *On Patience* 16 – 'resurrection of flesh and spirit'), universal judgement (often invoked as motive for conduct – e.g. *Apology* 45; *Testimony of the Soul* 2) and a renewed earth. There will be a millennial kingdom (*Against Marcion* 3.24.3–6). Hell is eternal punishment, not annihilation (*On the Resurrection of the Flesh* 35). In the resurrection the bodies of the righteous will be remade by God so as to remove blemishes and defects (*On the Resurrection of the Flesh* 57).

Impact

Montanism was attractive to Tertullian as confirming his views on martyrdom, marriage, fasting and forgiveness. His strict position on disciplinary matters such as remarriage, clothing of males and females, penitential practice and fasting did not prevail in the mainstream of the Church and except for forgiveness of post-baptismal sins may have been lost causes already in his time. His stand against Christian participation in warfare touched on a question becoming more pressing for many in his day. Then, as often since, leading thinkers found military service inconsistent with Christian teaching, but many Christians nonetheless entered the army.

Tertullian's high evaluation of martyrdom was part of the ethos of the North African Church for some time to come. His strong negative view of pagan entertainments (*On Shows*) was shared by other Christian ethicists, but many Christians then and later ignored the counsels of their teachers and attended the theatrical performances, the gladiatorial contests in the arenas and the chariot races in the circuses. It is notable that two authors who seem to have such contrasting personalities and approaches to intellectual questions as Tertullian and Clement of Alexandria shared a common viewpoint on moral questions.

The argument over reconciliation to the Church of those who fell into serious sin involved contrasting views of the nature of the Church: the Church of the pure or the Church as a mixed body of saints and sinners. The interpretation that the Lord through giving the keys of the kingdom of heaven to Peter gave them to the whole Church (*Antidote for the Scorpion's Sting* 10.8) was contested by the clergy who claimed for themselves the authority to reconcile to the Church. Tertullian understood that the Church was built on Peter (*Prescription against Heretics* 22; *On Monogamy* 8), but Peter's opening the doors of the kingdom was done through preaching baptism (*On Modesty* 21).

His prerogatives passed to spiritual persons, so 'the church will forgive sins', but it is the 'church of the Spirit' not 'the church of bishops' (ibid.). It is a somewhat curious development that the 'laxist' position on church discipline was more often associated with a hierarchical view of the Church and a more 'rigorist' position was championed by the advocates of the priesthood of the laity.

Tertullian's doctrinal arguments against Marcionites and Gnostics solidified the orthodox position that carried the day. His interpretations of the Trinity and the nature of Christ over against the Monarchian view provided the arguments and a vocabulary for the way along which theological thought would proceed in the Western Church during the following centuries.

The story repeated by Jerome (*Lives* 53) that Cyprian daily read from Tertullian, requesting of his secretary, 'Bring me the master', seems to derive from a reliable source. Through Cyprian a 'catholicized' Tertullian passed into the heritage of the Western Church.

Academic study of Tertullian

The study of Tertullian has been approached from four major directions:

The legal background of Tertullian

The degree to which legal training has shaped the form and content of his work is debatable.[17] Legal terminology and procedures are certainly prominent in Tertullian's writings, but these features do not seem to be sufficient to establish that he received special training in the law. The legal cast that shaped later Western Christianity came in large part from two influences: the general Roman contribution of law to civilization, and the Christian appropriation of the Old Testament interpreted as a law book for the Church. Tertullian's argument on behalf of the Old Testament against Marcion and his use of legal language in theology contributed to these developments but were more of a reflection of the influence of Roman and Mosaic law on society and the Church than themselves formative factors.

The philosophical background of Tertullian[18]

Despite his negative statements about philosophy, the attitude of always seeking (curiosity) it encouraged and its inherent limitations as a human enterprise, Tertullian was much influenced by philosophy, especially Roman Stoicism. Some of this influence was unconscious (an unacknowledged philosophy is the most dangerous kind), but much of his use of philosophy was deliberate

---

[17] J. K. Stirnimann, *Die Praescriptio Tertullians im Lichte des römischen Rechts und der Theologie*, Paradosis 3 (Freiburg, 1949); G. Bray, "The Legal Concept of Ratio in Tertullian," *Vigiliae Christianae* 31 (1977), 94–116.

[18] C. DeLisle Shortt, *The Influence of Philosophy on the Mind of Tertullian* (London: Stock, 1933); H. B. Timothy, *The Early Christian Apologists and Greek Philosophy* (Assen: Van Gorcum, 1973), 40–58.

and employed to make his own points. Tertullian's indebtedness to law and professed aversion to philosophy contrasts with the Eastern (particularly Alexandrian) theological development and is indicative of the different paths Western and Eastern theology would take.

The history of language and semantics[19]

Tertullian's substantial body of works and his rich literary skills have prompted many studies of his vocabulary and his place in the history of Latin literature in general. Philologists and linguists still mine his works in ways that throw light on his theology as well.

Rhetoric[20]

As indicated, Tertullian is best understood as a rhetorician, and the most fruitful recent studies of him have concentrated on this aspect of his work. He wrote as an advocate in order to win arguments, and so could adopt different approaches according to the issue at hand and the arguments of his opponents. Appreciation of the strategies in argument employed by ancient rhetoricians goes far toward accounting for the many seemingly contradictory positions expressed by Tertullian. The caution that this approach requires before taking everything he said at face value should not lead to a dismissal of his arguments as 'mere rhetoric' nor detract from recognizing the rich capacity of his mind to embrace paradox.

These approaches add to the perennial interest in Tertullian for his thoughts on the fundamental Christian doctrines and for the information he provides on the history of church life.

Conclusion

Although it is to be doubted that Tertullian himself went into schism, he shared characteristics of sectarian movements throughout Christian history: concern (almost legalistic) with externals of dress, makeup and hair styles (*On the Dress of Women, On Veiling Virgins, On the Pallium*); refusal of government office and military service (*On Idolatry* 17; 19; *On the Crown* 11); the call to responsible voluntary commitment, seen especially in his rejection of infant baptism (*On Baptism* 18); taking Church discipline very seriously (*On Repentance* 9); the principle of interpretation that what is not commanded is forbidden (*On the Crown* 2); emphasis on the Holy Spirit (*On the Soul* 9); and eschatological speculation (*Against Marcion* 3.25).

These features, however, should not overshadow Tertullian's enormous importance for the development of the major Christian doctrines of the

---

[19] See Braun in the bibliography.

[20] In addition to Sider in the bibliography, on individual works see Sider, "Tertullian *On the Shows*," *Journal of Theological Studies* n.s. 29 (1978), 339–365; G. D. Dunn, *Tertullian's Adversus Iudaeos: A Rhetorical Analysis* (Washington, DC: Catholic University of America Press, 2008).

Trinity and Christology and his contributions to understanding the less authoritatively defined doctrines of human nature (the soul), sin, salvation, sacraments and eschatology.

In our time of post-Christendom when reflection on the relation of Church and civil government is once more in flux, it is instructive to see Tertullian in relation to the positions expressed about the relation of Christians to the Roman state in pre-Constantinian times. Some voiced a radical rejection of the Roman government (Hippolytus, *Commentary on Daniel* 2.12; 3.20–25; 4.9; *On Christ and Antichrist* 25; 28; 33; Tatian, *Oration* 28; 35; Minucius Felix, *Octavius* 25.5). Others saw civil government as a negative good, restraining evil (*1 Clement* 60–61 – prayer for the empire as preserving order; Ignatius, *Romans* 6 – Christians have nothing to do with the kingdoms of the earth, but persecution gives opportunity to witness by martyrdom). A more nuanced view was that governments, although ordained by God, were under intermediaries (angelic powers) that might either serve God or rebel; obedience was due until government became anti-Christ (Justin, *1 Apology* 57 – demons administer affairs and instigate persecution; *2 Apology* 5; 7 – Rome is to be obeyed because persecution is not really from Rome). Similar was the view that there are two realms, but the *Logos* instead of the divisive demons rules over all (the apologists stressed that Christ taught obedience – Justin, *1 Apology* 17; Theophilus, *To Autolycus* 1.11; Christians help rulers and people by their prayers and good deeds – Origen, *Against Celsus* 8.73–75; and Christians preserve the world from destruction – Aristides, *Apology* 16; *Epistle to Diognetus* 6). An even more positive assessment of the empire affirmed that it was the agent of providence for bringing Christianity into the world and provided the framework for spreading Christianity (Melito, in Eusebius, *Church History* 4.16.6ff.; Origen, *Against Celsus* 2.30).

Where does Tertullian fit? He sometimes expressed his opposition to pagan society, idolatry and Roman persecution by negative words about the empire that sound like the first position described above (*To the Nations* 2.1 – rejection of the Roman 'customs of the ancestors'; *Apology* 21.24 – Christians cannot be Caesars; 38.3 – nothing more alien to Christians than affairs of state; *On Idolatry* 18 – secular powers are alien to God; *On Clothing of Women* 2.12 – Rome is the harlot of the Apocalypse). In another direction, his argument in the *Apology* 30–33 fits the last line of thought above that aims at an empire converted to Christ which would unify Christianity and the Roman state.[21] He found a place for the Roman empire in the divine purpose.

[21] Richard Klein, *Tertullian und das Römische Reich* (Heidelberg: C. Winter, 1968) – Tertullian's goal was an empire converted to Christianity; R. F. Evans, "On the Problem of Church and Empire in Tertullian's *Apologeticum*," *Studia Patristica* 14 (1976), 21–36 – Tertullian's deepest convictions were eschatological and not accommodative; J. C. Fredouille, "Tertullien et l'Empire," in *Aufstieg und Niedergang der römischen Welt* (Berlin: De Gruyter), 2.27.3. On a wider topic J. C. Fredouille, *Tertullien et le conversion de la culture antique* (Paris: Études Augustiniennes, 1972), shows that Tertullian preserved his pagan cultural heritage within his Christian perspective.

This one topic illustrates the possibility of clarifying current issues by examining the multi-faceted thought of Tertullian on matters of perennial concern.

Bibliography

Editions

J. W. Ph. Borleffs et al. (eds), *Q. S. Fl. Tertullianus*, Corpus Christianorum Series Latina, vols 1–2 (Turnhout: Brepols, 1954).

J. Waszink (ed.), *De anima* (with comm.; Amsterdam: Mulenhoff, 1947).

J. H. Waszink and J. C. M. van Winden (eds), *De idolatria* (Leiden: Brill, 1987).

Translations

E. Evans (ed.), *Adversus Praxean* (London: SPCK, 1948); *De Oratione* (London: SPCK, 1953); *De carne Christi* (London: SPCK, 1956); *De resurrectione carnis* (London: SPCK, 1960); *De baptismo* (London: SPCK, 1964); *Adversus Marcionem*, 2 vols, Oxford Early Christian Texts (Oxford: Clarendon, 1972).

S. Thelwell and P. Holmes, *Latin Christianity: Its Founder, Tertullian*, Ante-Nicene Christian Library, vols 7, 11, 15, 18 (Edinburgh, 1885); reprint *Ante-Nicene Fathers*, vols 3–4 (Peabody, MA: Hendrickson, 1995).

G. D. Dunn, *Tertullian* (London: Routledge, 2004), introduction with translation of *Against the Jews, Antidote for the Scorpion's Sting* and *On the Veiling of Virgins*.

Studies

T. D. Barnes, *Tertullian: A Historical and Literary Study* (Oxford: Oxford University Press, 1971; reprint with postscript, 1985).

R. Braun, *Deus christianorum: Recherches sur le vocabulaire doctrinal de Tertullien*, 2nd edn (Paris: Études Augustiniennes, 1977).

H. R. Drobner, *The Fathers of the Church: A Comprehensive Introduction*, trans. S. S. Schatzmann (Peabody: Hendrickson, 2007) 153–164.

T. P. O'Malley, *Tertullian and the Bible: Language, Imagery, Exegesis* (Nijmegen: Dekker & Van de Vegt, 1967).

E. Osborn, *Tertullian, First Theologian of the West* (Cambridge: Cambridge University Press, 1997).

D. Rankin, *Tertullian and the Church* (Cambridge: Cambridge University Press, 1995).

R. D. Sider, *Ancient Rhetoric and the Art of Tertullian* (Oxford: Oxford University Press, 1971).

A. Viciano, *Cristo Salvador y Liberador del hombre: Estudio sobre la soteriología de Tertuliano* (Pamplona: Universidad de Navarra, 1986).

D. E. Wilhite, *Tertullian the African* (Berlin: De Gruyter, 2007).

7

Perpetua

SARA PARVIS

Introduction

The attractions of Perpetua as an early church writer are well known and clear. To begin with, she is a woman writer in an age in which women are very seldom heard from directly. In addition, she is one of the earliest Latin Christian writers, a contemporary of Tertullian's, and a very useful alternative witness to the state of Christianity in the Carthage of his day. Furthermore, she and the narrative within which her diary survives provide important evidence for the context and spread of Montanism, the charismatic, prophetic movement mainly based in Asia Minor. But perhaps most importantly of all, she provides us in her diary with the first example of Christian autobiography; sketchy though it is, she gives us the sort of glimpse of her private life and the way she constructs her Christian identity that we will not see again until Augustine.

The *Passion of Perpetua and Felicity*

Most, though not quite all, of what we know about Perpetua comes from the composite document known in Latin as the *Passion of Perpetua and Felicity* (one or two plausible details appear only in the Greek version, the *Martyrdom of Perpetua and those put to death with her in Africa*).[1] This document contains Perpetua's prison diary, including her accounts of four revelatory dreams; an account by Saturus, another of the condemned Christians, of a vision of his; and a wraparound narrative which includes a brief description of all the arrested Christians, the death of Secundulus in prison, Felicity's childbirth two days before the executions, and the executions themselves, together with an exhortatory introduction and concluding paragraph.

Carthage at the turn of the second and third centuries after Christ contained, like other Christian communities in the Latin-speaking West at the period, a notable proportion of Greek speakers. In Saturus' dream vision, Perpetua speaks in Greek to Optatus the bishop and Aspasius the presbyter. Given the

---

[1] Both versions are included in the *Sources chrétiennes* edition (ed. Jacqueline Amat), with a French translation of each. Herbert Musurillo (*The Acts of the Christian Martyrs*) includes only the Latin, with an English translation. Details of these editions are in the bibliography. I generally follow Amat's text, though the translations are my own.

existence of an early Greek text, which seems to preserve some details better than the extant Latin versions, the question arises as to the original language of the *Passion*, and of each section within it.

The Latin text of the wraparound narrative, introduction and conclusion is generally now considered to be the original. The author is sometimes held to be Tertullian, both because this section has some stylistic similarities with his writings, and because (as we shall see) it shows affinities with Montanism.[2] A further reason sometimes adduced is that a different author would raise the number of highly educated Christians in Carthage beyond a plausible total; writers of Tertullian's class and ability must surely have been rare in Christianity of this period. However, intelligent and literate people tend to attract other intelligent and literate people, and it has been pointed out that Tertullian misrepresents the *Passion* by stating that Perpetua saw only her fellow martyrs in heaven in her vision as her passion approached (*De Anima* 55.4).[3]

In the case of Perpetua's own narrative, both Greek and Latin have been championed as the original language. Her name (Vibia Perpetua) and local position (*honeste nata* implies her father was of the decurion class) suggest a Latin-speaking family established in North Africa for several generations, at least.[4] On the other hand, Saturus' vision of her speaking Greek to the Carthaginian church leaders would seem to imply that she was fluently bilingual, unless this is an example of dreamer's paradox. As her brother was called Dinocrates, it is possible that her mother was Greek. Louis Robert has argued that the imagery in Perpetua's fourth vision, her kick-boxing match in the amphitheatre, is much more technically accurate in the Greek version, and reflects the Pythian Games which would have taken place in Carthage in the previous winter, while the Latin version mixes in imagery from a gladiatorial contest, a completely different occasion. Robert sees this as clear proof that Perpetua originally dictated her diary in Greek.[5] But Jan Bremmer has pointed out that for a dream to conflate imagery from two settings is nothing unusual, especially since neither of the settings is in any case the event in which she is actually going to fight her real battle (which is against the wild beasts).[6] No one who knows sports fanatics could be surprised that

---

[2] For a good summary of late nineteenth- and early twentieth-century discussion of the question of Tertullian's authorship, see Rex D. Butler, *The New Prophecy & 'New Visions', Evidence of Montanism in* The Passion of Perpetua and Felicitas (Washington: Catholic University of America Press, 2006) 49–52.

[3] See Timothy David Barnes, *Tertullian, A Historical and Literary Study* (2nd edn; Oxford: Clarendon Press, 1985), 265. Tertullian's claim here would seem to fit Saturus' vision better than Perpetua's (cf. *Passion* 11.9). It is possible, however, that Tertullian interpreted as martyrs the white-robed figures seen by Perpetua in her first vision (*Passion* 4.8). For further arguments excluding Tertullian as the author of the *Passio* narrative and introduction, see René Braun, *Approches de Tertullien* (Paris: Institut d'études augustiniennes, 1992) 287–299.

[4] See Jan N. Bremmer, 'Perpetua and Her Diary: Authenticity, Family and Visions', in Walter Ameling (ed.), *Märtyrer und Märtyrerakten* (Wiesbaden: Franz Steiner Verlag, 2002) 77–120, at 87.

[5] Louis Robert, 'Une vision de Perpétue martyre à Carthage en 203', *Comptes rendus de l'Académie des Inscriptions et Belles-Lettres* (1982) 228–276, esp. 253–276.

[6] Bremmer, 'Perpetua', 113–18.

a later translator, particularly a Greek, would feel himself compelled to correct a woman's wrong rendering of the details of a famous Greek sporting contest, no matter how much esteem he held her in.

Other details tell strongly in favour of Latin as the original language of Perpetua's diary as well as the wraparound narrative, in particular arguments from the differences of Latin prose rhythm of the different sections of the *Passio*, which make no sense in a translation.[7] These stylistic differences are also strong arguments for the authenticity of the two first-person narratives by Perpetua and Saturus. The latter has, however, been argued to have been itself originally composed in Greek, again because of stylistic differences, this time in the Greek version.[8] It is, perhaps, difficult to see why Saturus would have noted the singularity of Perpetua speaking Greek in a narrative which was itself written in Greek, but on the other hand the existence of memorials from the martyrs in two different languages would explain why the *Passion* seems to have been circulated from early on in both those languages.

For both versions do seem to be early. The detail (only found in the Latin) that the martyrs were to be made to fight in honour of the birthday of Geta Caesar, Septimius Severus' younger son (*Passion* 7.8), must date from the first decade or so of the third century, since Geta was killed by his brother Caracalla in December 211, and then subjected to *damnatio memoriae*, making any information about his birthday impossible to come by at a later date.[9] On the other hand, the Greek narrative also includes an important detail that looks to be authentic: that the catechumens were arrested in the city of Thuburbo Minus (*Martyrdom* 2.1).

Perpetua's life and death

It is when we look at Perpetua's life as it emerges from the *Passion* that we begin to have a sense of how extraordinary is the window she opens for us. Perpetua is in her twenty-second year during the time covered in this document, the last weeks of her life. She is one of a group of young catechumens who are together when they are arrested (*Passion* 2.1–3). Their catechist, Saturus, is not with them at the time, but later gives himself up to be martyred with them.

The little group is interestingly diverse. Felicity and Revocatus are slaves, perhaps married to one another (she is described as his *conserva*). It has been suggested that the catechumens all come from the same household; Saturninus and Secundulus could be friends, or hangers-on (perhaps Perpetua's foster brothers, or the sons of a freed servant of the previous generation), or may themselves be servants of some sort. In any case, they seem to be lower down

[7] For a good summary of the earlier literature on this topic, see Butler, *New Prophecy*, 45–48. For more recent treatments, see Bremmer, 'Perpetua', 81–82.
[8] See Åke Fridh, *Le problème de la* Passion *des saintes Perpétue et Félicité* (Gothenburg: Acta Universitatis Gothoburgensis, 1968).
[9] See Barnes, *Tertullian*, 263–265.

the social scale than Perpetua. She clearly stands out for reasons of birth as well as character.

Perpetua herself is described as well born, well educated and married (*honeste nata, liberaliter instituta, matronaliter nupta*). Her own diary soon tells us she is a mother as well, of an infant at the breast (3.6–9). Her husband is nowhere to be seen, nor is he mentioned in the course of the narrative. This may mean they are divorced; however, he makes no attempt to claim his child either, which is perhaps more surprising. His death would have led us to expect some interest in the child from members of his family. Perhaps he himself became a Christian, was repudiated by his family, and then died; or perhaps Perpetua's child is not his. In any case, she is exceptionally close to her own family, her mother, two brothers, and maternal aunt. Even in the case of her non-Christian father, painful though their relationship has become, it is clear that at least in the past they have been very dear to one another.

This arrest of catechumens, Christians preparing for baptism over what may be intended to be two or three years, seems to imply a policy on the part of the authorities (at whatever level) of specifically targeting converts to Christianity rather than long-standing Christians. On the face of it, such a policy would seem to have a good chance of success. Catechumens will not yet be fully integrated into the community; they will be unsure of themselves, and perhaps unsure of their loyalty. They need not even necessarily describe themselves as Christians when the fatal question ('Are you a Christian?') comes; arguably, they are not Christians yet. They can, perhaps, be easily scared off. But the authorities have reckoned without Perpetua.

Perpetua and her companions are exactly the sort of catechumens to ruin such a policy. Despite the hardships of the stifling, overcrowded, pitch-dark prison into which they are thrown, even the gently reared Perpetua quickly adjusts. The circle support one another in prayer and by means of Perpetua's visions, the wider Christian community supports them by furnishing the necessary bribes to allow them periodic spells in a better part of the prison, and their morale is high. Called to trial, all confess, including Perpetua, to being Christians, despite her father's attempts to persuade her otherwise. Brought into the amphitheatre before the beasts, they display courage and resolution; in Perpetua's case, as we shall see, she gets the better of everyone involved in her death. Perpetua and her companions have made a mockery of judicial attempts to make an example of them, or so the narrative would have us believe; they have proved that even novice Christians can die an exemplary death.

The theological context of the *Passion*

The anonymous editor of the *Martyrdom* tells us:

> If the former examples of faith served both as a witness to the grace of God and for the bringing about of the upbuilding of humankind, and they were set forth in letters precisely because of this, so that by reading them, re-presenting as it were the events, God might be honoured and humankind

be comforted, why should not also new documents fitting to both these ends be produced? At least for this reason, that they too will sometime be old and necessary for those who come after, though in their own present time they are reckoned to be of less authority because of this presumed respect for antiquity. But let those who judge the one power of the one Holy Spirit on the basis of times and ages consider this: that the more recent things are to be thought the greater, precisely because they are the newest, in accordance with the superiority of grace that has been decreed for the last ages of the world.

'For in the latter days, the Lord says, I shall pour out from my Spirit on all flesh, and their sons and daughters shall prophesy; and on my slaves and maidservants I shall pour out from my Spirit; and the young shall see visions and the old shall dream dreams.' [Acts 2:17–18]

Therefore we too, who both acknowledge and honour the promise of new prophecies and equally the new visions, and reckon the rest of the deeds of power of the Holy Spirit to be for the use of the Church (to which the same Spirit was sent to administer all gifts to all, as the Lord distributes to each), necessarily both write and celebrate them in reading for the glory of God, lest any weakness of faith or despair should deem that the grace of the Godhead dwelt only among those of old, whether in the dignity of martyrdoms, or in that of revelations, since God always works those things which he promised as a witness to unbelievers and as a benefit to believers.

The document that the anonymous editor goes on to present does in fact beautifully illustrate the Acts quotation paraphrasing Joel 2:28. We see Perpetua and Saturus prophesying, the former that they will be condemned to death (4.10), the latter that only the leopard and not the other beasts will attack him (19.4; 21.1–2). We see the slaves Felicity and Revocatus bravely face their martyrdom, and Felicity miraculously give birth to her child a month early, so she can die with her fellow Christians, and not later, on her own, with only criminals for company (15.1–7). The young woman, Perpetua, sees visions, as does Saturus, who is likely to be senior in some sense, as he is catechist to the little group of *adulescentes catechumeni*.

But the argument of the editor has given many scholars pause, because it employs the technical vocabulary of Montanism, otherwise known as the 'New Prophecy'.[10] Against the general drift of antique thought, which held that long-standing customs and long-hallowed texts were venerable and recent ones highly suspect, Montanism taught that the Holy Spirit was speaking anew through three prophets from small villages in Phrygia, two of whom were women.

Montanism's most famous adherent was Tertullian. Despite his apparent misogyny, he was happy to accept the prophetic visions of the New Prophecy women Priscilla and Maximilla, as well as local female visionaries in Carthage.

---

[10] For the claim that the whole *Passion* – including wraparound narrative, Perpetua's diary and Saturus' vision – is Montanist to the core, see Butler, *New Prophecy*. On Montanism in general, see Christine Trevett, *Montanism: Gender, Authority and the New Prophecy* (Cambridge: Cambridge University Press, 1996).

For as far as he was concerned, the Holy Spirit was preaching discipline and an end to laxity: no remarriage, even after the death of a spouse, more rigorous fasting, and veils down to the waist for females, not the light head-coverings typical of Roman women. If, as has been claimed above, he is not the author of the *Passion*, he still provides an important witness to the nature of Montanism in Carthage, and hence to the milieu in which the introduction to the *Passion*, at least, may be situated.[11]

It is sometimes argued that Montanism brought about the closing of the New Testament canon, precisely because of the kind of argument used by the editor of the *Passion*: new revelations and prophecies are at least equal to, if not greater than, former ones, and should be written down and shared for general edification. However, before we relegate Perpetua to the realms of schism or even heresy, we should pause and note an important question: not the familiar one of 'Why were the Montanists condemned?', but 'When were the Montanists condemned?'

It is now largely agreed, since Douglas Powell's article 'Tertullianists and Cataphrygians', that the Montanists long co-existed as part of the Carthaginian church before they were expelled, which may not even have happened during Tertullian's lifetime. The sect known as the Tertullianistae encountered by Augustine at the beginning of the fifth century would in that case not have been started directly by him, but would only have taken their inspiration from him. There were certainly clear divisions in the Carthaginian church, as Saturus' vision bears witness (13.1–6), but they had not yet become irrevocable.[12]

However, even those who accept that this was the situation in Carthage well into the third century generally think that Montanism had been well and truly condemned in Asia Minor in the 170s, and in Rome shortly after-wards.[13] Yet this depends simply on Eusebius of Caesarea, and the anti-Montanist tracts he quotes from (which are themselves difficult to date; only his anonymous anti-Montanist pamphlet gives clear signs of coming from the early days of the movement). Despite all our reasons to mistrust Eusebius (and we know that he hated the kind of theology the Montanists represent), scholars are still timid about questioning his universalizing *obiter dicta*, especially when they appear to give us a picture of an overweening, repressive Catholic Church. Butler tells us that 'the larger church and its representatives harassed the Montanists wherever they thrived',[14] but it is far from clear that the 'larger church' in Asia Minor was in agreement over the New Prophecy in its early stages. The zealous bishops mentioned in Eusebius'

---

[11] On Tertullian's Montanism, see Barnes, *Tertullian*, 130–142; Douglas Powell, 'Tertullianists and Cataphrygians', *Vigiliae Christianae* 29 (1975) 33–54; Trevett, *Montanism*.

[12] In Saturus' vision, the angels tell Optatus, the bishop of Carthage, to correct his layfolk, because they behave like crowds coming home from the chariot races, fighting over the different teams (13.6).

[13] This is the position of Trevett, *Montanism*, which is also implicitly adopted in Butler, *New Prophecy*.

[14] Butler, *New Prophecy*, 22.

early anonymous anti-Montanist tract are few (Zoticus of Cumana and Julian of Apamea are mentioned),[15] and matched by large centres where Montanism was enthusiastically welcomed (Thyateira, Ancyra). It is clear that the New Prophecy was the subject of heated debate in the late 170s, but it is not obvious that a majority of local bishops condemned the movement at this point; Irenaeus (who at least had local links) would appear to be defending it well into the 180s. Serapion of Antioch, at the turn of the century, is still having to make a concerted effort to get a synod to condemn the movement, while the Roman condemnation may also have been very recent.

I think we can argue, therefore, that the kind of local condemnation of the Montanists in the province of Asia in the 170s that Eusebius presents in Book V of his *Ecclesiastical History* was neither as widespread nor as complete as he and some of his sources pretend. This is perhaps reflected in the introduction to the *Passion*, which depicts the gifts of the Spirit as given universally for the use of the Church. There is a defensive edge to this passage, certainly, but both that defensiveness and Saturus' vision of Perpetua making peace in Greek between the bishop Optatus and the presbyter Aspasius suggest a community under strain, but not yet torn apart irrevocably. If this was true in Carthage, it may still have been true in the churches of Asia Minor also.

What we are left with, then, is an Irenaean vision of a Spirit doing deeds of power in all Christians, for all Christians, and for a witness to unbelievers. And this precisely matches the theology of Perpetua that emerges from her sections of the narrative.[16]

Perpetua's theology

If the editor of the *Passion* can easily be dismissed as a Montanist, Perpetua can be and often is dismissed as neurotic, indeed, a wilful suicide. The kind of pop-Freudian psychological analysis proposed by E. R. Dodds in his *Pagans and Christians in an Age of Anxiety* is at one level horribly plausible. Rebellion against her father would seem to be Perpetua's driving impetus. Her dreams are full of obvious phallic symbols (the serpent lifting his head (4.7)) and

---

[15] In Eusebius, *Historia Ecclesiastica* 5.16.17.

[16] Butler has argued that the visions of Perpetua have too many features in common with Montanism for her to have been anything but a Montanist. He produces some interesting parallels with Tertullian's writings, though the influence could as easily be Perpetua's on Tertullian as vice versa. But the features he picks out can all be paralleled in 'mainstream' late second-century Christian works, including those of Irenaeus and Athenagoras. Butler's analysis ultimately depends on the assumption that by the early third century the mainstream church would not have allowed a woman to do the things Perpetua is described as doing. But what Perpetua does – having private visions and praying in private – is actually perfectly innocuous. She neither preaches nor prophesies publicly, nor does she baptize – all of which the mainstream *Acts of Paul and Thecla* describe Thecla as doing.

breast-feeding fantasies (4.9–10), not to mention one of Antiquity's clearest examples of penis envy (10.7). These things are clearly there in Perpetua's dreams, which is one of the things that makes them so believable.[17] But Perpetua's own theology will, I believe, serve as the best answer to the criticisms implied by these observations, that she is 'really' choosing martyrdom for some motive other than her commitment to Christianity.

Perpetua's doctrine of God is spelled out in a conversation with her father. Here, in one of several passages where he is trying to persuade her to give in to the authorities, he acts like an ancient caricature of a woman, weeping and kissing Perpetua's hand and falling at her feet, unable to accept her fate. She, meanwhile, is grieved for him, because 'alone of all my kin, he would not rejoice at my passion' (5.6). Modern sensibilities are with Perpetua's father, but ancient ones, at least in theory, would have been with her position, when she says '*Hoc fiet in illa castata quod Deus voluerit; scito enim nos non in nostra esse potestate constitutos, sed in Dei*': 'Let what God wills happen on that tribunal; for know that we have not been placed in our own power, but in that of God.' It is Perpetua who shows courage and resolution in the face of the threat of death, and a sense of Providence while her father pleads for her to think of his reputation.

We might flesh out her doctrine further from the content of her dreams, although, or perhaps even because, it is difficult to tell whether the ageing, grey-haired figure in her first dream is meant to be Christ or the Father (4.8). The grey-haired shepherd welcomes her as his child, and feeds her quasi-Eucharistic curds into her cupped hands. Saturus has a similarly ambivalent vision of a white-haired man with a youthful face (12.3).

Her doctrine of Christ can be summed up by her claim '*fabulari cum Domino*', 'to chat with the Lord' (with connotations of sitting around swapping stories), 'from whom I had experienced such great benefits' (4.2). All Perpetua's divine relationships, like her human ones, have a familial ring to them in her accounts. Even when Christ appears to her as a *lanista*, a gladiator-trainer, he still kisses her and calls her 'daughter' when she wins her fight (10.13).

Despite the editor's interest in the Holy Spirit, Perpetua describes her visions as coming from the Lord rather than the Spirit, although she may not intend to make a very clear distinction. When she does mention the Spirit, it is at her baptism, and the Spirit dictates to her what to seek in her post-baptismal prayer (3.5; cf. Rom 8:26).

Her view of her own Christian calling, and of the Christian community, is simple but powerful. The very first point she makes in her own section of

---

[17] Bremmer, 'Perpetua', 95–96, criticizes Patricia Cox Miller (*Dreams in Late Antiquity*, Princeton: Princeton University Press, 1994) for neglecting Perpetua's own interpretation of her dreams, and replacing the 'premises of the past' by the 'prison of the present'. He is right that the conclusions of pop-Freudianism are banal, but he misses the important point that if the dreams work well in an entirely different interpretive system from any the ancients would have recognized, that is surely good evidence that they are real, rather than invented, dreams.

the narrative (3.1–2), before she is even baptized, is that the name of Christian describes completely what she is. There is no other name by which she can now be called, so that when she finally says the fatal words '*Christiana sum*' to Hilarianus the procurator, they are now no more than a simple statement of fact, a confession not only of the name of Christ, but of her own nature.

The most striking feature of Perpetua's theology, however, is the way she sees herself within the context of a divine family, which also includes her family in the flesh. The shepherd calls her 'child' (4.9), the gladiator-trainer calls her 'daughter' (10.13), and the narrator sees her as the '*matrona Christi*', as the '*delicata Dei*' (18.2). Meanwhile, she is alternately grieved for and delighted by the various members of her family in the flesh. She is conscious of her father's affection for her, even when he pushes her to rejoice in his absence (3.4). She worries about and then breastfeeds her baby (3.6–8). She tries to comfort her mother and brother, and shares her hope with her catechumen brother, who seems to see her as a kind of spiritual 'big sister' (3.8, 4.1–2), as well, probably, as a literal one. Her concern for her family extends to her dead brother Dinocrates, whom she wants to see restored to childlike playfulness (8.4), a playfulness and certainly a childlike quality she seems to share.

This 'building the family of God' quality appears still more strongly when we look at the impact of Perpetua's character on those around her. And this brings us to one of the most interesting points about Perpetua as she emerges from the *Passion*. Her own diary is almost infantile, full of straightforward emotions of happiness and sadness, fear and grief, desire to comfort others and be welcomed by them. But the real impact of her personality appears in the accounts of the others, the narrator and Saturus.

In the case of Saturus, so far as we can tell from his own dream, Perpetua is the only one of his catechumens he is really interested in (though perhaps he is returning the compliment of his own appearance in her dreams). He and she are welcomed into heaven by martyrs, angels, elders and the white-haired fresh-faced man, and even more welcomed by the bishop and presbyter of the community they have left behind them (13.1–2). The two throw themselves at the feet of Perpetua and her catechist, begging them to make peace between them, and lamenting their departure. Although both Saturus and Perpetua are addressed by them and embrace them, Perpetua seems to be accorded the lead role in the peacemaking in Saturus' vision. Her childlike character is also alluded to, though, in the elders' command to her to 'play' (12.6), and her speaking of her own hilarity before and after death (12.7).

But it is the narrator who presents her most clearly as an extraordinary woman. Perpetua herself presents herself at moments as a tough and determined character, trampling on the serpent's head and kick-boxing with the Egyptian. But for the narrator, she is the '*sanctissima Perpetua*' (16.1), '*tanta femina*' (21.10), whom evil spirits fear. She defeats all those with whom she comes in contact. The tribune shuts the party up for fear of magical attempts to release them (16.2). Perpetua stares him in the face and demands better treatment, which she gets (16.4). While walking into the amphitheatre, she forces all onlookers to lower their gaze before the vigour of her own (18.2). She demands the right for the Christians not to be dressed in the robes of priests of Saturn and priestesses of Ceres while in the arena, and once again obtains her request (18.6). '*Agnovit iniustitia iustitiam*' – this was the concession Justin Martyr tried so hard for, probably in vain.

The planned big spectacle with the women in the end falls flat. Perpetua and Felicity are brought out nearly naked, but the crowd, ferocious in their treatment of the men, demand and get better treatment for the women; they are given dresses to wear (20.2–3). A maddened cow tossed the two of them around, but Perpetua sits up, fixes her dress, fixes her hair, gets up and goes and lifts up Felicity, and stands with her hand in hand in the middle of the arena (20.6). And in that gesture her theology of the family of God is most perfectly encapsulated. The young *matrona*, well born, and liberally educated, who chose to throw her lot in with slaves and criminals and be their mother and sister and daughter, is to be brought down by the Roman judicial and gubernatorial system, as a class traitor and a family traitor, and made an example of. But she brings the judicial system down, and brings her companions up, lifting Felicity from the dust to stand beside her, undefeated, *matrona* and slave together. And thus they defeat the crowd too, whose harshness is overcome, so they are called over to the Sanavivarian Gate – the gate to the amphitheatre known locally as the 'gate of health and life' (20.7). She preaches to the other catechumen and to her brother one last time, telling them to stand in the faith, love one another and not be scandalized by her death (20.10), and then they are all called back into the middle to be finished off. They walk there of their own accord, and embrace with a final kiss of peace (21.7). Perpetua even has to guide the dagger of the novice gladiator to her throat, so incapable are her enemies of showing any resolution against her.

If Perpetua is not the early church's greatest theologian, what she has going for her is yet something fairly rare: we have convincing portraits of both her family and her public life, and they add up. The indomitable, loving, caring, playful character we meet in her diary and her dreams is the indomitable, loving, caring, playful character we meet in Saturus' dream and the narrative of her passion, though inevitably in different measures. It was a character which clearly brought a great deal to the Carthaginian church she was joining, short as was her time as a baptized Christian. And in her notion of the family of God, which she both fervently believed in and passionately tried to build, I think we do find a genuine and characteristic theology. Perpetua and her narrator clearly both believed they belonged to a charismatic church, full of visions and deeds of power, as well as prophecy and the call to bear witness with one's life. But it may be that other aspects of Perpetua's theology are still more striking, and still more indicative of some of the lost theological voices of the early church.

Bibliography

Editions

Jacqueline Amat, *Passion de Perpétue et de Félicité, suivi des Actes*, Sources chrétiennes (Paris: du Cerf, 1996).

Herbert Musurillo, *The Acts of the Christian Martyrs*, Oxford Early Christian Texts (Oxford: Oxford University Press, 1972) 106–131.

Studies

Timothy David Barnes, *Tertullian, A Historical and Literary Study* (Oxford: Clarendon Press, 1971; 2nd edn, 1985).

Jan N. Bremmer, 'Perpetua and Her Diary: Authenticity, Family and Visions', in Walter Ameling (ed.), *Märtyrer und Märtyrerakten* (Wiesbaden: Franz Steiner Verlag, 2002) 77–120.

Rex D. Butler, *The New Prophecy & 'New Visions', Evidence of Montanism in* The Passion of Perpetua and Felicitas (Washington: Catholic University of America Press, 2006).

Gillian Cloke, '*Mater* or Martyr: Christianity and the Alienation of Women within the Family in the Later Roman Empire', *Theology and Sexuality* 5 (1996) 37–57.

E. R. Dodds, *Pagan and Christian in an Age of Anxiety, Some Aspects of Religious Experience from Marcus Aurelius to Constantine* (Cambridge: Cambridge University Press, 1968), chapter 2 ('Man and the Demonic World').

R. S. Kraemer and S. L. Lander, 'Perpetua and Felicitas', in *The Early Christian World*, Philip F. Esler (ed.), 2 vols (London: Routledge, 2000), vol. 2, 1048–1068.

Sara Maitland, *The Martyrdom of Perpetua* (Evesham: Arthur James, 1996) [with commentary and Shewring's translation of 1931].

Judith Perkins, *The Suffering Self, Pain and Narrative Representation in the Early Christian Era* (London: Routledge, 1995) 104–123.

D. Potter, 'Martyrdom as Spectacle', in *Theater and Society in the Classical World*, ed. Ruth Scodel (Ann Arbor: University of Michigan Press, 1993) 53–88.

J. Rives, 'The Piety of a Persecutor', *Journal of Early Christian Studies* 4 (1996) 1–25.

Louis Robert, 'Une vision de Perpétue martyre à Carthage en 203', *Comptes rendus de l'Académie des Inscriptions et Belles-Lettres* (1982) 228–276; reprinted in Robert, *Opera Minora Selecta*, vol. v (Amsterdam: Hakkert, 1989), no. 130, 791–839.

Joyce E. Salisbury, *Perpetua's Passion, The Death and Memory of a Young Roman Woman* (London: Routledge, 1997).

Christine Trevett, *Montanism: Gender, Authority and the New Prophecy* (Cambridge: Cambridge University Press, 1996).

8

Origen

REBECCA LYMAN

Introduction

Origen was a controversial spiritual teacher, biblical scholar and priest in the early third century in Alexandria and Caesarea. He produced an unprecedented number of commentaries, homilies, a major apology and the first comprehensive theology. Reading scripture allegorically was the primary means of encountering the living Word, and therefore the accessible way of transformation for all Christians. The son of a martyr, he was later tortured for his faith. Pronounced a heretic after his death, yet also continually defended and read for his theological brilliance and exegetical insight, he remains an uneasy ancestor for Christians as unfailingly faithful and original.

He came of age during a transitional period of pre-Nicene Christianity as smaller house churches and charismatic teachers gave way to larger assemblies and clearer lines of clerical authority and theological orthodoxy. Although he was very well educated in scripture and philosophy, he never mentioned the urbane Clement of Alexandria as a teacher, though he knew his work; given Origen's critical stance toward contemporary culture, Henry Chadwick famously contrasted them as the 'Liberal Puritan' and the 'Illiberal Humanist'.[1] As a tireless scriptural commentator, speculative theologian and devoted teacher, Origen embodied intellectually the intense sectarian faith of the third-century church of martyrs and converts. Shaped by debates with rabbis, 'Gnostic' Christians and philosophers, as well as tempered by conflicts with bishops and less intellectually gifted Christians, he developed his own optimistic cosmology of salvation through the incarnate Word.

Life

In his *Ecclesiastical History* Eusebius of Caesarea devoted most of the sixth book to the life and writing of Origen. This was originally part of an apology written on behalf of Origen after his death by the teacher of Eusebius, Pamphilus. The account like any ancient biography of a revered thinker is not intended to be objective, and often borders on hagiography; by contrast

---

[1] H. Chadwick, *Early Christian Tradition and the Classical Tradition* (Oxford: Oxford University Press, 1966).

an account by the heresiologist Epiphanius several decades later is almost entirely hostile. In addition we have two letters of Origen and an account of his teaching by a student in Caesarea, later identified as Gregory Thaumaturgus. These documents together with his many writings make Origen one of the better-known figures in the period before Nicaea. The outline of Origen's life is accepted by most scholars, though certain episodes remain controversial because of conflicting sources.[2] He was born into a Greek-Egyptian Christian family of some means around 185, and was well educated in scripture as well as Greek literature, philosophy and science. Alexandria was the second city of the Roman Empire in size and importance, and a cultural and economic crossroads including Greek, Egyptian, Jewish and Indian thought. According to Eusebius, Origen's father recognized his precocious intellect early and taught him great amounts of scripture as well as traditional Hellenic texts, often gazing upon him while he slept, and kissing the divine genius in his breast. Since as a child Isaac Newton measured the wind by leaping into it, we need not entirely doubt Origen was a gifted child, even if the story centres on the charismatic nature of his abilities.[3] The second story from his teenage years underscores another trait of Origen, that is, zeal. His father was arrested during the persecutions under Septimius Severus and was eventually martyred around 203. According to Eusebius, Origen was wild to follow his example, but his mother prevented this by hiding his clothes. Brilliance, zeal and modesty were thus early characteristics of intellectual charism as told by Eusebius; according to Epiphanius these qualities were precisely what got Origen into eventual trouble through intellectual speculation.[4]

Unlike the dramatic conversion story of Augustine's misspent youth, Origen's life seemed marked by consistent and deepening commitment to God through study. After his father's death and the confiscation of family property, he became the sole support of his family, and continued his education through the patronage of a wealthy woman. Although a notorious heretic was also resident in her household, Eusebius assured us that Origen never joined him for prayer, which is an interesting insight on early ecumenism. Origen trained as a *grammateus* in order to teach Greek literature, learning traditional Alexandrian arts of textual criticism, word study and interpretation. In addition he studied philosophy with Ammonius Saccas, a famous Platonist, though the traditional connections between Origen and Plotinus must be

---

[2] P. Nautin provided a critical review of Eusebius and his sources in *Origène: Sa vie et son oeuvre* (Paris: Beauchesne, 1977). H. Crouzel took a more traditional approach in *Origen* (Edinburgh: T&T Clark, 1989), 1–87. J. Trigg provides a helpful recent synthesis in *Origen* (London: Routledge, 1998), 3–66.

[3] *HE* 6.2.10–11. On the charismatic nature of the stories see P. Cox Miller, *Biography in Late Antiquity: A Quest for the Holy Man* (Berkeley, CA: University of California Press, 1983). Newton's story of his childhood is in R. Westfall, *Never at Rest* (Cambridge: Cambridge University Press, 1980), 62.

[4] *HE* 6.2.5; Epiphanius, *Panarion* 64.1–5.

revised.[5] He also learned Jewish exegesis including the work of Philo, perhaps through his Hebrew teacher whom he mentions with gratitude as opening his eyes to the unity and depth of the Bible.[6] After some of his students and companions were martyred during a renewal of persecution, Origen decided to devote himself exclusively to studying scripture and an ascetic lifestyle; he sold his secular books. This event through the lens of Eusebius seems to be a Christian form of a philosophical conversion in the third century. Spiritual and intellectual life were considered as one in Antiquity, marked by the intense study of texts, a circle of students and ascetic living. A teacher (*didaskalos*) therefore was a spiritual guide as much as an intellectual mentor.[7] At this time Origen allegedly castrated himself either through drugs or an operation; this was an extreme, but not unknown, practice. Curiously, Eusebius sympathetically defends the story, but Epiphanius doubts it. Origen later rejected the practice in his exegesis of Matthew 19:12, so scholars remain divided as to whether this was an actual ascetic choice or a later slander.[8]

Significantly, the Bishop of Alexandria, Demetrius, officially appointed Origen to be a catechist, which seems to mark not the existence of a formal 'Christian School' as often claimed in Alexandria but rather the increasing control of Christian teachers by the bishop for the first time. In the wake of the exegetical debates with Valentinus and other Christian thinkers, the orthodox communities increasingly restricted and tested teaching authority. In this century not only Origen but also widows would be censured for their teaching; the right of laity to preach or speak would also be debated as communities were increasingly organized on more clerical lines.[9] Recent scholarship has increasingly focused on the importance of texts, teachers and exegesis in establishing and maintaining Christian identity in Late Antiquity, so Origen was claiming a central and significant, if shifting, role within the Alexandrian church. His dedication to sophisticated reflection as well as the instruction of the less educated in the assembly was not an easy task, and earned him consistent charges of heterodoxy and elitism over the course of his life. As Henri Crouzel commented, '... a more elitist attitude would have brought him more serenity and real disdain would have brought him more rest'.[10]

In addition to the catechetical school, he created an advanced school in Christian exegesis and instruction to train students in philosophy, including

[5] See comments by M. Edwards, *Origen against Plato* (Aldershot: Ashgate, 2002), 53–55.

[6] Nautin discusses his identity in *Origène*, 132–33.

[7] P. Hadot, *Philosophy as a Way of Life* (Oxford: Blackwell, 1995); R. Valantasis, *Spiritual Guides of the Third Century* (Minneapolis, MN: Fortress, 1991).

[8] See discussion by J. McGuckin in *The Westminster Handbook to Origen* (Louisville, KY: Westminster John Knox, 2004), 6–7.

[9] U. Neymeyr, *Die Christlichen Lehrer im Zweiten Jahrhundert* (Leiden: Brill, 1989), 95–105; H. von Campenhausen, *Ecclesiastical Authority and Spiritual Power* (Stanford, CA: Stanford University Press, 1969), 238–64.

[10] Crouzel, *Origen*, 115; G. af. Hällström, *Fides simpliciorum according to Origen of Alexandria* (Helsinki: Societas Scientiarum Fennica, 1984).

mathematics and astronomy. In a later letter Origen described the use of Greco-Roman wisdom as the 'spoils of the Egyptians' which could be drawn upon with care after proper instruction to understand and explore Christian wisdom.[11] He also began his prodigious life's labour of producing over two thousand works. This was aided by Ambrose, a patron who paid for scribes to copy his lectures into papyrus; these writings and their corruption both aided and damaged his reputation.[12] Origen completed the *Hexapla*, a comparative table of Greek and Hebrew versions of the Old Testament, *On First Principles*, which was both a complete theology and a declaration of his theological and exegetical foundations, and began his *Commentary on John* in response to a Gnostic commentary by Heracleon and also a *Commentary on Genesis*. He travelled widely, going to Rome to hear one of the leading theologians of the day, Hippolytus, and also to Athens. He was sought out by others including meeting in Antioch with the mother of the emperor, Julia Mammaea. During a journey to Caesarea, he was ordained by the local bishop. Motivated by jealousy and anger over a violation of his own authority, Demetrius objected to Origen's ordination as illegal. Charges of heterodoxy as well as references to castration emerged, and an Egyptian synod deprived him of his priesthood.[13]

As a result Origen left Alexandria in 234 with his library and set up a new school in Caesarea. His continued interaction with the local rabbinic community over textual and exegetical issues revealed a mutual influence and rivalry.[14] For his patron Ambrose, he wrote treatises on prayer and martyrdom as well as continuing his *Commentary on John*. In 248 he wrote a lengthy response to the philosophical critic of Christianity, Celsus. Not surprisingly, he was controversial again in Caesarea because of his use of Hebrew scriptures and his complex cosmology which included teaching on pre-existent souls. The majority of his extant homilies date from this time and range from extemporaneous to prepared speeches; they may reveal a shifting emphasis from speculation to more spiritual devotion.[15] The transcription of a dialogue concerning the suspect views of a bishop (*Dialogue with Heraclides*) revealed Origen in the role of theological examiner whose subtlety at times confounded as much as clarified. During the persecution of Decius in 250, Origen was imprisoned and tortured. He eventually died as a result. His library was

---

[11] *Letter of Origen to Gregory* 3.2.
[12] On scribes and control of texts see Kim Haines-Eitzen, *Guardians of Letters: Literacy, Power, and Transmitters of Early Christian Literature* (Oxford: Oxford University Press, 2000); Origen complained about an altered discussion being circulated by a heretic in a letter preserved by Jerome quoted in Crouzel, *Origen*, 20.
[13] Crouzel reviews the varied accounts in *Origen*, 21–23.
[14] Paul Blowers, 'Origen, the Rabbis and the Bible: Toward a Picture of Judaism and Christianity in Third Century Caesarea', in C. Kannengiesser and W. Petersen (eds), *Origen of Alexandria: His World and His Legacy* (Notre Dame, IN: University of Notre Dame Press, 1988), 96–116; M. Hirschman, *A Rivalry of Genius: Jewish and Christian Biblical Interpretation in Late Antiquity* (Albany, NY: State University of New York Press, 1996).
[15] M. Harl, *Origène et la fonction révélatrice* (Paris: Seuil, 1958), 362.

preserved and expanded by Pamphilus and Eusebius. His tomb was visible in Tyre until the twelfth century.

Writings

With the aid of his patrons and scribes, Origen may have been one of the most prolific writers in Antiquity.[16] Although the majority of his work is lost or fragmented – a 'smoldering ruin' is a recent apt description[17] – we possess an astonishing range of material from scriptural exegesis to theology to pastoral works. This diversity of genre, breadth of material, fragmented condition, contested theological legacy and his own method of tentative or multiple conclusions has led modern scholars to proceed cautiously in their interpretation of his work. Many of the criticisms of his theology were based on what he must have concluded from certain premises rather than what he actually taught. De Lubac commented that the safest course was to watch Origen work rather than assume particular techniques or outcomes.[18]

Scripture: commentaries and homilies

Devoted to scripture as the incarnate revelation of transcendent divine truth, Origen was primarily a biblical exegete, and the majority of his extant works are commentaries or homilies about the Old and New Testaments. Especially in the past two centuries with the prevalence of the historical critical method as the highest tool of biblical exegesis and continuing suspicion about his philosophical interests, Origen as an allegorist has often been criticized, if not scorned, for overly spiritual and arbitrary interpretations.[19] Recent attention to diverse literary methodologies both in Antiquity and throughout Christian tradition has revised this assessment to recover Origen's literary methodologies and interest in the spiritual abundance of a text. A single historical reading was never the point of his work. As set out in his explanation of scripture in *First Principles* 4, the plain style, confusing stories and hidden wisdom gave rise to many distortions and mythologies from those who would interpret only on a literal level to those who invent additional gods. Only scripture itself can be the guide to seeking the hidden divine wisdom; the places that appear to have little significance can be places to investigate deeper doctrines. These 'stumbling blocks' give the exegete the clue to search for a higher meaning. For Origen legitimate exegesis combines apostolic doctrine with the charismatic reading of scripture, but not all might agree with his understanding of the first or the second, that is, his exegesis of the nations as the

---

[16] Crouzel reproduces and discusses the list of Origen's works in a letter of Jerome, *Origen*, 37–59.

[17] McGuckin, *Handbook*, 25.

[18] H. de Lubac, *Histoire et Esprit* (Paris: Editions du Cerf, 1950), 34.

[19] See the introduction of Trigg to the new edition of R. P. C. Hanson, *Allegory and Event* (Louisville, KY: Westminster John Knox, 2002), i–xxv.

descent of souls.[20] However, this doctrinal model prevents the division of the Testaments as in Marcion or the blindness toward the prophecy of Christ by Jews. All levels of scripture are important to the task. Just as human beings were complex layers of different aspects of created existence, so was the Bible: 'For just as a man consists of body, soul and spirit, so in the same way does the scripture, which had been prepared by God to be given for human salvation.'[21] Equally important, scripture as the divine Word has a unity and a sacramental presence, 'containing outward forms of certain mysteries and images of divine things'.[22] This divine presence seeks the reader as much as the reader seeks God: 'The whole Word of God indeed, that which was with God in the beginning, is not many words, for it is not words; for it is one word subsisting under many notions, every one of which notions is a part of the whole word.'[23]

Trained in the traditions of Alexandrian grammar as well as in allegorical exegesis, Origen then created a body of work with consistent attention to the sophisticated exegetical techniques of his day as well as to his own process of spiritual ascent. In Late Antiquity communities of philosophers, Jews and Christians focused on texts and formed around teachers, so that Origen reflected this culture, and profoundly shaped it for those who came after him through his commenting on practically all biblical texts for spiritual progress.[24] He wrote scholia, commentaries and homilies: 21 homilies are extant in Greek and 120 in Latin translation. Sizeable portions of his commentaries on John, Matthew, Romans and the Song of Songs remain, along with numerous catenae. Origen's most famous product of textual criticism in the tradition of the school of grammar in Alexandria is not extant: the *Hexapla*, a copy of Old Testament translations and versions in Greek and Hebrew in six columns.

Origen's practice of exegesis in his commentaries and homilies integrated contemporary practices with Christian spirituality. He included the grammarian's attention to words and the proper reading of a text as well as the allegorical or figural analysis of the hidden wisdom. Words, once established through textual criticism, had important and complex etymologies, and could be linked to other words in other parts of scripture to reveal new insights. From these links and narratives, the exegete began to reflect on the moral meaning of the text and how this could teach the discipline and virtue of the soul from the particular context. Throughout these moves Origen's own understanding of God and the economy of salvation forms the background

---

[20] *Princ* 4.3.10–12.
[21] *Princ* 4.2.4.
[22] *Princ* Pref 8.
[23] *Philocalia* 5.4 in M. Edwards, 'Christ or Plato? Origen on Revelation and Anthropology', in L. Ayres and G. Jones (eds), *Christian Origins: Theology, Rhetoric and Community* (London: Routledge, 1998), 20.
[24] A. Grafton and M. Williams, *Christianity and the Transformation of the Book: Origen, Eusebius and the Library of Caesarea* (Harvard, MA: Belknap Press of Harvard University Press, 2006), 86–132.

for understanding issues of divine activity or human behaviour. Finally, one could then seek the layer of interpretation that was the spiritual meaning of the text; this revelation of divine knowledge or insight about the means of divine presence drew one closer to God.[25]

As recently described by Mark Edwards, Origen 'is not presenting us with a single reading, ecclesiastical or spiritual, but as it were with a hermeneutic rainbow, spanning the interval through which the soul must fly through the wings of knowledge'.[26] Origen's care in distinguishing the readings and the levels was a means of nourishing the entire person or an entire congregation in this exercise of soul-making, linked to asceticism, repentance, openness to God. This emphasis on multiplicity and process is important since Origen has sometimes been faulted for not moving systematically through one or two levels of the text. However, the major point of Origen's exegesis was the transformation of the individual as a whole, so that moral and spiritual teaching worked reciprocally in order to strengthen both virtue and vision.[27] The scripture as a whole in its varied levels therefore was a model of spiritual transformation just as the Word itself in its incarnation and presence in teaching was also an instructor.[28]

Stylistically, Origen appears as one always in pursuit of new insight through the immediacy of the text at hand. Within his method rarely can a text be uninteresting or unimportant. He is like a theological rock climber who is anxious to move from point to point in pursuit of a deeper meaning now revealed by the Logos. Less skilled climbers found it hard to keep up or had less confidence in the narrow crevices as a place of support, but Origen's example of confidence, utility and humility in spiritual exegesis inspired many from the Cappadocians to Bernard of Clairvaux: 'What does it profit me to say that Christ has come to earth only in the flesh he received from Mary, if I do not show that he has also come in my flesh?'[29]

On First Principles

Modelled on contemporary philosophical and theological works, Origen set out in 220 in Alexandria to expound apostolic teaching as comprehensively as possible with reference to cosmology, anthropology and eschatology as well as exegesis. Michael Williams has argued that rather than debate our understanding of 'Gnosticism' as a pejorative label for constructions of salvation which may have included dualism or divine election, we should understand a larger philosophical crisis of the second century in which arguments about

---

[25] Trigg discusses Simonetti's analysis of three principles of utility (spiritual use), ideology (relation to Christ) and structure (ascent from sensible to intelligible levels) in *Origen*, 35.

[26] Edwards, *Origen against Plato*, 142–43.

[27] E. A. Dively Lauro, *The Soul and Spirit of Scripture within Origen's Exegesis* (Leiden: Brill, 2005), 239.

[28] K. J. Torjesen, *Hermeneutical Procedure and Theological Method in Origen's Exegesis* (Berlin: De Gruyter, 1986).

[29] *Hom Gen* 3.7 quoted in Crouzel, *Origen*, 76.

the relation of the transcendent god to the material world were cast into cosmological form with a emphasis on mediation.[30] Origen's own work which addresses creation, fall, incarnation, the nature of the soul and the restoration of creation fits into such a crisis, and self-consciously with regard to both philosophers and other Christians including 'Gnostic' systems and Marcion's separation of the gods of the Old and New Testaments. In the preface Origen noted the diversity of opinions among Christians, set out the apostolic teaching of the church, and then outlined questions that remained unanswered. In his view these mysteries in apostolic tradition as in scripture were deliberate lures to encourage the search for God. Other questions such as human free will or the creation of the world had been affirmed by the church but not clearly explored or explained. His intention was then to set out a 'single body of doctrine' from scripture and reflection.

The structure of the work is complex, and echoes philosophical treatises on underlying principles of being. The preface set out the rule of faith, and the following part from 1.1 to 2.3 examined the three groups of the principles: God with the Son and Holy Spirit, the rational creatures, and the world. The second section from 2.4 to 4.3 answered the problems set out in the discussion of the rule of faith in the preface. The final section 4.4 was a new treatment of the three principles set out in the first section.[31] The contents and structure combine philosophical analysis and exposition as well as the economy of salvation from the life of the Trinity to the restoration of all in a final eschatology. As often noted the work was not intended to be a systematic theology, but rather an exploratory piece of foundational principles. In several places Origen suggested answers to questions for the sake of conceptual clarity rather than a final answer, such as the controversial pre-existence of souls as a means to ensure free will.[32] The text has been preserved mainly in a Latin translation by Rufinus, who in places updated some of Origen's expressions to match his own contemporary orthodoxy. This has been supplemented by excerpts from the *Philocalia* in Greek, notably Book 3 on free will. More controversial are Greek fragments from a variety of sources, some hostile, which were placed in the text by P. Koetschau in his 1913 edition, and consequently translated into English by G. Butterworth.

Against Celsus; On Prayer; Exhortation to Martyrdom

Around 170 a Greco-Roman philosopher Celsus wrote a polemic, 'True Word', perhaps against the Word theology of Justin Martyr. This was the first and most extensive attack against Christian life and teaching which signalled some success in early Christian attempts to gain a hearing in the larger

---

[30] M. Williams, *Rethinking 'Gnosticism': An Argument for Dismantling a Dubious Category* (Princeton, NJ: Princeton University Press, 1996).
[31] For discussion of the structure of the work see Crouzel, *Origen*, 45–57, and Trigg, *Origen*, 18–35.
[32] *Princ* 2.8.4.

intellectual environment. Celsus portrayed Jesus as a magician, and Christians as disloyal toward the traditional religion and society of the Empire as well as credulous and ignorant. The work only exists through portions quoted by Origen in his refutation, but Celsus knew the New Testament and defended a conservative monotheism. Commissioned by his patron Ambrose, Origen's response in eight books contains most of his extant quotations or allusions to classical literature, and reveals his own theological interests more broadly than the ideas of Celsus. The major contrast he drew was between the human wisdom of philosophers and the revealed truth of scripture, though he was not afraid to address issues such as contradictions between gospels or weaknesses of the apostles. Origen expanded many of the earlier apologetic points that the very rustic character of the Bible or of the Christian movement testified to its divine origins and power. Christianity therefore by its accessibility and antiquity was revealed to be the truth.

Origen's works on prayer and martyrdom were also addressed to his patron Ambrose, and are a combination of textual analysis of scripture, theological argument and spiritual encouragement. The treatise on prayer included reflections on providence, formulae of prayer, including the Lord's Prayer, and an assurance as to the importance of human participation over against fatalism. He noted that prayer should be addressed to the Father through the Son. Not surprisingly, Origen as the son of a martyr outlined the importance of Christians remaining faithful to their baptism and standing steadily against persecution.

Theology

Divine goodness and human freedom

Like many theologians of his era, Origen was profoundly concerned with the question of theodicy, that is, why do bad things happen to good people if God is the good and just creator of all existence? For some the answer to this question lay in the imperfect limits of material being that prevented knowledge of the transcendent good, and therefore the inevitable existence of error and chaos. Fatalism was a persistent belief as well that events and fortunes were predetermined. Within Christian circles these contemporary questions had been addressed in several ways in the light of scripture. Marcion had taught that Jesus was the messenger of the hidden good God, and his mission was to deliver believers from the tyranny and injustice of the God of the Old Testament. This mediator and demiurge was falsely claiming worship through a system of harsh legalism. Other teachers such as Basilides or Valentinus also affirmed the transcendence and perfection of the original and good deity by identifying the God of the Old Testament with an inferior mediator, a demiurge, who was defeated and replaced by the incarnation of the Son. The Son revealed the hidden gospel of salvation that allowed individuals to awaken to their kinship with the original and hidden God, and therefore be finally reunited with an original perfection that had been ruptured in a cosmic fall. Material being seems to have been a sign of blindness and imperfection, so that created existence was catastrophic; salvation therefore was focused on spiritual awakening, and appeared to be an election theology in which only some persons recognized gnosis and therefore gained salvation.[33]

Origen's own account of creation, fall, Incarnation, and final eschatology was a sophisticated response to these models of divine life and human salvation in the light of contemporary philosophy and biblical exegesis. As argued most recently and strongly by Mark Edwards, Origen was not a Platonist, but a theologian brilliantly adapting contemporary forms in his cosmology. He accepted the apostolic teachings of one God, material creation, fall and human free will as foundational to his understanding of salvation. Building on these theological axioms, Origen ambitiously portrayed existence itself as the economy that revealed and contained the negotiation between divine love and human redemption. The spiritual necessities of goodness and freedom were then discussed over the contemporary metaphysical grid and vocabulary of the spiritual and material. While this process was outlined most clearly in *First Principles*, the basic pattern of creation and eschatology remains consistent through his exegetical works.

As set out in the first book of *First Principles* God as revealed in scripture was transcendent, incorporeal and creator of all existence. Origen is determined to protect God from material images in scripture that would compromise his transcendence or perfection. God is simple, invisible and incorporeal. In contrast to Marcion, God is not only just but also good, and the original good (Mark 10:18) of which the Son is the image. Through the Word, God created the world, and through providence continues to work for the benefit of humanity.[34] God as Trinity reflected distinct spheres of activity as Father, Son and Spirit, but shared a common harmony and will.[35]

Following the definitions of Justin and Irenaeus about the freedom of human beings developed over against 'Gnostic' theologians, Origen asserted that humans were all created in the image of God as free and in proximity to God. 'Predestination gives glory to God, but destroys our freedom,' he commented.[36] In a controversial move he described this original intimacy as spiritual, that is, appropriate to intimacy with the incorporeal nature of God, and the movement away therefore as toward material existence. Most crudely, Origen has appeared to look like a Gnostic in which a fall into bodies was a sign of sin, and therefore a dualist; or he is a Platonist affirming the pre-existence of souls without any biblical warrant. More sympathetically, we can see Origen recasting the fall story of Genesis into a cosmological explanation

---

[33] For a sympathetic and critical review of 'Gnostic' dualism or fatalism see Williams, *Rethinking 'Gnosticism'*.

[34] God's kindness and goodness in *Or* 29.13–14; creation in *Princ* 1.3.3.

[35] *Cel* 8.13; *Princ* 1.3.5.

[36] *Com Gen* = *PE* 6.11.

(demythologizing or remythologizing depending on your point of view): souls were created free, but turned away from God through boredom or neglect and fell into differing degrees of distance from God.[37] Angels are those who clung most closely, demons are those farthest away. What is highly significant here is the dynamic nature of bodies and evil based entirely on free will. In Origen's scheme there is no predestination to a certain nature or gap between humans and God apart from the will. The function of the economy of the Incarnation is to reverse this motion through the education and transformation of the will in order to restore souls to God. Origen is extremely careful to say that the teaching of pre-existent souls is a hypothesis since scripture gives no clear answer.[38] This emphasis on will rather than nature allows Origen to make the highly controversial claim that the possibility exists that even the devil could return, since it is only his will which separates him from God.

Critics of Origen, ancient and modern, found this account to be unnecessarily speculative and abstract. The definition of God as incorporeal seems to drag biblical history into heavenly cycles of error and away from biblical narratives or history. The focus on the origin and progress of the soul as free-willed may give less credence to the doctrine of grace. In Origen's defence we may return to a third-century context in which cosmological structures were the source and form of identity and debate. The point was not merely a coherent system, though he was later read and criticized on the basis of such connections, but rather a stretching and opening to the possibilities of divine life. The defence of divine goodness and human freedom was therefore an essential part of his exegetical work in teaching the means of moral progress and spiritual transformation. Judas' failure for example was not his betrayal of Jesus, but his despair; he doubted divine mercy, and did not turn again to God to be forgiven and strengthened.[39] For the Christian the process of drawing near to God was part of the movement of the universe: 'As sons of a patient God and brothers of a patient Christ, let us be patient in all that may happen to us.'[40]

Revelation and Incarnation

In Origen's optimistic cosmology of the incorporeal good God and the fallen human beings, the revelation and Incarnation of the Logos had a central epistemological and soteriological place. Following the structure of the Logos theology of the earlier Apologists, Origen in his exegetical works develops a rich and intimate exposition of the vibrant work of the self-communication of God through the many facets of the revealing Word in scripture and the Incarnation. In comparison to the simplicity of God the Father, the Son is the

---

[37] *Princ* 1.3.8.
[38] *Princ* 2.8.4. Edwards argues that Origen attributes only an instantaneous pre-existence, *Origen against Plato*, 160.
[39] *Comm Jo* 32.19.
[40] *Ex Mart* 43.

multifaceted revelation in order to reach the varied levels of comprehension. The titles (*epinoia*) of the Son as Wisdom, Vine, Shepherd or Door corresponded to the levels of spiritual growth of individuals.[41] The Son is the visible image of God, the mediator, and origin of all. If the Son is the subordinate agent of the Father, he shares his divinity through eternal generation.

The Incarnation is the supreme revelation of the love of God in becoming visible and accessible to all human beings. With regard to his humanity, Origen reiterates the full humanity in the Incarnation of soul and body. The human soul of Jesus was the only soul that did not fall away in the pre-cosmic disaster, but in fact clung to the Word in love: 'Since the faculty to choose good and evil is within all, this soul which is Christ's chose to love righteousness, and by its great love cling unchangeably and inseparably.' This love transformed the soul, like iron in fire, and fused it to the Word. When the Word took flesh, he had a human soul with independent will and a body.[42] What is at stake here is human freedom and authenticity, that is, when we read scripture we can trust the obedience, the fear and the love of Jesus. Origen asked ironically, 'Was Christ also subject to fate according to the movement of the stars by his birth, and therefore did and suffered these things?'[43] Jesus demonstrated the perfect human will, because of his fusion with the divine Word. In this sense he is the exemplar of the goal of all humanity. Origen wanted to read the life of Jesus in scripture as a harmony of notes played constantly together, so that one may separate out aspects, but the fulness of the mystery is in the totality of the chord. Because human beings are created in the image of the Word, who is the image of God, the conformity of souls and minds to the pattern of the Word will eventually restore humanity to union with God.

The accommodation of the Word in various forms and through the centuries is therefore the story of God's constant work of redemption. The multiplicity of scriptural names reveals the various ways in which truth may be apprehended, and then ascent will clarify and simplify. The Word is alive in the text as the teacher:

> if such there is who is constrained by love for the Word of God, if at any time it is in the thick of an argument about some passage – and everyone knows from his own experience how when one gets into a tight corner like this, one gets shut up in the straits of propositions and enquiries, if any time some riddles or obscure sayings of the Law or the Prophets hem in the soul, if the soul should chance to perceive the Logos to be present, and should afar catch the sound of his voice, immediately she is uplifted.[44]

To unravel what is tangled, to unfold and to discern the obscure through one's own ability is to be kissed by the Word.[45] The Word, in Origen, portrays

---

[41] *Com Jo* 1.119f; 19.37.

[42] *Princ* 2.6.5.

[43] *Comm Gen.*

[44] *Homily on Song of Songs* 2.

[45] *Comm on Song of Songs* 1.1.

the pedagogical nature of the universe through revelation and by example through which God patiently reunites the creation to himself.

Christian life as restoration with God

In the *City of God*, Augustine accused Origen of relegating material existence to a prison, and therefore making human life a penitentiary.[46] This reading of Origen's cosmology reflected not only the distortions of the Origenist controversy, but also Augustine's discomfort with Origen's focus on human transformation and freedom in concert with divine grace and revelation. The shape of Origen's cosmology is indeed pedagogical, but the energy of the cosmos through the persistence of free will and the tutelage of the Word is driven by a great hope and faith in divine love. For Origen the pursuit of wisdom as union with God was the main drive of his life. Within his writing the external world has little attraction or diversion for him. There are no long meditations on beauty or music or friendship as in Augustine, but rather the passionate searching through the puzzle of the text or the theological problem; the pleasure is in the process of the study of the text and the world. Theology therefore is like wine that makes us happy; heaven will be the place where we learn where each star is placed, and can converse daily with the Word.[47] Origen's own pleasure in study and God may be glimpsed in the devotion of his students, and their transforming intimacy: 'Therefore a spark – the love which is both toward the same holy and beloved logos ... and toward this man who is his friend and mouthpiece – being thrust into the midst of our souls was lit and burned.'[48]

The goal of the process of soul-making in the embodied state was the maturation of the soul from the original image of God to divine likeness. By endurance, discipline, and grace all may become 'begotten of God'; while they do good works, the spirit of God dwells within them, and the slave changes into the disciple, the brother of Christ, and finally the son.[49] The controversial aspect of Origen's vision of persuasive grace is whether he taught universalism in the eventual reconciliation of the creation with God. He has been accused, and praised, for such a teaching, and the evidence is complicated by the fragmentary state of *First Principles*. He affirms a final restoration, yet does not seem to state clearly that all creation will be resolved through this, given the persistence of free will; he also suggested a possibility of remedial punishment or a school for souls.[50] Origen's main focus was on the particularity of the process of healing and advancement for each individual, so that in due course all would be securely reunited with God; like Irenaeus he affirmed the ability to progress into loving intimacy with God.[51] In line with arguments about suspected reincarnation or cycles of worlds, his pedagogical vision was

---

46 *Civ Dei* 11.23.
47 *Com Jo* 1.208; *Princ* 2.11.4–5.
48 *Panegyric* 6.83, in Valantasis, *Spiritual Guides of the Third Century*, 25–33.
49 *Com Jo* 20.33; *Cel* 1.57.
50 *Princ* 3.5.7; 3.6.1; *Com Jo* 28.8.
51 *Princ* 2.11; 3.6; 4.4; *Hom Numbers* 27.5.

often overlooked for the possible consequences of his foundational principles of freedom and love. Origen seems to affirm no repetition of worlds, and clarifies the matter of restoration as a suggestion or a hope.[52]

Legacy of Origen

Origen's original theology and exegesis did not survive beyond him in any comprehensive way, though his work negatively and positively set the standard for several centuries with regard to Christology, anthropology, cosmology and exegesis. His account of the two natures of Christ united through the human soul may have been an important background to the later Arian controversy as well as his subordination of the Son to the Father and affirmation of eternal generation.[53] Origen's fluid and optimistic anthropology was readily adopted by some ascetics such as Antony, the Cappadocians or Evagrius Ponticus, and vilified by others such as Epiphanius. The Origenist controversy which spanned from West to East, including the translators of Origen, Rufinus and Jerome, as well as monks in Egypt, pointed toward his spiritualization of the body as a grievous error.[54] Yet, his belief in the dynamic cosmology of reunion with God was modified and centralized in the Cappadocians, and through them into later Christian tradition to the hymns of Charles Wesley. Exegetes who condemned his excesses of allegory found his voluminous works indispensable, even if his influence created a shift from allegory to contemplation (*theoria*).[55] His official condemnation at the Second Council of Constantinople in 553 by Justinian settled the question for many on the negative side of the balance sheet. Unfortunately, many of the positions were not actually held by him, but were developed by others in response to his thought long after his death.

Charles Williams once commented that Origen 'is suspected of a great orthodoxy'.[56] There are curious divisions within Christianity as a charismatic as well as dogmatic movement which makes Origen repeatedly both a hero and a villain. Origen has been celebrated for being a heretic, which he never wished to be and as a universalist, which he never explicitly claimed, and as a reincarnationalist which he explicitly denied. He breaks rather than fits our categories in his adventurous orthodoxy and spiritual intellectualism. Over the past century scholars such as Daniélou and Crouzel have consistently defended his orthodoxy through careful historical study and reconstruction of texts, if others such as Nautin have also affirmed Origen's spiritual independence and intellectual ambition. If theology is faith seeking understanding then his seemingly audacious attempts to understand the origin of the soul or the final reunion of all souls are errors of spiritual zeal as much as

---

[52] *Princ* 1.6.3.
[53] R. Lorenz, *Arius Iudaizans?* (Freiburg/Göttingen: Vandenhoeck & Ruprecht, 1980).
[54] E. A. Clark, *The Origenist Controversy* (Princeton, NJ: Princeton University Press, 1992).
[55] Trigg, *Origen*, 65.
[56] C. Williams, *The Descent of the Dove* (New York: Pellegrini & Cudahy, 1939), 37.

intellectual curiosity. When Erasmus famously commented that there is more of Christian philosophy in one page of Origen than in ten of Augustine, he may have been referring to the immediacy of Origen's hermeneutical encounter with the Word through the text.[57] A fitting analogy to Origen's work to reveal and teach the wisdom of God may be Wynton Marsalis's comments about Louis Armstrong:

> He was chosen to bring the feeling and the message and the identity of jazz to everybody ... He could play the trumpet better than anybody. He could play higher with more dexterity than anyone else. And the thing that made him so great as a musician is that he heard what everybody was playing. And not only did he hear what they were playing, he heard what they were trying to play ... and all that he played ... Then, he was always himself.[58]

Bibliography

Selected editions and translations of Origen of Alexandria

A complete list of the many Greek and Latin editions of Origen together with the modern critical editions may be found in J. McGuckin (ed.), *The Westminster Handbook to Origen*, 41–44. These abbreviations pertain to the following entries: *SC* = *Sources chrétiennes* (Paris, Editions du Cerf); *FC* = *The Fathers of the Church* (Washington: Catholic University of America Press); *ANF* = *The Ante-Nicene Fathers* (Edinburgh, 1868–69; reprint Grand Rapids, MI, 1979).

On First Principles

The critical edition, with French translation, is *Traité des Principes*, ed. H. Crouzel and M. Simonetti (*SC* 252, 253, 268, 269, 312). There is unfortunately no recent English translation. The Butterworth version is best, but should be used cautiously with regard to Greek fragments included by Paul Koetschau (*Origenes Werke V, De principiis* [GCS 22, 1. Aufl. 1913]): Origen, *On First Principles*, trans. G. W. Butterworth (London: SPCK, 1973).

Against Celsus

The critical edition, with French translation, is *Contre Celse*, ed. M. Borret (*SC* 132, 136, 147, 150, 227). The best English translation remains Henry Chadwick, *Contra Celsum* (Cambridge: Cambridge University Press, 1953).

Commentaries

On Ephesians: The Commentaries of Origen and Jerome on St Paul's Epistle to the Ephesians, trans. R. Heine (Oxford: Oxford University Press, 2002).
On John (*SC* 120, 157, 222, 290): a new English translation appears in *FC* 80, 89; Books 1–6 in *ANF* 10.

---

[57] Chadwick cites the reference in *Early Christian Thought*, 170.
[58] Geoffrey Ward, *Jazz: A History of America's Music* (New York: Knopf, 2000), 117–18.

On Matthew Books 10–11: SC 162; English translation in *ANF* 10.

On Romans: Commentarii in Epistulam ad Romanos. Romerbrief-Kommentar, ed. T. Heither (Freiburg, 1990); English translation in *FC* 103, 104.

On Song of Songs: SC 375; English translation in Ancient Christian Writers 26: *Song of Songs: Commentary and Homilies*, trans. R. P. Lawson (London: Longmans, Green & Co., 1957).

Homilies

Genesis (SC 7; FC 71); *Exodus* (SC 16; FC 71); *Leviticus* (SC 286, 287; FC 83); *Numbers* (SC 29); *Joshua* (SC 71; FC 105); *1 Kings* (FC 97); *Song of Songs* (SC 37); *Jeremiah* (SC 232, 238; FC 97); *Luke* (SC 87; FC 94).

Collections

Origen, *An Exhortation to Martyrdom, Prayer and Selected Works*, trans. Rowan A. Greer (New York: Paulist Press; London: SPCK, 1979).

Origen, *Treatise on the Passover and Dialogue with Heraclides*, trans. R. Daly (New York: Paulist Press, 1992).

Origen, trans. J. W. Trigg (London: Routledge, 1998): collection of homilies and selections from the *Commentary on John*.

Origen, Spirit and Fire: A Thematic Anthology of His Writings, ed. H. Urs von Balthasar and trans. Robert J. Daly (Washington: Catholic University of America Press, 1984).

Selected studies

H. Chadwick, *Early Christian Thought and the Classical Tradition* (Oxford: Oxford University Press, 1966).

E. Clark, *The Origenist Controversy* (Princeton, NJ: Princeton University Press, 1992).

H. Crouzel, *Origen: The Life and Thought of the First Great Theologian*, trans. A. S. Worrall (Edinburgh: T&T Clark, 1989).

H. Crouzel, *Théologie de l'image de Dieu chez Origène* (Paris: Aubier, 1956).

N. De Lange, *Origen and the Jews* (Cambridge: Cambridge University Press, 1977).

E. A. Dively Lauro, *The Soul and Spirit of Scripture within Origen's Exegesis* (Leiden: Brill, 2005).

M. Edwards, *Origen Against Plato* (Aldershot: Ashgate, 2002).

C. Kannengiesser and W. Petersen (eds), *Origen of Alexandria: His World and His Legacy* (Notre Dame, IN: University of Notre Dame Press, 1988).

J. McGuckin (ed.), *The Westminster Handbook to Origen* (Louisville, KY: Westminster John Knox, 2004).

P. Nautin, *Origène: Sa vie et son oeuvre* (Paris: Beauchesne, 1977).

K. Torjesen, *Hermeneutical Procedure and Theological Method in Origen's Exegesis* (Berlin: De Gruyter, 1986).

J. Trigg, *Origen* (London: Routledge, 1998).

9

Cyprian of Carthage

J. PATOUT BURNS

Introduction

Thascius Caecilianus Cyprianus was elected bishop of Carthage in 248 CE, the millennium of the city of Rome. Two years later, the first systematic imperial persecution of religious dissent shattered the peace and unity of the Christian church. Bishops were executed or exiled; some Christians stood fast and suffered; others failed under trial; many escaped by subterfuge or flight. The church divided over how to reintegrate the apostates and schismatics, and to control the confessors. Renewed persecution threatened and then materialized. Through the decade of his episcopate, Cyprian organized and guided the North African church to face these challenges. Shortly after his own execution in September 258, his *martyrdom* was recorded, his *Life* written, his treatises and letters collected. He quickly became the venerated patron of African Christianity and his thought its guide in negotiating the transition from persecuted to established church in the fourth century. His theology places the episcopal college at the centre of the church, as the guarantor of its unity, purity and sanctifying power. His thought proved a troublesome guide for the African church as it negotiated the transition from persecuted to established church.

Biography

In 248 CE, the Christian community in Carthage elected Cyprian its bishop. This wealthy, unmarried aristocrat, trained as a rhetorician, had become a Christian a scant two years earlier. The laity seems to have overridden the objections of a majority of their presbyters in choosing him as bishop over more senior candidates.[1] In ascending to office as bishop of Carthage, Cyprian assumed the leadership not only of the bishops of Proconsular Africa but also of all Latin Africa.

In December 249, the Emperor Decius decreed that every citizen should join him in offering homage to the immortal gods, whose graciousness secured the peace and prosperity of the empire. While Decius required participation

---

[1] Pontius, *Life of Cyprian*. For fuller accounts, please see the introductions to G. W. Clarke's translations of Cyprian's letters in *ACW* and *CCL* 3D:679–90.

in the Roman ceremonies, he did not specify the renunciation of other religious practices or loyalties. Christian bishops were targeted for early action when enforcement began in January 250. Fabian of Rome died in prison, Dionysius of Alexandria was hunted down, and Cyprian of Carthage withdrew into exile. By the time the deadline for compliance with the edict arrived, a significant portion of the laity and some of the clergy had obeyed or found a legal subterfuge for avoiding the sacrifice itself. Those who persistently refused the commissioners' demand were initially deprived of property and sent into exile; later they were subjected to coercive torture. Some died as martyrs, other were worn down and failed, still others persisted in confession and were eventually released.[2]

From his place of exile outside the city, Cyprian attempted to govern the shattered community through letters and messengers. He ordered those who failed voluntarily or under torture to undertake penance and insisted that none of the fallen could be admitted to communion before God had granted peace to the church as a whole. Cyprian authorized the presbyters to confer the church's peace and communion on any dying penitents. He began preparing for general consultations of clergy and laity after the persecution in order to establish a policy for restoring the repentant to communion.

At Carthage, imprisoned confessors and the resident presbyters responded differently to the appeals of Christians who had failed. In expectation of entering into glory through martyrdom, some confessors granted letters of peace to the lapsed. They promised to intercede with God to win forgiveness for their sin of apostasy and they recommended that the bishop readmit the penitent to the church's communion. Some of the imprisoned confessors claimed that they had been authorized by martyrs to issue letters of peace in their names. Contrary to Cyprian's orders and perhaps the confessors' intentions, some of the clergy immediately admitted these sinners to communion. The confessors eventually declared a general amnesty for all who had failed. Cyprian sharply rebuked the rebels, recognizing a threat to the authority of the bishop and the unity of the church.[3] Cyprian's attempts to control the church in Carthage led to an open division of the community and the exclusion of five presbyters, a deacon and their lay supporters. Some of these persisted and eventually elected their own bishop as a rival to Cyprian.[4]

Cyprian was able to return to Carthage shortly after Easter 251. He began the process of restoring his battered community by delivering an exhortation to repentance (*On the Lapsed*) and a lecture on the unity of the church (*On the Unity of the Catholic Church*). In each of these, he insisted that the lapsed could regain salvation only through the church's ritual of repentance supervised by

---

[2] The situation in Carthage is recorded in the contemporary *Letters* 5–6, 10–20.
[3] *Letters* 16, 21–23, 27, 33.
[4] *Letters* 41–43, 45, 59.

the legitimate bishop, who had received the power of forgiveness from Christ through succession from the original bishops, the apostles. A few months later, a council of bishops gathered in Carthage agreed to require further penance only of those who had actually sacrificed. Those who used legal stratagems to evade both a public confession of Christ and the idolatrous sacrifice were to be admitted immediately. Those who had sacrificed, in contrast, were to continue the regimen of repentance with the promise that they would be admitted to communion as death approached.[5] At that same meeting, the bishops were informed of a disputed episcopal election in Rome. The presbyter Novatian challenged the election of Cornelius on the grounds that he followed a moderate policy on reconciling the lapsed, similar to that the Africans had just adopted. The African bishops justified their recognition of Cornelius on procedural grounds. Cyprian sent an adaptation of his *On Unity* to some of the opponents of Cornelius, which convinced them to return to his communion.[6] Novatian then sent a representative to establish a church in Carthage which excluded permanently all who had compromised during the persecution.[7] Cyprian, then, faced both a laxist and a rigorist rival in Carthage.

When the African bishops met again under Cyprian's presidency in May 253, they faced not only the organized opposition of the laxists but also the threat of renewed persecution by the government of the new emperor, Galerius. They decided that any who had failed by sacrificing and had then submitted to the church's penitential discipline should be admitted to communion immediately, instead of readmittance being delayed until the time of death. They were, however, to be excluded from clerical office. In subsequent years, Cyprian and his colleagues supported attempts in Gaul and Spain to enforce a similar policy.[8]

The divisions of the church in Carthage and elsewhere in Africa raised a question which had been debated during the prior half-century: how should converts to the Catholic communion be received if they had originally undergone the ritual of Christian baptism outside the unity of that church? After some debate within Africa, Cyprian and his colleagues affirmed the policy which had been adopted some years earlier. Such persons had not been effectively baptized and must receive true baptism in the Catholic communion. Stephen, the bishop of Rome, strongly supported the opposite position, which the Africans had themselves followed at the beginning of the third century.[9] In a major council in September 256, the African bishops insisted on following their own policy, while recognizing the right of bishops in other regions to adopt a different practice.[10]

---

[5] *Letter* 55.
[6] *Letters* 44–54.
[7] *Letters* 51, 53, 59.
[8] *Letters* 57, 67, 68.
[9] *Letters* 69–75.
[10] *Judgments of the Eighty-Seven Bishops.*

In autumn 257, Cyprian was expelled from Carthage in the initial stages of the Valerian persecution. A year later, in anticipation of a formal trial, he returned and made formal confession of Christianity before the Roman authorities and his community in Carthage. He was executed on 14 September 258. As martyr-bishop of Carthage, he became and remained the greatest hero of the African church.[11]

Writings

According to the list provided by the deacon Pontius in the *Life of Cyprian*, he wrote twelve treatises, two of which are collections of scriptural texts. *To Donatus* was prepared for a friend shortly after Cyprian's conversion. *On the Dress of Virgins* followed, perhaps to deal with a problem of inappropriate conduct reflected in *Letter* 4. *On the Lapsed* was critical for the success of his episcopate; it addressed the necessity of repentance by those who had sinned by failing to confess Christ during the Decian persecution. *On the Unity of the Catholic Church* followed shortly thereafter, in response to the schism created by clergy supporting immediate reconciliation of all the fallen. This treatise underwent at least one revision which is evidenced by the survival of an alternate version of chapters 4 and 5. *On the Lord's Prayer* renews a treatise of Tertullian, *On Prayer*. Two or three treatises are associated with the outbreak of plague about 252 and a subsequent threat of persecution. *To Demetrian* addresses a pagan friend on the reason for human suffering; *On Mortality*, and *On Work and Alms* are exhortations to the Christian community in response to the plague. Two treatises on moral topics followed perhaps four years later, *On the Good of Patience* and *On Zeal and Envy*.

The collection of eighty-two surviving letters stretches through the whole of Cyprian's episcopal career. Thirteen of these were written to Cyprian and three do not include Cyprian as either writer or recipient. Six were sent jointly with other bishops, though they may have been composed by Cyprian himself. Twenty-four of Cyprian's own letters are addressed to the clergy and people of Carthage from his place of exile during the Decian persecution. As might be expected he wrote regularly to the church of Rome: eleven letters to its bishops (Cornelius, Lucius, Stephen), three to the presbyters and deacons who governed that church during the Decian persecution, and three to confessors who supported the schism of Novatian. A few of the letters are quite short while others, such as *Letters* 55 and 73, are equivalent to treatises, dealing with the efficacy of the rituals of penance and baptism. In all cases, this collection of letters provides detailed information on the practice of Christianity in Africa which is unparalleled for any other area in the middle of the third century.

---

[11] *Acta Proconsularis.*

In addition to these, the *Judgments of the Eighty-Seven Bishops* records the deliberations of a council of bishops over which Cyprian presided on 1 September 256. It dealt with the controversy over baptism performed in heresy or schism and insisted on the African practice of baptizing anew any convert from these deviant forms of Christianity.

Theology

The range of theological issues on which Cyprian wrote remained quite narrow in comparison with his predecessor, Tertullian, whose work he read and used. His theology developed in response to conflicts over practice within the church. Three questions dominated his episcopate: the unity and unicity of the church; the purity of the church; and the efficacy of the church's ritual actions. In dealing with each of these, Cyprian's efforts centred on the episcopal office, which he held and exercised, in contrast to Tertullian's focus on the laity. Finally, Cyprian was forced to move beyond the scripture in developing his theology.

The unity and unicity of the church

Cyprian insisted that the church was a social organization whose clearly defined and defended boundary separated it from the idolatry and pollution of both imperial Roman culture and deviant forms of Christianity. The sanctifying power of Christ was exercised only within the community, through its differentiated offices and layered membership. Within a local Christian community, the bishop was the principle of unity, acting as God's agent in governing and sanctifying, with the assistance of other clergy. Although the bishop was elected by the community, Cyprian insisted that its decision realized the selection which God had made; anyone who opposed the bishop, therefore, was defying God. A bishop served for the remainder of his life and could be removed from office only if he had broken his relationship with God by serious sin, and, even then, only by the judgement of his fellow bishops.[12]

Though elected by his congregation, a local bishop was ordained to his office and inducted into the episcopal college by the bishops of neighbouring churches. Christ himself had organized the episcopal college by conferring upon the twelve apostles a single power to sanctify and govern the church. This body had been expanded with the success of its mission of evangelizing and had continued in time by replacing its members as they died or were removed from office. Each bishop governed a local community but shared responsibility for the universal church with his colleagues in the episcopate. This collaboration was exercised not only in ordaining new bishops but in regional meetings to determine and enforce common policies

---

[12] *Letters* 33, 43, 45, 59, 66; *On Unity.*

on emerging issues, and in regular consultation through letter and messenger between the bishops of major cities who served as conveners for their regions. Cyprian's surviving correspondence provides evidence of this collaboration within Africa and with the overseas churches in Spain, Gaul, Italy and Cappadocia. Cyprian allowed that regional groups of bishops could follow different practices within the unity of the universal church; he expected, however, that an individual bishop would generally adhere to the commonly adopted policy of his region. He insisted, in opposition to the bishop of Rome, that no one bishop had been entrusted by Christ with supervision of either a fellow bishop or the universal church. Peter represented the unity of the episcopal college but his office was exercised by each and every local bishop. During Cyprian's time, the bishops of Africa met in provincial synods and occasionally in plenary councils. Universal councils of the episcopal college would become possible only in the fourth century, with the support of a Christian emperor.

Holiness was made available to the members of each local church through its bishop's sharing in the common power to sanctify bestowed upon the episcopal college by Christ himself. For Cyprian, this power was conferred first upon Peter (Matt 16:19) and then upon all the apostles together (John 20:22–23) to show that it was a single power shared by all. Only those bishops actually joined into the unity of the episcopal college shared the power. Moreover, the identification of the power with the gift of the Holy Spirit (John 20:22) indicated that anyone who had proven unworthy of the indwelling of the Holy Spirit could not receive, retain or exercise the power. Its bishop guaranteed the holiness of the local church; he regularly delegated this power to presbyters and deacons. During the period between the death of a bishop and the ordination of his successor, these clergy jointly exercised the bishop's power.

The social boundary defined by the ritual of baptism and maintained by the rituals of excommunication and penance identified the church's communion, separating and protecting it from the demonic realm of idolatry and sin. Outside the unity of the church's universal communion or in opposition to the congregation gathered around a local bishop, no one could be sanctified and saved. Heretical or schismatic Christian communities were established by demonic attacks on the unity of the church, and as such they were functionally idolatrous. Normally, incorporation into a local Christian community was socially evident but in exceptional instances, such as the martyrdom of an unbaptized catechumen or the death of an unreconciled penitent, the union might be only intentional. The members of Cyprian's community, however, demanded the security of actual participation in the eucharistic communion before the time of death.

Cyprian understood the unity of the church as layered. The local communities were differentiated by types of membership ranging from the catechumen or penitent anticipating admission to the eucharistic communion through the faithful, the clergy and the bishop. The episcopal college was undifferentiated and egalitarian; every bishop enjoyed the same status, though some might function as leaders and coordinators for their regions. The cohesion of the episcopal college was the foundation of the unity of the universal church; it joined together all the local communities. The unity of the church was not, however, the result of human co-operation: it was a created expression of the indivisible unity of the Trinity. The church was, moreover, identified with Christ himself. To separate from the church was to deny Christ; to adhere to the church to confess Christ.

The purity of the church

To retain its identity, the church had to protect itself from the contagion of idolatry and other forms of sin. This was accomplished through the rituals of baptism and penance which purified the members seeking admission and those who failed after being admitted. Cyprian trusted the ritual of baptism performed in the church to forgive the sins of the convert and to bestow the gift of the Holy Spirit. If baptism was omitted through a misunderstanding of its necessity – as was the practice of some bishops – participation in the eucharist could accomplish the same purpose.[13]

The problem which Cyprian and his colleagues had to face was that of significant failure after baptism, particularly by denial of Christ either through participation in an idolatrous ritual or leaving the unity of the true church for a rival communion. Within the unity of the church, the contagion of sin was spread only by consent; the holiness of the eucharistic celebration prevented involuntary communication of guilt or pollution from one member to others. Tolerating known sinners, however, would have made the entire community complicit in their failures and thus guilty of their sin. Baptism could not be repeated, so another means of purification was developed. The rituals of public excommunication, penance and satisfaction could cleanse the sinner and protect the community: both involved acknowledging and repudiating the sinful action; the penitent mourned the sin and was supported by the prayers of the community in petitioning God for forgiveness; only after a prolonged period was the sinner allowed to return to the communion. Because of the rejection of sin they required, these rituals were effective in protecting the community from contagion, even if they could not guarantee the repentance of the sinner and the forgiveness of God.

The sinfulness of the clergy represented a particular danger to the purity of a church. The power to sanctify which the bishop received through the episcopal college and made available to his clerical associates was identified with the gift of the Holy Spirit. As such, it was incompatible with serious sin. A sinful bishop, therefore, would lose the power to sanctify and could no longer exercise it on behalf of his community by celebrating baptism or the

---

[13] *On the Lapsed; Letters* 33, 49, 55, 57, 67.

eucharist. Tolerating such a leader would alienate the local community from God and even pollute any episcopal colleagues who failed to exclude and replace the sinner. Because a penitent's purification and standing before God could not be securely known, such persons were not allowed to retain or to be placed in clerical office. Once reconciled, sinful clerics could, however, be allowed to communicate among the laity without threatening the purity and holiness of the church.

The efficacy of ritual actions

Cyprian and his community believed that ritual actions were powerful, for good or ill. They trusted that within the unity of the church, the baptismal washing would cleanse from sin and that the imposition of the bishop's hands would confer the gift of the Holy Spirit. Idolatrous rituals were also effective in polluting anyone participating in them: in determining the penance necessary after the Decian persecution, distinctions were made between those who had actually come into contact with the meat and wine of the imperial sacrifice – without or even against their wills – and those who had escaped by a legal stratagem. Cyprian reported that some of the former were seriously injured by contact with the eucharistic elements.

Only bishops participating in the episcopal college had access to the power of sanctification which was operative in the rituals of baptism, eucharist and penance which they performed in their local congregations. Cyprian asserted that bishops who were outside the unity of the episcopal college lacked this power and that their actions were empty or even harmful to the recipients. Some bishops had been excluded and replaced by their colleagues because they were judged sinful and unworthy; others had created, joined or been elected in a schismatic movement, which rebelled against the unity of the church. Cyprian implied that bishops whose sins were still hidden were also incapable of sanctifying through ritual action, though in practice he never suggested a remedy to this situation, other than the removal of the unworthy minister once God had revealed his sinfulness.

The ritual of baptism performed in the unity of the church removed all sins and conferred the gift of the Holy Spirit. These two effects were inseparable, even if the imposition of the bishop's hands for the conferral of the Spirit had to be omitted when a dying person was baptized by a presbyter or deacon in the bishop's absence. The ritual was never to be repeated: if a person baptized within the church later sinned gravely, even by entering a schismatic communion, purification had to be attempted through the rituals of penance. When performed outside the unity of the church, however, baptism was empty and meaningless; it even polluted the recipient in the same way that contact with idolatry would have. A person originally attempting baptism in a schismatic or heretical community had not, Cyprian insisted, actually been baptized and purified because the minister acting outside the unity of the church had no power to do so. Such converts to the unity of the church must submit to its effective baptism before being allowed to join the eucharistic communion. In Cyprian's memorable phrase, 'No one can have God for Father without having the Church for Mother.'

The earlier practice of the African church – against which Tertullian had argued – was to accept any baptism performed in the name of Jesus or the Trinity. That practice had been changed by a council under Agrippinus, one of Cyprian's predecessors as bishop of Carthage. Opinion remained divided in Africa, however, as is evident both in the contemporary *Treatise on Rebaptism* which defended the earlier practice and in the series of letters Cyprian wrote to convince colleagues of his position. In addition, the Roman church rejected Cyprian's policy and only reluctantly tolerated its continued implementation.[14]

The efficacy of the eucharistic ritual was clearly affirmed in Cyprian's writings. As has been noted already, he claimed that some of those who approached or received it after contact with idolatrous sacrifices suffered physical harm. The Christians of Carthage seem to have believed that they would be found acceptable to Christ and gain salvation only if they died as members of the eucharistic fellowship. When Cyprian initially refused to promise such readmission to penitents who had failed during the persecution, many supported the laxist communion which offered immediate admission. A rigorist schism led by Novatian in Rome continued to deny readmission to such penitents, even at the time of death; it met with little success in attempting to establish itself in Africa.

Cyprian's interpretation of the eucharist focused on its function as an alternative to the Roman imperial cult and its joining the believers together as the body of Christ. He used priestly and sacrificial language to describe the action and its role in preparing Christians to confess Christ. In defending his own decision to allow the penitents to rejoin the communion in anticipation of renewed persecution, for example, Cyprian asserted that the eucharistic drinking of the blood of Christ strengthened Christians to witness and shed their own blood for Christ. In a subsequent exchange, he insisted that wine rather than water had to be used for the eucharist because its inebriating quality symbolized the power of Christ's blood. Cyprian also appealed to the efficacy of the eucharist in uniting the church. The bread symbolized the joining of Christians into the body of Christ; the mixing of water and wine, their inseparable union with Christ. In the face of schism, he stressed the importance of gathering the entire community for the eucharistic celebration, even though this departed from the model of the Lord's Supper and involved only a sharing of small amounts of bread and wine rather than the full *agape* meal. The uniting of the community in Christ became the major function of the eucharist.[15]

The efficacy of the penitential ritual in forgiving major sins committed after baptismal cleansing was much disputed in the period immediately following

---

[14] *Letters* 69–74.
[15] *Letters* 57, 63.

the Decian persecution. Cyprian initially followed a policy like that of the Roman rigorist, Novatian, by declining to offer reconciliation to any apostates, even after extended penance. The laxists in Carthage may have shared this view and relied instead on the intercessory authority of Christian confessors and martyrs to gain Christ's forgiveness. After consultations, the bishops of both Africa and Italy first decided to offer reconciliation to penitents at the time of their deaths. A few years later and in anticipation of a renewal of persecution, they decided to readmit all who had submitted to the regimen of penance within the church.

Unlike baptism, penance could effect the forgiveness of sins only by petition: its efficacy depended on the repentance of the sinner, the intercession of the church and the judgement of Christ. Cyprian argued that the bishops could not judge the sincerity of the repentance; the disposition of the heart might not correspond to the penitential actions. Nor could they presume the willingness of Christ to forgive, especially when he had threatened to deny those who denied him. The church's intercession was, therefore, necessary but insufficient to secure the purification of the sinner. Thus the bishops decided to admit penitents to communion so that they could be presented to Christ with the full support of the church. The ritual was, as has been noted above, effective in preserving the church from complicity in sin and pollution by the sinner: the rituals of penance indicated the community's repudiation of the sinful action and insistence on the code of morality.

The role of scripture

When Cyprian defended the decision which he and his colleagues had made to allow the penitent lapsed to return to the communion of the church, he remarked that they had been unable to determine the proper course of action on the basis of scripture. They had brought forward various passages but found that none of them offered adequate guidance for the decision they were facing. They turned then to considerations of pastoral practice. Could they reasonably and responsibly direct the sinners to undertake the penitential discipline for the remainder of their lives with the stipulation that they would not be readmitted to the church's communion even at the time of their deaths? They could themselves expect that in response to such a policy the penitents would either join the laxist communion which promised the intercession of the martyrs or give up all hope of salvation to enjoy what remained of their earthly life. In his discussion of the eucharist, Cyprian also indicated that the church had moved beyond the precedent of the evening eucharist in order to maintain the full assembly, which was also judged necessary for the meaning of the eucharist to be fulfilled. He then looked for divine confirmation of the decisions in the life of the church: many of those reconciled in anticipation of death received the divine gift of health as well as forgiveness.[16]

---

[16] *Letters* 57, 63.

Impact upon the historical setting

Cyprian's policies and his theological justification for them had an enormous impact on the development of Christianity in Africa. He offered a coherent and scripturally based explanation of the church and its organization which placed central importance on the episcopal office. Although the problems consequent upon the theory, particularly those arising from the presence of unworthy bishops, were already becoming evident in Cyprian's own day, the African church would struggle for nearly two centuries to assimilate and adapt his theory.[17]

The status of the church as the sole mediator of salvation was already well established among Christians in Africa. It was evident in the pressure exerted by the penitents and their supporters to guarantee their readmission to communion before their deaths. The schismatic communions presented themselves as the true church by claiming a more powerful sanctifying authority than their rivals, the intercessory power of the martyrs and confessors. The difficulty was that this appeal allowed the martyrs, who were not accountable to the membership of the church, to dispense with the disciplinary procedures which controlled access to communion. Permitting a person who had abandoned Christ and the church in time of stress to return to full membership without any public repentance would undercut the standards of conduct which defined the holiness of the church and thereby erased the boundary separating a holy church from a sinful culture. Such a church could not have maintained the plausibility of its claim to being holy and able to transmit holiness to its members, to being the necessary and effective instrument of salvation. By locating the necessary holiness of the church in the episcopal college, Cyprian's theology allowed the community to readmit sinners among the laity through rituals which effectively maintained its protective boundary. His use of the episcopal college as the agent of unity also provided a foundation for the later insistence that only a universal communion could claim to represent Christ and make his saving power accessible.

Cyprian had insisted that the power to sanctify through sacramental action – baptism, eucharist, penance – was transmitted through time from Christ through the episcopal college to the local bishop of a Christian community. This theory brought the great advantage of justifying the readmission to the church communion, after extended penance, of Christians who had sinned in ways which might have jeopardized the identity of the community and its relationship to God. As long as these were only tolerated among the laity rather than being honoured by clerical office, the church's access to sanctifying power was secure. Because that power was identified with the indwelling of the Holy Spirit, it would be lost by any bishop who sinned against the Spirit by blasphemy against God, apostasy against Christ or schism against

---

[17] *Letters* 68, 1; *On the Lapsed* 6.

the church. The holiness of the church depended upon its bishop avoiding such sins or upon his being promptly removed and replaced when his failure became known. Were a sinful bishop tolerated by his own congregation he would not only deprive it of sanctifying power but would pollute it with his guilt. Were he tolerated by his colleagues, that would implicate the episcopal college itself and could deprive other churches of access to the Spirit's gifts.

The difficulty of maintaining the holiness of the church was already evident during Cyprian's episcopate. He explained that God had allowed the systematic persecution in order to force unworthy bishops into open sin and thereby remove them from office. He and his colleagues had to decide which of the contenders for the episcopal office in Rome was attempting to divide that church. They had to withstand the efforts of a dismissed African bishop to regain his office and support congregations in Spain in freeing themselves of unworthy bishops. They joined the campaign of Gallic bishops to remove a dissenting colleague.[18]

Over the longer term, the problem would be not with bishops who were known to be unworthy but those whose status was uncertain. After the Diocletian persecution, for example, charges were made against many bishops which could be neither proven nor disproven to the satisfaction of the interested parties – not all of whom were acting in good faith. Cyprian's theology did not offer an explanation of the efficacy of the ritual action of a bishop who was not obviously unworthy, whose sin was unknown to his congregation and colleagues. He held that within the communion of the church, one could be contaminated only by consent. Still, he could not explain how a minister deprived of the Holy Spirit by secret sin could exercise the power to sanctify: how those he baptized might be purified and saved; how his eucharistic celebration joined a community to Christ.[19] After the division of the African church after the Diocletian persecution, the Roman bishop Miltiades insisted that the unity of the church must take precedence over the holiness of individual bishops in guaranteeing the efficacy of the rituals. The theologians serving both parties to the conflict between Caecilian and Donatus would have to restrict, supplement or replace Cyprian's explanation of the holiness of the church.

As has already been noted, Cyprian's teaching that true baptism could be conferred and received only within the unity of the true church met with strong resistance even in his own time. He had to answer numerous objections from his colleagues in Africa and required the support of bishops in the eastern Mediterranean to uphold his practice of rebaptizing against the opposition of the Roman bishop, Stephen.[20] In the division of the African church after the Diocletian persecution, the Caecilianist party agreed to

---

[18] *On the Lapsed* 6–7; *Letters* 44, 59, 67, 68.
[19] *Letter* 66 deals with these questions but with such irony that shows Cyprian did not take the question seriously.
[20] *Letters* 69–74 and 75 from Firmilian of Caesarea to Cyprian.

follow the Italian and Gallic policy of recognizing any properly performed baptism, even if conferred in heresy or schism. They thereby won the support of the overseas churches against their Donatist opponents but hampered themselves in Africa by abandoning the legacy of Cyprian. Even the Donatists, however, made occasional concessions and did not always insist on rebaptizing converts to their communion.

His explanation of the role of the episcopate in the structure of the church may have been Cyprian's most significant theological contribution. The African church had understood the apostle Peter as a prototype of the local bishop, as is evident in the arguments for episcopal power to which Tertullian responded as well as in the initial version of Cyprian's treatise *On the Unity of the Catholic Church*. Under pressure, Cyprian moved to a more general theory, in which Peter served as an indicator or symbol of the unity of the episcopal college, all of whose members were equal in their sharing of the power to sanctify and responsibility for governing the universal church. This development provided a justification for the authority of episcopal synods not only to discipline their members but also to determine policy and practice when new challenges arose. In Cyprian's time, episcopal councils were limited in their regional scope and forced to undertake broader consultation by letter. Once the resources of the empire became available to the church, however, larger meetings – exemplified by those at Arles in 314 and Antioch in 324 – became possible. These were quickly followed by councils which could claim to be universal. Cyprian's defence of episcopal collegiality stood, in the west, as a check on the authority of any one bishop over his colleagues.

Ongoing contribution

Cyprian played a major role in the transition from defending the purity of the church to understanding it as including confessed sinners who had failed to maintain their baptismal commitment. His locating the purity and holiness of the church in the episcopal college proved unworkable, however, and the issue had to be faced again in the Donatist controversy. Even then, however, the African church continued to refuse reconciliation after a second post-baptismal failure.

The role of the episcopal college in maintaining the unity and holiness of the church was first elaborated by Cyprian; it proved more flexible and useful than earlier appeals to continuity in the leadership of individual churches, such as Rome or the Pauline foundations. It also rested upon an assertion of both the equality of all bishops and the superiority of communal agreement to individual decisions. Thus Cyprian provided a justification not only for acceptance of episcopal councils but also for a refusal to sacralize the broader jurisdiction exercised by particular bishops, such as the metropolitans, patriarchs and popes. The western church's interpretation of the original version of Cyprian's *On Unity*, however, made it useful for defending the claims of the Roman bishop. Both versions continued to be used, for contrary purposes, and charges of forgery abounded.

Cyprian's insistence on the unity of the church as a universal communion and its role as the exclusive agent of salvation was broadly accepted. Its corollary, that no one could be saved outside the unity of that communion, played a more prominent role in African theology than in that developed in other parts of the Christian world. Its influence is evident in Augustine's doctrines of inherited guilt and of gratuitous election and predestination. The refusal to accept its other corollary, the inefficacy of sacramental action outside the unity of the communion, caused an incoherence in western theology. Augustine's solution to this problem was not fully compatible with those parts of Cyprian's understanding of the episcopal office which the European church would adopt and espouse.

Unlike Augustine's more complex and nuanced understanding of the church, the efficacy of its ministries and the authority of its governors, Cyprian's ecclesiology provided a theory for building the institutions of the western church, once the understanding of the bishop as agent of Christ had been developed in the fourth and fifth centuries.

Bibliography

Editions

Corpus Scriptorum Ecclesiasticorum Latinorum, vols 3.1–3 (Vienna, 1868–76).
Corpus Christianorum, Series Latina, vols 3, A–E (Turnhout: Brepols, 1972–2004).
Sources chretiénnes, vols 291, 440, 467, 500, 519 (Paris: Cerf, 1982–2008).

Translations

M. Bevenot, *St Cyprian: The Lapsed, The Unity of the Catholic Church* (New York: Newman, 1957).
G. W. Clarke, *The Letters of St. Cyprian of Carthage, Ancient Christian Writers* 43–44, 46–47 (New York: Newman, 1984–89).
E. Wallis, *Cyprian: Letters and Treatises, Ante-Nicene Fathers* 5:261–572 (Grand Rapids, MI: Eerdmans, 1981).

Studies

E. W. Benson, *Cyprian: His Life, His Times, His Work* (London: Macmillan, 1897).
M. Bevenot, *The Tradition of Manuscripts: A Study in the Transmission of St Cyprian's Treatises* (Oxford: Clarendon Press, 1961).
J. Patout Burns, *Cyprian the Bishop* (London: Routledge, 2002).
G. D. Dunn, *Cyprian and the Bishops of Rome* (Strathfield, NSW: St Paul's, 2007).
M. A. Fahey, *Cyprian and the Bible: A Study of Third-Century Exegesis* (Tübingen: J. C. B. Mohr, 1971).
M. M. Sage, *Cyprian* (Cambridge, MA: Philadelphia Patristic Foundation, 1975).

10

Hippolytus of Rome

ULRICH VOLP

Introduction

Hippolytus of Rome is an evasive figure and good for many superlatives, even though some of them will always remain a matter of dispute: first ever antipope, most quoted early church figure at the Second Vatican Council, only ever canonized antipope, first heresiograph, most important early heresiologist, first Christian exegete, first apocalyptic eschatologist without belief in the apocalypse, only Church Father represented by a contemporary female statue, martyr, villain and saint ... Those who deem this to be too many descriptions for only one person will find consolation in the suitable theories which multiply the Hippolytan figure in question: they provide a Hippolytus of Rome, a Josipe of Rome, a Hippolytus of Alexandria and one of Porto. As if this was not enough, some of the Hippolytan writings were and sometimes still are ascribed to other authors such as Irenaeus of Lyon,[1] or Origen.[2] However, it is reasonable to say that the literary production of the third century left an enormous corpus of Greek Christian writings known under the name of Hippolytus, which at the time was only surpassed in importance by Origen. The extant information about the life and work of this prolific early church figure has been the object of much examination during two equally productive centuries of Hippolytus-research. The amount of research is well justified, above all, by the information provided by Hippolytus' writings on heresy, that is, gnostic thought and other schools of thinking within and outside Christianity for which only a few other sources existed before the Nag Hammadi discoveries of the 1940s. The most prominent early church order and liturgy, the *Apostolic Tradition*, is also believed by many to have been written by Hippolytus, a theory which will have to be considered in more detail below.

There are a great number of writings attributed to one Hippolytus of Rome. According to the traditional nineteenth-century view they were all written by a presbyter-bishop involved in some major theological controversies in Rome at the beginning of the third century. If this is correct – and the following overview explores the plausibility of such claims – the corpus comprises the first major exegetical works by a Christian author, the first

---

[1] Cf. D. Minns, 'Irenaeus', *Exp Times* 120 (2009) 157–66.
[2] Cf. R. Lyman, 'Origen', *Exp Times* 120 (2009) 417–427.

elaborate Christian liturgy and the first systematic heresiology, but also constitutes an important witness of the dawn of the trinitarian controversy. Anyone interested in the beginnings of Christian 'theology' must therefore look into this diverse legacy from possibly the last Greek Church Father in the west.

Life

Biographical information can be gathered not only from the writings which have survived under Hippolytus' name, but also from some short notes in Eusebius[3] and other later writers. All of this information needs to be considered with some caution, albeit for a variety of different reasons. The sources of the later authors are usually not known, and not all of the writings ascribed to Hippolytus were necessarily written by him.

However, this is what has been the general understanding of his life since the middle of the nineteenth century, even if some of it has always remained dubious or uncertain and is still controversial: Hippolytus was born in or just before the year 170, possibly in Asia Minor or Alexandria. He became a member of the clergy of the Christian community in Rome and was presbyter when Zephyrinus was bishop (198/99–217). It is possible that he was made presbyter under Zephyrinus' predecessor Victor (189–98). However, he does not seem to have been on good terms with either of them, and Hippolytus' descriptions leave one wondering how strong the position of the Roman episcopate really was at the time. Photius claims Hippolytus to have been a disciple of Irenaeus,[4] and he probably had styled himself to be exactly that – and to have exceeded his 'teacher' in his heresiology. According to Jerome, Origen heard him preach and was suitably impressed.[5] It has been suggested that this occurred in Alexandria, not Rome, and that Hippolytus was part of a group of Novatianists there. Novatian (d. *c.* 258) and Hippolytus certainly shared similarly strict views on some ethical issues. It seems difficult, however, to reconcile this view with the biographical information given in the said sources.

When Calixtus was elected bishop in 217, Hippolytus seems to have become his fiercest opponent and maybe even bishop himself which, in retrospect, would have made him the first 'antipope'. This hypothesis, however, depends on the view that the Roman community had a fully developed monarchian episcopate in the early third century already which left no room for a competing presbyterate with a comparable degree of authority and power, a view which is anything but uncontested today.[6]

In any case, the controversy caused by Hippolytus is highly instructive about the situation of the Roman community at the time, but it also marks

---

[3] Esp. Eusebius, *Historia Ecclesiastica* 6.20.22.

[4] Photius, *Bibliotheca*, cod. 121.

[5] Hieronymus, *De Viris Illustribus* 61; cf. Eusebius, *Historia Ecclesiastica* 6.14.10, who describes Origen's visit to Rome when Zephyrinus was bishop there.

[6] Cf. e.g. A. Brent, *Hippolytus and the Roman Church in the Third Century: Communities in Tension before the Emergence of a Monarch-Bishop*, SVigChr 31 (Leiden/Boston/Cologne: Brill, 1995).

an important starting point for the century long controversies about the Trinity. Keywords of this debate such as patripassianism, monarchianism and ditheism stayed with theology for a long time. The dispute continued under the episcopate of Urban I (223–30) and Pontian (230–35), and both Hippolytus and Pontian were deported to the Sardinian mines by Emperor Maximinus Thrax in 235 where both died within a year.

The Hippolytan writings and the *Hippolytus question*

Hippolytus wrote his works in Greek, and if their author was indeed a Roman presbyter he must have been the last of the western Church Fathers to do so. This in itself would explain the wide circulation of his work in the east from where Syriac, Coptic, Armenian and Arabic translations have survived. Eastern authors such as Origen (d. *c.* 254), Epiphanius of Salamis (d. 403), Theodoret of Cyrrhus (d. *c.* 457) and western thinkers such as Gregory Baeticus (d. *c.* 392) and Ambrose (d. 397) show signs of his influence. However, these eastern roots in his thinking and writing continue to raise doubts about the credibility of his 'Roman' biography which has been outlined above.

Anyone trying to establish the exact scope of his work faces a singularly curious situation. There are three 'catalogues' of Hippolytan writings, one surviving in Eusebius' *Historia Ecclesiastica* 6.22, another in Jerome's *De Viris Illustribus* 61, and on an ancient statue of a figure, probably female, which the Roman community somehow connected with Hippolytus after his death, and which surfaced in a coemeterium at the Via Tiburtina in 1551 where his bones were said to be buried. The size of his work thus recorded is impressive by any standards. However, assigning the many works circulating under his name has been a difficult and controversial business ever since. Eusebius mentions a 'Hippolytus' in three instances without connecting the three at all. Even Jerome had some – for him rather untypical – doubts about the tradition he recorded, and he had to admit that he did not know where Hippolytus had been bishop.[7] It was as early as in the eighteenth century that a German scholar, Gottfried Lumper (d. 1800), wrote a first monograph, summarizing the different opinions on the matter and starting the *Hippolytus question*.[8] It was not to be the last one. In 1947, Pierre Nautin, for example, identified two different authors: Josipe (or Josippus/Josepus) of Rome, Roman presbyter and later one of two opposing Roman bishops, and an eastern bishop named Hippolytus.[9] The Nautin controversy focused on anti-heretical works, and indeed for a long time Hippolytus' work *Contra haeresin Noëti* seemed to be the key to this question. It is difficult to reconcile this work with the thinking exhibited by the *Refutatio, De universo,*

---

[7] Hieronymus, *De Viris Illustribus* 61: *Hippolytus cuisdam ecclesiae episcopus nomen quippe urbis scire non potui* (ed. Richardson, TU 14.35.16–17).

[8] G. Lumper, *Dissertatio de vita et scriptis Sancti Hippolyti*, PG 10 (Paris: Editions Garnier Frères, 1857) 271–394.

[9] P. Nautin, *Hippolyte et Josipe: Contribution à l'histoire de la littérature chrétienne du troisième siècle*, Études et textes pour l'histoire du dogme de la Trinité 1 (Paris: Les éditions du Cerf, 1947).

fr. ex libro de paschate, *Canon paschalis*, the *Syntagma, fr. de resurrectione et incorruptione*, *Contra Gaium*, the *Homilia in Psalmos, fr. in Gen., fr. in Pr.* (fr. 1–29, 54), let alone the *Apostolic Tradition*. Vincenzo Loi attributed these writings and the *Chronicon* to the Roman presbyter Hippolytus, but suggested *Contra haeresin Noëti* to have been written by an oriental bishop[10] – a modified theory which met with slightly more applause (partly because the three decades in between had managed to loosen up the front of the Roman hypothesis a little). However, Loi also assigned some other works such as *Demonstratio de Christo et antichristo*, *fr. in Cantium canticorum*, *De David et Goliath*, *De benedictione Jacobi*, *Canticum Mosis, fr. in Is.* and finally the important commentary on Daniel to this other-wise unknown bishop which generated more serious opposition.[11] To name just one more theory, J. A. Cerrato in his 1996 Oxford doctoral thesis[12] con-centrated on Hippolytus' exegetical commentaries and tried to prove the authorship of an oriental bishop through gathering external historical evidence regarding the locality of the commentaries, and through highlighting the 'eastern' thinking underlying these works – a claim that, again, is anything but new: Gelasius of Rome and some medieval manuscripts held similar views.

All these theories point to major inconsistencies which are hard to over-look, for example the different interpretations of the number '1000' or the diverse meanings of παῖς θεοῦ/pais theou. The list grows longer with every new scholarly work on the *Hippolytus question*. However, there are also some good arguments for maintaining the hypothesis of only one Hippolytus, despite all the obvious difficulties.[13] Hippolytus does not strike one as being the most consistent of thinkers, and most of these inconsistencies hardly apply to issues which are central to his argument. Also, the external historical evidence is inconclusive: there is just no way to tell whether more reliable sources were available to Gelasius (d. 496) who calls Hippolytus a 'bishop and martyr of a capital city of the Arabians' or to Apollinaris of Laodicea (d. *c.* 390) who spoke of him as 'the most holy bishop of Rome'.[14]

In retrospect, it seems surprising that for well over a century the *Hippolytus question* was regarded as solved by many. The Roman Catholic scholar Ignaz Döllinger, in his 1853 book on Hippolytus,[15] had presented the antipope-theory which immediately became the *communis opinio*: the author of the *Refutatio*, he claimed, was a schismatic Roman bishop of the early third century involved in a controversy with Kallistos, Urban and Pontian, a controversy which left traces

---

[10] V. Loi, 'La problematica storico-letteraria su Ippolito' and 'L'identità letteraria di Ippolito di Roma', in Istituto Patristico Augustinianum Roma (ed.), *Ricerche su Ippolito*, SEAug 13 (Rome: Institutum Patristicum Augustinianum, 1977), 9–16 and 67–88.
[11] Cf. J. Frickel, *Das Dunkel um Hippolyt von Rom* (Graz: Institut für Ökumenische Theologie und Patrologie, 1988).
[12] Published as J. A. Cerrato, *Hippolytus between East and West: The Commentaries and the Provenance of the Corpus* (Oxford: Oxford University Press, 2002).
[13] Cf. C. Scholten, 'Hippolytus II (von Rom)', *RAC* 15 (1991) 492–551.
[14] Cerrato, *Hippolytus* 84, thinks otherwise.
[15] J. J. I. von Döllinger, *Hippolytus und Kallistus* (Regensburg: G. J. Manz, 1853).

Figure 10.1 Sketch of the statue found in 1551

Biblioteca Nazionale 'Vittorio Emanuele III', Ms. XIII. B. 7, fol. 424. From: M. Guarducci, 'La statua di "Sant Ippolito" in vaticano', in *Atti della Pontificia Accademia Romana de Archeologia: Rendiconti* (1974f) 165–90, 168. Permission to reproduce sought.

in all of the Hippolytan writings which were thus proven to be Roman. Pieces written before or outside the controversy, he argued, would not have been affected. A number of scholars, some of them pupils of the great Adolf von Harnack who supported Döllinger's theory,[16] started collations and editions of Hippolytan works, and most of them are still unsurpassed today. By the end of the nineteenth century, a huge corpus of writings was attributed to Hippolytus Romanus, and when Goltz, Connolly and later Botte suggested him to be the author of the *Apostolic Tradition* (s.b.), this also soon became the *communis opinio*.

This Roman hypothesis, which was prevailing when the Nautin controversy started, relies partly on the evidence of the female statue mentioned earlier (Figure 10.1). The fact that it was found in a Roman cemetery seemed to support the antipope-theory. The inscriptions on the statue provide a list of some, but not all, of the Hippolytan writings, and can be firmly dated to the third century.[17] The statue was totally altered in the sixteenth century (Figure 10.2 overleaf)

---

[16] Harnack was also the initiator of Hans Achelis's first approach to the subject, which eventually resulted in the discovery of the *Apostolic Tradition*.

[17] Brent, *Hippolytus and the Roman Church* 115–203, suggests it to be simply a catalogue of the library of the Roman church, but this does not explain the lack of authors' names which would be expected from an ancient library catalogue.

Figure 10.2 Statue redesigned by Ligorio

From: H. Leclerq, Art. Hippolyte (Statue et Cimitière de Saint): DACL 6, 1 (Paris, 1925) 2419–83, 2421. Cf. also M. Guarducci, 'La statua di, Sant'Ippolito', in Istituto Patristico Augustinianum Roma (ed.), *Ricerche su Ippolito*, SEAug 13 (Rome: Institutum Patristicum Augustinianum, 1977) 17–30; Guarducci, *San Pietro e Sant'Ippolito: Storia di statue famose in Vaticano* (Roma: Istituto Poligrafico e Zecca dello Stato, 1991).

by the famous renaissance architect Pirro Ligorio (d. 1583), but both he[18] and the archaeologist and antiquities collector Fulvio Orsini (d. 1600)[19] left drawings (Figure 10.1) which demonstrate that it originally showed a female body with one naked breast, most likely the mythological amazon Hippolyta, mother of the mythological Hippolytus, a very common and fashionable subject in first–third century Rome.[20] The Roman community must have adapted a statue which for them represented Roma, *virtus* and σοφία/Sophia, and then decided to inscribe on it the works of their venerated martyr Hippolytus. However, why are the *Refutatio*, the commentary on Daniel and other works missing?

---

18 Neaple, Ms. XIII. B. 7, fol. 424.
19 Ms. Vat. Lat. 3439, fol. 124a.
20 M. Vinzent, 'Hippolyt von Rom und seine Statue', in A. M. Ritter, W. Wischmeyer and W. Kinzig (eds), *'Zur Zeit oder Unzeit': Studien zur spätantiken Theologie-, Geistes- und Kulturgeschichte. Festschrift Hans Georg Thümmel*, Texts and Studies in the History of Theology 9 (Mandelbachtal/Cambridge: Cicero, 2004) 125–34.

Whatever the answer may be, the *Hippolytus question* is still open and the question whether we are dealing with a single – eastern, western or perambulating – author, or two or even more authors, remains unsolved.

Beyond the *Hippolytus question*

The *Hippolytus question* has greater implications than many other learned disputes about authorships of ancient texts. This may be demonstrated by two examples taken from the vast material in question here: (1) the relationship between the *Refutatio* and the commentary on Daniel; and (2) the *Apostolic Tradition*.

1 The relationship between the *Refutatio* and the commentary on Daniel

The Hippolytan corpus of writings constitutes the most important source for the thinking of heretical groups at the time. His work *Refutatio omnium haeresium* tries to prove that the basic teachings of all the heretical groups came from outside the Christian revelation, especially from Greek philosophy and mythology. In his description of the various heresies Hippolytus refers to many texts now lost. Before the Nag Hammadi discoveries (but also proven by these texts),[21] his writings were considered the best source for gnostic thinking, more reliable than the antignostic polemics written by the likes of Irenaeus and Tertullian.

The Hippolytan commentaries on Daniel and on the Song of Songs are the oldest surviving Christian writings attempting to comment and interpret typologically the Old Testament in detail. However, they do not exhibit the kind of antagonisms and acrid polemics found in the *Refutatio*, so this leaves one wondering about the relation between the anti-heretical, polemical and 'agonistic' Hippolytus, the author of the *Refutatio*, on the one hand, and the exegete Hippolytus, on the other. If the *Hippolytus question* is decided in favour of a single author, there has to be some connection between these two very different groups of writings. Indeed, scholars such as Demetrios Trakatellis interpret the Hippolytan exegesis in the following manner. The commentary on Daniel (and especially on Dan 3), he says, is an 'agonistic speech' dominated by an attitude of competition and dispute.[22] It really is a *Refutatio* wrapped in some exegesis. If one looks very closely, there is certainly some tension perceptible. However, the overall tone can also be regarded as one of paraenesis and consolation rather than one of attack and even vengeance by which the *Refutatio* is dominated. Hence, it is not surprising that it has been

---

[21] M. Marcovich even perceives Hippolytus to be 'vindicated' by the Nag Hammadi findings and considers him to be 'one of the best extant heresiological sources for the study of Gnosticism': M. Marcovich, *Hippolytus, Refutatio omnium haeresium*, PTS 25 (Berlin/New York: De Gruyter, 1986) 7.

[22] D. Trakatellis, 'ΛΟΓΟΣ ΑΓΩΝΙΣΤΙΚΟΣ: Hippolytus' Commentary on Daniel', in L. Bormann (ed.), *Religious Propaganda and Missionary Competition in the New Testament World: FS Dieter Georgi*, NTS 74 (Leiden: Brill, 1994) 527–50, 528–41.

argued that Trakatellis overinterprets these 'agonistic' traces.[23] Moreover, if one takes a different stand on the *Hippolytus question*, other interpretations are possible and his reflecting on the date of the parousia and the hour of martyrdom can be seen in totally different contexts: Hippolytus may have written this piece in a time of persecution[24] or when faced with followers of Montanism – the latter would suggest itself especially if the text was written in Asia Minor rather than in Rome.

2 The *Apostolic Tradition*

The liturgical order for ordinations in the Roman Catholic Church, *De Ordinatione Diaconi, Presbyteri et Episcopi* (which was one of the outcomes of the Second Vatican Council)[25] includes a text which it presumes to have been written by Hippolytus who is also portrayed as authorizing the rule that ordination can only be administered by bishops. Both can be found in a text reconstructed by Bernard Botte OSB on the basis of earlier research by Hans Achelis, Eduard von der Goltz and R. Hugh Connolly, and which is since known as the *Apostolic Tradition* or simply 'TA'.

Achelis put together a number of different Coptic, Ethiopian and Arabic canons of the Alexandrinian synods (an Egyptian collection of different church orders) which he thought belonged to one very ancient church order and called this new collection 'Egyptian Church Order'.[26] Both von der Goltz[27] and Connolly[28] looked at this collection independently, and they came to the conclusion that this Egyptian church order was based on an even older text: the *Apostolic Tradition*, compiled in the early third century. The research following this discovery[29] suggested the following stemma showing the dependencies between the different sources, as shown in Figure 10.3.

The stemma shows the importance of this discovery: since only about half of the even older *Didache* is concerned with the order of the community and the liturgy and thus provides only some rudimentary guidelines in these matters, the newly discovered *Apostolic Tradition* constitutes the earliest elaborate church order, collection of prayers and liturgical instruction on which all of the other documents depend. The document was originally compiled

---

[23] K. Bracht, 'Logos parainetikos: Der Danielkommentar des Hippolyt', in K. Bracht and D. du Toit (eds), *Die Geschichte der Daniel-Auslegung in Judentum, Christentum und Islam: Studien zur Kommentierung des Danielbuches in Literatur und Kunst*, BZAW 371 (Berlin: De Gruyter, 2007) 79–97.

[24] This is the view taken by K. Bracht who speculates on a connection with the persecution under Septimius Severus in 202f.

[25] Cf. the apostolic constitution on the holy liturgy, *Sacrosanctum Concilium*.

[26] H. Achelis, *Die ältesten Quellen des orientalischen Kirchenrechts* 1, TU 6 (Leipzig: J. C. Hinrichs, 1891). Cf. H. Achelis, *Hippolytstudien*, TU 16.4 (Leipzig: J. C. Hinrichs, 1897).

[27] E. von der Goltz, *Unbekannte Fragmente altchristlicher Gemeindeordnungen*, Sitzungsberichte der Königlich-Preussischen Akademie der Wissenschaften zu Berlin 5 (Berlin: Königlich-Preussische Akademie der Wissenschaften, 1906).

[28] R. H. Connolly, *The So-called Egyptian Church Order and Derived Documents*, Texts and Studies: Contributions to Biblical and Patristic Literature 8.4 (Cambridge: Cambridge University Press, 1916).

[29] E.g. by Eduard Schwartz, *Über die pseudapostolischen Kirchenordnungen* (Strasbourg: Trubner, 1910).

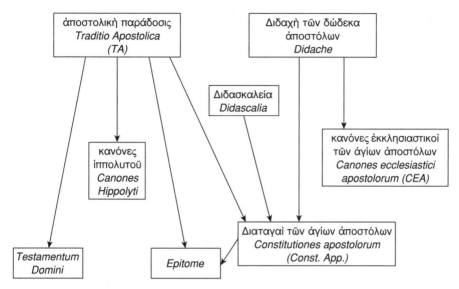

Figure 10.3 Early church orders

in Greek, but had to be reconstructed from the surviving Latin, Sahidic Coptic, Arabic, Ethiopic and Bohairic Coptic translations. Each translation has significant shortfalls and gaps, but the reconstructed *Tradition* provides detailed instructions for the Christian liturgy in connection with the eucharist, baptism and ordination. It assigns different rights and duties to bishops, presbyters and deacons, as well as confessors, readers, subdeacons, widows, virgins and catechumens. Most notable are the preserved prayer texts which experienced an unprecedented career during the twentieth century, both in the Roman Catholic and in many Protestant churches.

The complicated tradition from which the *Tradition* was extracted mentions the name 'Hippolytus' in three instances, especially in the *Canones Hippolyti* and in the *Epitome* of the *Const. App.* (cf. Figure 10.3) – and always in places where passages from the *Tradition* can be found. Since the catalogue on the side of the Hippolytan statue also mentions an ἀποστολικὴ παράδοσις/ Apostolike Paradosis, this was by many regarded as sufficient evidence to believe in Hippolytus' authorship of the *Tradition* itself. The exact title ἀποστολικὴ παράδοσις/Apostolike Paradosis does not appear in these texts, but the text is consistently called διατάξεις/Diataxeis. However, the idea that it represented some sort of 'Apostolic' tradition is clearly assumed – a claim which, of course, was anything but unusual in the early church. The same is true for the attribution of texts to important authorities, be they apostolic or not.[30] By the time these compilations were put together in the

---

[30] Cf. also *Apostolic Tradition* 43.

fourth and fifth centuries, Hippolytus had already become a name regularly used in such fashion.[31] The fact that the *Tradition* is the obvious result of a longer process and not the work of a single author also supports a theory according to which the attribution to Hippolytus could simply be the result of two periods of first 'apostolicizing' and then 'hippolyticizing' this document.[32] Nevertheless, the Hippolytan authorship seemed so convincing for many that it has even been used as an argument for the question of Hippolytus' own eastern origins.[33]

The impact of the *Hippolytus question* on the status of this document must not be underestimated. Without the early – pre-Constantinian – dating of this document and its attribution to a Roman(!) bishop its prominence in the modern debate cannot be understood. Moreover, today's perception of pre-Constantinian worship has largely been shaped by this document. The many issues surrounding the *Hippolytus question* thus also apply to our understanding of pre-Constantinian worship in general.

Hippolytus, the Antichrist and the apocalypse

The *Demonstratio de Christo et antichristo* and his *Commentarium in Danielem* reveal the exegete Hippolytus, a scholar who displays a great degree of originality and a choice of topics which makes him curiously stand out in patristic literature. The *Demonstratio* is a work of systematic exegesis in which the author connects New Testament references on the Antichrist with an allegorical exegesis of Old Testament texts. This results in a profound and somehow new image. Hippolytus portrays the Antichrist both as Christ's opponent and his imitator, mimic and impersonator. Hence, he is able to trace Satan's every step in analogy to Christ's existence. Similar approaches would only be taken up again in the Middle Ages.

At about the same time or possibly slightly later, Hippolytus the exegete wrote his commentary on Daniel which again shows how he struggled with a genre of theological scholarship which had yet to be invented. He follows the Greek text closely (Dan 13, however, is discussed in between Dan 1 and 3) and allows himself lengthy quotations. It is surprising how little allegorical exegesis he employs, his commentary on the Susanna tale in Daniel 13

[31] Cf. Theodoret, *Epistula* 145; Palladius, *Historia Lausiaca* 148; Cyrillus Scythopolitanus, *Vita Euthymii*.
[32] Cf. C. Markschies, 'Wer schrieb die sogenannte Traditio Apostolica? Neue Beobachtungen und Hypothesen zu einer kaum lösbaren Frage aus der altkirchlichen Literaturgeschichte', in Wolfram Kinzig, Christoph Markschies and Markus Vinzent, *Tauffragen und Bekenntnis. Studien zur sogenannten 'Traditio Apostolica', zu den 'Interrogationes de fide' und zum 'Römischen Glaubensbekenntnis'* (Berlin/New York: De Gruyter, 1999) 1–74. Cf. P. F. Bradshaw, M. E. Johnson and L. E. Phillips, *The Apostolic Tradition: A Commentary* (Minneapolis, MN: Fortress Press, 2002) 3.
[33] J. M. Hanssen, *La liturgie d'Hippolyte: Ses documents, son titulaire, ses origines et son charactère*, OrChrA 155 (Rome: Pontificiio Istituto Orientale, 2nd edn, 1995); L. Bouyer, *Eucharist: Theology and Spirituality of the Eucharistic Prayer* (Notre Dame, IN: University of Notre Dame Press, 1968).

constituting the exception to the rule.[34] Instead, the commentary is both tinctured by παράινεσις/paraenesis and consoling edification. He is also clearly interested in the correct understanding of eschatology: he seems to combat prophetic enthusiasm[35] as well as any attempt to calculate the exact hour of the apocalypse[36] in favour of a more rational and only mildly apocalyptic understanding of the millennium to come.

Hippolytus' exegetical works are of historical importance and capture the spirit of their own age, because they certainly pioneered a Christian form of reflecting on and discussing the testimony of the Holy Scripture – even if pioneering work and mastership can sometimes be two different kettles of fish.

The heresiographer Hippolytus as a new 'master of heresiology'

By contrast, the 'agonistic' Hippolytus of the *Refutatio* appears very different. The Roman Hippolytus, as he has been reconstructed by Döllinger, developed his theology in a community torn apart by serious theological differences. This is the Hippolytus who presents himself in the *Refutatio*. One of Hippolytus' major enemies was the Roman bishop Kallistos (Κάλλιστος/Calixtus; eponymous for the first-known Christian catacombs in Rome) for whom he felt deep hatred, and he made no attempt to conceal his feelings from the reader of the *Refutatio*.

Apart from a short passage in Eusebius,[37] *Refutatio* 9–10 provides the only information we have on Kallistos, but the picture given here is clear enough: Kallistos was elected bishop in 217 and faced by two divided theological factions of the Roman clergy. On the one hand, the proponents of a 'logos theology' followed the great Roman teacher Justin.[38] They fought for a theological line of thinking which allowed for a personalized concept of a λόγος/Logos independent from God the Father. On the other hand, there were some relentless advocates of a divine monarchy, of a strict unity of God. Hippolytus accused Kallistos of being one of them, and thus of promoting modalism, monarchianism or patripassianism:

> Thus, after the death of Zephyrinus, supposing that he had obtained [the position] after which he so eagerly pursued, he excommunicated Sabellius, as not entertaining orthodox opinions. He acted thus from apprehension of me, and imagining that he could in this manner obliterate the charge against him among the churches, as if he did not entertain strange opinions. He was then an impostor and knave, and in process of time hurried away many with him.

---

[34] Hippolytus, *In Dan. comm.* 1.12–33. This passage enjoyed a particular influence on the shaping of patristic ecclesiology. Cf. his commentary on Apoc 12 in *Demonstratio de Christo et antichristo*.

[35] Hippolytus, *In Dan. comm.* 4.18f.

[36] Hippolytus, *In Dan. comm.* 4.17.

[37] Eusebius, *Historia Ecclesiastica* 6.21.1f.

[38] P. Parvis, 'Justin Martyr', *Exp Times* 120 (2008) 53–61.

And having even venom imbedded in his heart, and forming no correct opinion on any subject, and yet withal being ashamed to speak the truth, this Calixtus, not only on account of his publicly saying in the way of reproach to us, 'You are Ditheists', but also on account of his being frequently accused by Sabellius, as one that had transgressed his first faith, devised some such heresy as the following. Calixtus alleges that the Logos Himself is Son, and that Himself is Father; and that though denominated by a different title, yet that in reality He is one indivisible spirit. And he maintains that the Father is not one person and the Son another, but that they are one and the same; and that all things are full of the Divine Spirit, both those above and those below. And he affirms that the Spirit, which became incarnate in the virgin, is not different from the Father, but one and the same. (Hippolytus, *Refutatio omnium haeresium* 9.7).[39]

In Hippolytus' eyes Kallistos thus failed to distinguish the persons of God the Father and the Son sufficiently. Hippolytus in turn was accused of being a 'ditheist', of being somone who actually worships two gods. The passage also mentions a certain Sabellius who taught a modalistic monarchianism according to which God was indivisible, and Father (creator and legislator), Son (redeemer) and Holy Spirit (God's presence among humanity) were nothing but three consecutive appearances of one God. Sabellius was excommunicated by 220 when Kallistos had declared this to be heretical. However, Hippolytus claimed that this was only a diversion in order to cover up Kallistos' own heretical thinking. Other theologians followed Hippolytus in his abhorrence of sabellianism: Tertullian,[40] Dionysius of Alexandria and Arius, to name just three. Moreover, the entire incident shows the new *geistesgeschichtliche* quality of the time: 'Theology' in the sense of a struggle over a precise and correct formula of the doctrine of God had – just – come of age. And this is perhaps the most important insight when reading the heresiology of Hippolytus.

Such reading, one has to add, leaves one with a distinct feeling of watching a process which is far from complete: Hippolytus' speculative approach to the doctrine of God was clearly alien to western thinking at the time, and it shows a great degree of uncertainty and incompleteness.[41] The *Refutatio* may be the first systematic attempt at a history of theology, a *Theologiegeschichte* – but it was not to be the most successful attempt. However, Hippolytus clearly outgunned Irenaeus in depth and broadness, and succeeded in pinpointing the very questions with which patristic theology was to stay and struggle for many years. It is in this light that the heresiograph Hippolytus should be given the credit he deserves – no matter how the *Hippolytus question* will be decided in the future.

---

[39] Transl. J. H. Macmahon, ANF 5.130.
[40] This presupposes that the Hippolytan ideas preceded Tertullian's *Adversus Praxean* which was probably written in 213. Cf. K. Bracht, 'Product or Foundation? The Relationship between the Doctrine of the Holy Trinity and Christology in Hippolytus' und Tertullian's debate with Monarchianism' (APB 18; Pretoria: Department of Ancient Languages, University of Pretoria, 2007) 14–31, 15f.
[41] Cf. esp. *Refutatio* 10.

Bibliography

Editions and translations

H. Achelis, A. Bauer, G. N. Bonwetsch, R. Helm, M. Richard and P. Wendland (eds), *Hippolytus Werke*, GCS 1/26/36/46/GCS.NF 7 (Berlin: 1896–2000).

B. Botte, *Hippolyte de Rome: La tradition apostolique d'après les anciennes versions* (SC 11bis; Paris: Les éditions du Cerf, 2nd edn, 1984).

R. Butterworth, *Hippolytus of Rome: Contra Noetum* (Heythrop Monographs 2; London: Heythrop College, 1977).

G. J. Cuming, *Hippolytus: A Text for Students. With Introduction, Translation, Commentary and Notes* (Grove Liturgical Study 8; Bramcote, Notts: Grove Books, 2nd edn, 1991).

R. Garitte, *Traités d'Hippolyte sur David et Goliath, sur le Cantique des cantiques et sur l'Antéchrist* (CSCO 263; Louvain: Secrétariat du Corpus SCO, 1965).

M. Lefèvre, *Hippolyte, Commentaire sur Daniel* (SC 14; Paris: Les éditions du Cerf, 1947).

M. Marcovich, *Hippolytus, Refutatio omnium haeresium* (PTS 25; Berlin/New York: De Gruyter, 1986).

M. Simonetti, *Contro Noeto* (Biblioteca patristica 35; Bologna: EDB, 2000).

Secondary works

B. Botte, *La tradition apostolique de Saint Hippolyte: Essai de reconstitution* (LWQF 39; Münster: Aschendorff, 1963).

A. Brent, *Hippolytus and the Roman Church in the Third Century: Communities in Tension before the Emergence of a Monarch-Bishop* (SVigChr 31; Leiden/Boston/Cologne: Brill, 1995).

J. A. Cerrato, *Hippolytus between East and West: The Commentaries and the Provenance of the Corpus* (Oxford: Oxford University Press, 2002).

M. Guarducci, *San Pietro e Sant'Ippolito: Storia di statue famose in Vaticano* (Rome: Istituto Poligrafico e Zecca dello Stato, 1991).

K. Koschorke, *Hippolyts Ketzerbekämpfung und Polemik gegen die Gnostiker: Eine tendenzkritische Untersuchung seiner 'Refutatio omnium haeresium'* (Göttinger Orientforschungen 6; Wiesbaden: Harrassowitz, 1975).

V. Loi, 'La problematica storico-letteraria su Ippolito' and 'L'identità letteraria di Ippolito di Roma', in Istituto Patristico Augustinianum Roma (ed.), *Ricerche su Ippolito* (SEAug 13; Rome: Institutum Patristicum Augustinianum, 1977) 9–16 and 67–88.

P. Nautin, *Hippolyte et Josipe: Contribution à l'histoire de la littérature chrétienne du troisième siècle* (Études et textes pour l'histoire du dogme de la Trinité 1; Paris: Les éditions du Cerf, 1947).

C. Osborne, *Rethinking Early Greek Philosophy: Hippolytus of Rome and the Presocratics* (London: Duckworth, 1987).

C. Scholten, 'Hippolytus II (von Rom)', *RAC* 15 (1991) 492–551.

11

Gregory Thaumaturgus

MICHAEL SLUSSER

Introduction

Gregory Thaumaturgus was a third-century bishop in Pontus in northern Asia Minor. Regarded by the later Cappadocian Fathers as one of the greatest of their forebears in the Christian faith, he has left behind a few writings, a legend full of miracles, and now also a 'Bermuda triangle' of critical questions.

Who is Gregory Thaumaturgus?

Saint Gregory Thaumaturgus, 'the Wonderworker', is little known to people today. If I mention him, someone may exclaim, 'Oh, I've heard of him. Wasn't he Saint Basil's brother, or his best friend?' No, that was Gregory of Nyssa or Gregory Nazianzen. Others think that he was Pope Gregory I, who like Gregory Thaumaturgus was known as 'the Great', or Gregory of Tours. One person even identified him as the Apostle of Armenia, Saint Gregory the Illuminator, which was a good guess, since he too had strong connections to Cappadocia. Gregory of Agrigentum and Gregory of Elvira seem to be even less known than our Gregory. Obscure or not, Saint Gregory Thaumaturgus is probably the namesake of these other Gregories, either directly or indirectly.

Gregory was bishop of Neocaesarea (modern Niksar) on the borders of Cappadocia and Pontus in northern Asia Minor during the 250s and 260s, and possibly even a little earlier. He was famous in his own time, as the large number of later Gregories attests, but it is not as if he has a great deal of competition for historical fame in that period. During the fifty years between 235 and 285, that is, between the end of the Severan dynasty and the arrival of Diocletian, 'there were at least eighteen "legitimate" emperors, and far more if one counts the numerous usurpers of the period'.[1] Documentation from that period (even about the emperors themselves) is scarcer than from the more settled periods before and after. We know of our Gregory through references

---

[1] J. F. Matthews in *The Oxford Classical Dictionary*, 3rd edition, edited by Simon Hornblower and Antony Spawforth (Oxford: Oxford University Press, 1996), s.v. 'Rome (history)', 1331.

in Eusebius of Caesarea's *Ecclesiastical History*,[2] in Rufinus' expansions to that history,[3] in Jerome's *de viris inlustribus*, his *Letter* 70, and his commentary on Ecclesiastes,[4] as well as mentions in Basil of Caesarea's *On the Holy Spirit* and his *Letters* 28, 204, 207 and 210,[5] and of course the panegyric on Gregory preached by Gregory of Nyssa[6] in Neocaesarea, probably on 19 November 379.[7] The other references to Gregory, such as those in the histories of Socrates[8] and Sozomen,[9] are at least partially dependent on these, and indeed a dependence can be traced even within this brief list.[10] As for what we may learn from Gregory's own writings, the issue is complicated by the fact that there was no ancient corpus of his works; each text has a separate history of transmission.[11]

If one takes these external data as reliable, Gregory was originally from Pontus, where he later became bishop. As a young man, he spent several years in Berytus and nearby Caesarea in Palestine, where he studied with Origen over a period of several years – five or eight, depending on how one reads Eusebius. Upon his departure to return to Pontus, he delivered an *Address of Thanksgiving*[12] in the presence of his master Origen. At some point, either while he was in Palestine or after his return, he wrote a *Metaphrase on Ecclesiastes*,[13] in which he gives that book a Christian spin. After he became bishop of Neocaesarea, he made at least two trips to Antioch in Syria to participate in church councils that were convened to deal with the bishop of Antioch, Paul of Samosata. On one of those trips, he was accompanied by a brother named Athenodorus. I believe that those external data are reliable, but they are being challenged.

---

[2] Eusebius, *Ecclesiastical History*, 6.30 and 7.14; hereafter abbreviated *HE*. The translation used here, unless otherwise specified, is that by J. E. L. Oulton in the Loeb Classical Library (London: William Heinemann, 1964).

[3] Rufinus, *Historia ecclesiastica* 7.25.

[4] Jerome, *de viris inlustribus* 65; *ep.* 70.4; *Comm. on Eccles.* 14.

[5] Basil, *de Spiritu Sancto* 29, §74; *ep.* 28.1–2; 204.2; 207.4; 210.5.

[6] Gregory of Nyssa, *de vita Gregorii Thaumaturgi*, edited by Gunther Heil. *Gregorii Nysseni sermones*, part 2, Gregorii Nysseni Opera, vol 10.1 (Leiden: Brill, 1990), 17–19 (= PG 46.912D–913A).

[7] Stephen Mitchell, 'The Life and *Lives* of Gregory Thaumaturgus', in *Portraits of Spiritual Authority*, edited by Jan Willem Drijver and John W. Watt (Leiden: Brill, 1999), 99–138 (115).

[8] Socrates Scholasticus, *Historia ecclesiastica* 4.27.

[9] Sozomenus, *Historia ecclesiastica* 7.27.

[10] Benedetto Clausi, 'L'altro Gregorio. Intorno alla tradizione agiografica latina sul Taumaturgo', in *Il giusto che fiorisce come palma: Gregorio Taumaturgo fra storia e agiografia*, edited by B. Clausi and V. Milazzo (Rome: Institutum Patristicum Augustinianum, 2007), 185–223.

[11] There may be a partial exception to this in the transmission of the *Metaphrase on Ecclesiastes* and *To Philagrius* together in a characteristic extension of some of the manuscripts of Gregory Nazianzen's works.

[12] Grégoire le Thaumaturge, *Remerciement à Origène, suivi de la Lettre d'Origène à Grégoire*, edited and translated by Henri Crouzel, Sources chrétiennes 148 (Paris: Éditions du Cerf, 1969). Crouzel's introduction to this volume, though dated, was as close as there was to being a monographic study of Gregory at that time. His text is based on *Des Gregorios Thaumaturgos Dankrede an Origenes, als anhang der Brief des Origenes an Gregorios Thaumaturgos*, edited by Paul Koetschau, Sammlung ausgewählter kirchen- und dogmengeschichtlicher Quellenschriften 9 (Freiburg and Leipzig, 1894).

[13] *PG* 10.988–1017.

Nautin's challenge to the general consensus

The late Pierre Nautin gives a *much* shorter account of Gregory Thaumaturgus: 'In the end, the only thing that we know for certain about Gregory Thaumaturgus is that he was bishop of Neocaesarea in Pontus at the time when the young Eusebius saw him.' He continues, 'Everything else is conjecture by Eusebius and other hagiographers; let each make use of it as he sees fit, according to his own standards on historical matters.' Nautin recognizes only two standards, either the 'precritical' attitude that held sway up till the publication of his book *Origène* in 1977 or the 'critical' attitude that he himself uses.[14] Of the written works generally attributed to Gregory, Nautin accepts (but with unspecified reservations) only the *Canonical Epistle* and the lost *Dialogue with Gelianus* referred to by Basil.

What of the *Address of Thanksgiving*, which up to now has been a central piece of Gregory Thaumaturgus' dossier? Nautin ascribes it to another student of Origen's of whom nothing is known except his name, 'Theodore'. Such was Nautin's confidence in this assertion that in the index of cited works at the back of his 1977 book he lists Theodore, without quotation marks or question mark, as the author of the *Address of Thanksgiving*.[15] He has persuaded some to this view: some Italian scholars have accepted that attribution to the point of listing 'Teodoro/Gregorio' among the pre-1500 names in the indices to recent books,[16] while other scholars have decided to treat the authorship of the *Address* as an open question.

Nautin's hypothesis is that Eusebius found the name 'Theodore' in the title of the *Address of Thanksgiving*, and that Theodore was the student of Origen who delivered the *Address*. Then Eusebius found 'Gregory' in the letter of Origen to a student of that name that is preserved in the *Philokalia*.[17] There is no evidence that it was written to Gregory Thaumaturgus or to the author

---

[14] Pierre Nautin, s.v. 'Grégoire dit le Thaumaturge', *Dictionnaire d'histoire et de géographie ecclésiastiques* by Alfred Baudrillart (Paris: Letouzey et Ané, 1912); the fascicle in which this article appears came out in 1987, but from the bibliography it apparently was written some years before. It draws on and summarizes material from Nautin's earlier book, *Origène. Sa vie et son œuvre* (Paris: Beauchesne, 1977).

[15] *Origène*, 469. In his 1947 monograph, *Hippolyte et Josipe. Contribution à l'histoire de la littérature chrétienne du troisième siècle*, Nautin proposed to assign some of the writings of Hippolytus, notably his *Refutation of all heresies*, to a certain 'Josipe'; the only place where I have seen Josipe (or Josippus) listed among ancient authors is in the indices to Nautin's own *Origène* and *Le Dossier d'Hippolyte et de Méliton* (Paris: Éditions du Cerf, 1953). Other authors do not seem to have followed his lead; see most recently V. Saxer, s.v. 'Josipe, prétendu écrivain ecclésiastique romain du début du IIIe siècle', *Dictionnaire d'histoire et de géographie ecclésiastiques* 28, 273–74.

[16] Clausi and Milazzo, *Il giusto che fiorisce come palma*, 298; there are also entries for 'Gregorio (il) Taumaturgo' and 'Gregorio (il) Taumaturgo (pseudo)' on page 296; also *La biografia di Origene fra storia e agiografica*, edited by Adele Monaci Castagno (Turin: Pazzini, 2004), 327, which lists 'Teodoro, Discorso di ringraziamento' in the index of ancient authors.

[17] This text from the *Philokalia*, Chapter 13, is conveniently available in Henri Crouzel's 'Sources chrétiennes' edition of the *Address of Thanksgiving*, 185–95, and is translated in the Appendix of my *St Gregory Thaumaturgus: Life and Works*, Fathers of the Church 98 (Washington: Catholic University of America Press, 1998), 190–92.

156

of the *Address of Thanksgiving*, but Nautin thinks that Eusebius guessed that the addressee was our Gregory. This is speculation on Nautin's part, and Marco Rizzi, who favours Nautin's hypothesis in other respects, thinks that this proposal has been definitively disproved.[18] Later, when Eusebius reported on the letter from the Antiochene council of 264 against Paul of Samosata,[19] Nautin thinks that he used that guess to explain why the famous bishop Gregory from Pontus, whom Eusebius had once seen when he was a lad[20] and who had attended that council, is not named in the council's letter: there is a 'Theodore' in that letter[21] and this must be none other than Gregory. Nautin, as he continues to read Eusebius' mind, thinks that it was on the strength of that guess that Eusebius and Pamphilus, when they came to copy the *Address of Thanksgiving* into the manuscript of Origen's *Against Celsus*, replaced the name Theodore in its title with the better-known Gregory. Later, toward the end of the fourth century at the earliest, the epithet Thaumaturgus was added.[22]

As the reader can see, Nautin constructs his hypothesis on a number of assumptions of his own:

1 Eusebius *must* have been familiar with Origen's letter to a certain Gregory, the letter preserved in the *Philokalia*.

2 Because both Gregory and Athenodorus are described in Eusebius' *Ecclesiastical History* as 'strongly enamoured of Greek and Roman studies',[23] this Gregory must have been the addressee of the *Philokalia* letter.

3 Because, although Eusebius has heard that Gregory was at the Council of Antioch against Paul of Samosata, the letter from that council does not name Gregory, he must be referred to in that list (which is explicitly not exhaustive, which is declared to be names of clergy from the region of Antioch itself, and which includes at least one named presbyter, Malchion)[24]

---

[18] Marco Rizzi, 'Intervento', in *La biografia di Origene fra storia e agiografia*, 31. He cites Eric Junod, who has pointed out that at only two places in the *Philokalia* do its compilers, Gregory of Nyssa and Basil of Caesarea, omit a full textual reference to the work which is about to be cited: here and in Chapter 27. Junod says, 'This silence makes us doubt that the addressee of the letter was the Wonderworker. For if he had been the addressee, how could Gregory and especially Basil not have known? The latter was in contact with the community of Neocaesarea, and he had a special veneration for the memory of its bishop.' See Junod, 'Particularités de la Philocalie', in *Origeniana*, edited by Henri Crouzel, Gennaro Lomiento and Josep Rius-Camps (Bari: Istituto di Letteratura Cristiana Antica, 1975), 186–87.

[19] Eusebius, *HE* 7.28.1.

[20] Eusebius, *HE* 6.30, 'Among these as especially distinguished we know to have been Theodore, who was the selfsame person as that renowned bishop in our day, Gregory, and his brother Athenodore.' Other translations are equally emphatic: '... Theodore – who was none other than that illustrious bishop of our own day, Gregory ...' (G. A. Williamson); '... Théodore, qui portait aussi le nom de Grégoire, l'évêque célèbre de notre temps ...' (G. Bardy).

[21] Eusebius transmits a letter in *HE* 7.30 that mentions the names of some of those who took part in a council at Antioch against Paul of Samosata; the fourteenth name is 'Theodore'.

[22] For a trenchant critical response to Nautin's hypothesis, see Henri Crouzel, 'Faut-il voir trois personnages en Grégoire le Thaumaturge?' *Gregorianum* 60 (1979): 287–319.

[23] *HE* 6.30.

[24] *HE* 7.30.2.

by a different name. Someone named Theodore is named in this list, so Nautin assumes that Eusebius takes this Theodore to be Gregory of Neocaesarea under his other name.

4 Eusebius must have had the *Address of Thanksgiving* in mind when he wrote of the two brothers, Gregory and Athenodorus, that they 'continued with' Origen for 'five whole years',[25] since the foreign student who gave the *Address* also stayed a long time with Origen.[26]

5 The *Address* must originally have been titled 'Of Theodore to Origen ...'; otherwise Eusebius would have had no reason to mention Theodore in *HE* 6.30 at all.

6 The later mention of a 'Theodore' at the Council of Antioch, the alleged presence of Gregory at that Council, and the fact that in his youth Eusebius had encountered two bishops from Pontus named Gregory and Athenodorus, leads Nautin to conclude that Eusebius must have identified the 'Theodore' that he thinks originally stood at the beginning of the *Address* with the Pontic bishop he had seen perhaps thirty years earlier.

This series of conjectures loses power to convince with each successive undocumented inference to which Nautin requires the reader to assent.

How later scholars have reacted to Nautin's challenge

A conference on Gregory held in Italy in 2002 shows the extent to which Italian scholars have either subscribed to Nautin's hypothesis or at least have decided to treat the authorship of the *Address of Thanksgiving*, and consequently the whole picture of Gregory Thaumaturgus, as an open question.[27] Marco Rizzi gave a paper in which he tried to work out the background of its author from indications internal to the *Address* itself. His hypothetical 'Theodore' would have been from Syria, probably from Antioch, although Laodicea, on the coast south of Antioch, is a possibility. Theodore's brother-in-law may even be known to us: Caius Furius Sabinus Aquila Timesiteus, procurator for Palestine in 232.[28] At the same conference, Clementina Mazzucco provided an exhaustive catalogue of the internal hints that the *Address of Thanksgiving* offers about its author.[29] It is striking

---

[25] *HE* 6.30.

[26] In *Address* 1.3, the speaker says that he has not written or delivered a formal rhetorical address for eight years. Nautin, *Origène*, 82, explains the discord between five and eight as due to Eusebius' forgetfulness of the exact number, but there is no reason to accept this conjecture in preference to any other, for example, Alberto C. Capboscq, 'Aspekte der Paideia bei Gregor dem Wundertäter', in *Frühchristentum und Kultur*, edited by Ferdinand R. Prostmeier (Freiburg: Herder, 2007), 279–91 (285), who thinks that Gregory studied law for three years before coming to Caesarea.

[27] *Il giusto che fiorisce come palma*.

[28] Marco Rizzi, 'Ancora sulla paternità dell' *Encomio di Origene*. Spunti geografici e storico-sociali', in *Il giusto che fiorisce come palma*, 73–85, especially 80–83 and, on the brother-in-law, n. 13.

[29] Clementina Mazzucco, 'La componente autobiografica nel *Discorso di ringraziamento* attribuito a Gregorio il Taumaturgo', in *Il giusto che fiorisce come palma*, 101–38.

that her independent reading of the internal evidence does not confirm Rizzi's picture at any point.

Rizzi's volume containing the *Address of Thanksgiving* had already signalled his views.[30] He proposes a two-stage development of the text: sections 1–20, 73–126 and 127–32 would be written additions to a much briefer oral version and would have had as their purpose to give Christianity greater appeal to that class in the eastern regions of the Empire who were becoming more hellenized. At the same Staletti conference, Giulia Sfameni Gasparro agreed that the speech was probably not delivered exactly as we have it in written form, but expressed reservations about Rizzi's proposal of blocks of added text.[31]

A number of the scholars at that conference are so far persuaded by Nautin's arguments that they consider the identity of the author of the *Address* an open question, but they do not follow Rizzi by speculating about a precise identification. Manlio Simonetti, who has been considering the authorship of the *Address* for a long time,[32] gives a typically complex and nuanced answer. While granting that Eusebius may have had evidence that Theodore and Gregory were one and the same,[33] and while confessing that in his old age he does not care for radical solutions,[34] Simonetti says that it is simpler to say that Gregory and Origen never met than to figure out how Gregory came to write so many works that are non-Origenian in character.[35] In the end, despite his having given many reasons to doubt whether Gregory had anything to do with Origen or the *Address*, Simonetti says that he finds it hard to subscribe to a radical solution wholeheartedly.[36] Sfameni Gasparro says that she prefers to suspend judgement on the authorship of the *Address*, although she then proceeds to point out some serious weaknesses in Nautin's hypothesis.[37] Mazzucco agrees to treat the authorship of the *Address* as an open question, but without evident enthusiasm.[38]

In the rest of the scholarly world, one finds a variety of positions in the most recent literature. Christoph Markschies has little time for the Nautin hypothesis that Eusebius conflated Theodore and Gregory into a single figure;

---

[30] Gregorio il Taumaturgo, *Encomio di Origene*, introduzione, traduzione e note di Marco Rizzi (Milan: Paoline, 2002), 84–85.

[31] See Giulia Sfameni Gasparro, 'Origene "uomo divino" nell' *Encomio* del discepolo di Cesarea', in *Il giusto che fiorisce come palma*, 155–56 and 140, n. 6. Likewise, Marcelo Marin voices doubts about Rizzi's literary analysis in his essay in the same volume, 'Pittura e scrittura. Osservazioni sul prologo dell' *Encomio di Origene* (§8)', in *Il giusto che fiorisce come palma*, 87–99 (87, n. 1).

[32] For example, in Simonetti, 'Una nuova ipotesi su Gregorio il Taumaturgo', *Rivista di storia e letteratura religiosa* 24 (1988): 17–41.

[33] Manlio Simonetti, 'Gregorio il Taumaturgo e Origene', in *Il giusto che fiorisce come palma*, 19–30 (25).

[34] Ibid., 26.

[35] Ibid., 28.

[36] Ibid., 30: 'Si tratta comunque di soluzione radicale, che ho difficoltà io stesso a sottoscrivere *toto corde*.'

[37] Sfameni Gasparro, 'Origene "uomo divino"', 142–46.

[38] Mazzucco, 'La componente autobiografica', 103, with n. 10.

as he remarks with some asperity, there are similar examples of ancient notables with two names, such as '*Caecilius Cyprianus, qui et Thascius*, and not least *Origenes, qui et Adamantius*'.[39] Stephen Mitchell dismisses doubts about the authorship of the *Address* with the remark that 'there are no strong grounds for scepticism'.[40] Others who recently take Gregory's authorship as assured include Anders-Christian Jacobsen[41] and Alberto C. Capboscq.[42] A few scholars have voiced sympathy with Nautin's challenge to the authorship of the *Address* by Gregory. Joseph W. Trigg thinks that Gregory was likely the author, but in a footnote says that the attribution is open.[43] Much more radical is Gilles Dorival, who suggests that Nautin did not go far enough when he separated Theodore and Gregory; there may also have been two different *Addresses of Thanksgiving*! For him, the author of the *Address* cannot be identified with Theodore, Gregory Thaumaturgus or another Gregory, but was simply an anonymous student of Origen.[44]

A defence of a more traditional Gregory Thaumaturgus

Someone who is not convinced by Nautin's hypothesis need only suppose that, when Eusebius in *HE* 6.30 speaks of 'Theodore, who was the selfsame person as that renowned bishop in our day, Gregory', he is correct in claiming that Gregory had two names. Nautin has condemned that supposition as 'precritical', but by comparison with his own chain of conjectures that are supported only by further conjectures it seems at least as critical. With no hypothetical 'Theodore' to carry all the conjectural burdens that Nautin placed on him, one can proceed to deal with the other critical issues concerning Gregory and the texts associated with him in the same way one would deal with other ancient materials.

In my book, *St Gregory Thaumaturgus: Life and Works*, I said in the Introduction, 'In this volume I have taken what may be termed a "maximalist" position with regard to Gregory's writings.'[45] Even to someone who does not espouse the Nautin hypothesis that no doubt sounds like an uncritical position,

[39] Christoph Markschies, *Origenes und sein Erbe: Gesammelte Studien* (Berlin: De Gruyter, 2007), 59, n. 111.
[40] Mitchell, 'The Life and *Lives* of Gregory Thaumaturgus', 101, n. 11. He thinks that 'we must accept as truthful' Gregory's account of his own development in the *Address*: ibid., 103.
[41] Anders-Christian Jacobsen, 'Apologetics in Origen', in *Three Greek Apologists. Drei griechische Apologeten*, edited by Anders-Christian Jacobsen and Jörg Ulrich (Frankfurt-am-Main: Peter Lang, 2007), 11–47 (24).
[42] Capboscq, 'Aspekte der Paideia'.
[43] Joseph W. Trigg, 'God's Marvelous *oikonomia*: Reflections of Origen's Understanding of Divine and Human Pedagogy in the *Address* Ascribed to Gregory Thaumaturgus', *Journal of Early Christian Studies* 9 (2001): 27–52 (28 and n. 7).
[44] Gilles Dorival, 'Est-il légitime d'éclairer le *Discours* de remerciement par la *Lettre à Grégoire* et réciproquement? Ou la tentation de Pasolini', in Monaci Castagno, *La biografia di Origene fra storia e agiografia*, 9–26 (20).
[45] *St Gregory Thaumaturgus: Life and Works*, translated by Michael Slusser, 5.

even though I exclude from my list on critical grounds the famous *Creed* from Gregory of Nyssa's *Life of Gregory Thaumaturgus* (see below for the reasons), *To Tatian on the Soul*, the *Letter of Origen to Gregory*, and a fragmentary *Glossary on Ezekiel*. I prefer to take into account all the works that are attributed to him by external attestation, provided they appear to be contemporary with him and not later works sheltering under his august name.[46] Such a corpus of writings may present us with a Gregory who challenges our preconceptions, but I want to try to understand that Gregory, if he can be understood. Otherwise I fear that by 'cutting him down to size' *a priori* as it were, I would be forcing him to conform to modern scholarly presuppositions.

It is not as if we know very much about Christian theology in the mid-third century. We do not know what Gregory Thaumaturgus must have thought, given his time and background, so to try to construct a list of his works on the basis of expectations is surely to move from the less known to the better known, *ignotum per ignotius*. That approach would *a priori* ensure that we would not encounter in Gregory anyone new and unexpected. It is better and more critical, in my opinion, to take the widest collection of what, from external testimony, may plausibly be his works and see what they add up to, rather than to impose a Procrustean framework based ultimately on nothing more than our preconceptions. The text-critical maxim *lectio difficilior potior* has an analogous application in connection with this issue. Then if inconsistencies or even incoherences show up in the writings thought to be Gregory's, maybe one or more of them is not by him; on the other hand, from our point of view he may not be a consistent thinker, or he may be consistent but we may not grasp what he was trying to do or who his audiences were. In the case of Gregory, I think that the writings that we have can be seen together as one man's work, rather as the stars in the constellation Orion suggest a single figure.

What does external attestation tell us about Gregory's works? The best attested as belonging to Gregory is the *Metaphrase on Ecclesiastes*, which is assigned to him by Jerome in *de viris inlustribus* 65 and by Rufinus in his appendix to Eusebius' *Historia ecclesiastica* 7.28. Jerome, in his own commentary on Ecclesiastes, quotes the *Metaphrase* and describes its author as 'the holy man Gregory, bishop of Pontus and hearer of Origen'.[47] The Greek canonical tradition also credits Gregory with a *Canonical Epistle*, which deals with moral issues that arose after an invasion of the Goths.[48] A third writing, *To Philagrius*,

---

[46] There were many such, as one can see from the *Clavis Patrum Graecorum* I, where the entry for Gregory runs 1763–94.

[47] PG 10.1000A.

[48] In the *Pedalion*, the standard compendium of Greek church laws, the *Canonical Epistle* comes in a section devoted to partial lists of canons derived from particular Fathers (after canons of the apostles and those of general and regional councils), between letters of Dionysius of Alexandria and Peter of Alexandria.

poses more problems: it is ascribed to our Gregory in the Syriac tradition,[49] but it appears in Greek manuscripts among the writings of Gregory Nazianzen (*ep.* 243) and Gregory of Nyssa (*ep.* 26), addressed to 'Evagrius'. The subtitle to the Greek version is odd: 'on consubstantiality'. I discount the subtitle as an anachronistic addition, since the text makes no reference to consubstantiality. I accept the attribution in the Syriac transmission to Gregory Thaumaturgus as a *lectio difficilior*, since it is easier to see how 'Philagrius' could be converted to the well-known name 'Evagrius' than the reverse. Likewise the editors of the Greek letters of the other two Gregories deny that it can be by them.[50] The identification is helped by the fact that, in the manuscript tradition of Gregory Nazianzen, *ep.* 243 generally appears in an appendix and nearly always close to Gregory Thaumaturgus' *Metaphrase on Ecclesiastes*, and in the manuscript tradition of Gregory of Nyssa it is usually associated with Nyssa's *Life of Gregory Thaumaturgus*.[51]

Another work that I would include in Gregory's *oeuvre* is the dialogue *To Theopompus on the Passibility of the Impassible God*.[52] Like *To Philagrius*, this text has come down to us in Syriac, but unlike it no Greek original has been discovered. Luise Abramowski expressed doubt as to its authenticity, because Philoxenus of Mabbug quotes a few words as coming from 'one of the true teachers, the holy Gregory'. Since Gregory Thaumaturgus in the fourth century was usually called 'the Great', Abramowski suggests that perhaps there was another third-century Gregory known as 'the Teacher'.[53] But our Gregory also went by that epithet; in his *Life* by Gregory he is designated 'the Teacher' seven times, as well as the more frequent epithet, 'the Great'.

Before proceeding to consider the *Address of Thanksgiving*, I should like to note that these texts attributed to Gregory Thaumaturgus by external testimony (*Metaphrase on Ecclesiastes*, *Canonical Epistle*, *To Philagrius* and *To Theopompus*), along with the fragment of a *Dialogue with Gelianus*,[54] are texts that Manlio

---

[49] Brit. Mus. add. 14597, fol. 119 and 12170, fol. 246v–247r. See Johannes Baptista Pitra, *Analecta sacra spicilegio Solesmensi* (Paris: Ex publico Galliarum typographeo, 1883), 4:100–103, 360–63.

[50] Georgius Pasquali, *Gregorii Nysseni epistulae*, Gregorii Nysseni Opera 8.2 (Berlin: Weidmann, 1925), ii; Paul Gallay, *Saint Grégoire de Nazianze: Lettres* I (Paris: Les Belles Lettres, 1964), xxi.

[51] See my *St Gregory Thaumaturgus*, pp. 29–32, and 'The "To Philagrius on Consubstantiality"', of Gregory Thaumaturgus', *Studia Patristica* 19, edited by Elizabeth A. Livingstone (Leuven: Peeters, 1989), 230–35.

[52] The text is found in Brit. Mus. add. 12156, fol. 122r–129v. See Pitra, *Analecta sacra spicilegio Solesmensi*, 4:103–20, 363–76.

[53] Luise Abramowski, 'Die Schrift Gregors des Lehrers "Ad Theopompum" und Philoxenus von Mabbug', *Zeitschrift für Kirchengeschichte* 89 (1978): 273–90.

[54] Basil, *ep.* 210.5: 'And they made an attempt by letter also against Anthimus, Bishop of Tyana, who is of one mind with us, to the effect that Gregory had said in his Exposition of the Faith that the Father and the Son in thought are two, in person one. But the fact that this was said, not dogmatically, but controversially in the dialogue with Aelianus [*v.l.* Gelianus] . . .'. The citation from Gregory cannot be more than ten Greek words.

Simonetti recently found at least relatively plausible as authentic works of Gregory Thaumaturgus.[55]

Unlike several of the scholars named above, I attribute the *Address of Thanksgiving to Origen* to Gregory Thaumaturgus, depending mainly on the external attributions. Jerome lists it among his works,[56] and Jerome claims to have had excellent access to the library at Caesarea, specifically to the remains of the work of the martyr Pamphilus.[57] Rufinus, who translated part of Pamphilus' *Apology for Origen*, does not mention the *Address of Thanksgiving* in his excursus on Gregory Thaumaturgus in *HE* 7.25, but he may not have had as good access to the sources in Caesarea as Jerome had.[58] Socrates Scholasticus says that Pamphilus the Martyr mentions Gregory in his own *Apology for Origen* and that the *Address of Thanksgiving* was included in the same manscript with Pamphilus' *Apology*.[59] It has never been attributed to any other author until Pierre Nautin hypothesized his otherwise unknown 'Theodore'.

A special problem is posed by one other text, the *Creed* that Gregory of Nyssa places in his *Life of Gregory Thaumaturgus*.[60] Despite the work of Luise Abramowski,[61] Simonetti is not ready to exclude it from the corpus of Gregory Thaumaturgus' writings, although he admits to doubts about its authenticity.[62] Gregory of Nyssa says that this *Creed* contains the initiation into the mystery of the truth uttered by John the Evangelist at the request of the Blessed Virgin Mary during a waking vision experienced by Gregory Thaumaturgus. After reciting it, Nyssa adds, 'Whoever would like to be convinced of this should listen to the church, in which he proclaimed the doctrine, where the inscriptions of that blessed hand are preserved to this very day', and he compares

---

[55] Simonetti, 'Gregorio il Taumaturgo e Origene', 23: 'questo frustulo di *Gel* è il testo di più sicura paternità gregoriana' (This fragment of *Gel* is the text whose Gregorian authorship is most secure); 29: 'gli scritti che riportiamo a Gregorio con sicurezza (*Gel. Metafrasi*) o con maggiore probabilità (o, forse, minore improbabilità) (*Teop Fil*)' (The writings that we assign to Gregory with certainty [*Gel. Metafrasi.*] or with greater probability [or perhaps less probability] [*Teop Fil*]); 20: 'resta fuori discussione la *Lettera canonica*, la cui autenticità non è stata mai seriamente revocata in dubbio' (The *Canonical Epistle*, whose authenticity has never seriously been questioned, remains beyond discussion).

[56] *de viris inlustribus* 65; he also describes Gregory as *Origenis auditor*, 'one who heard Origen', *comm. in Eccles.* 4, a point that he could have got from Eusebius.

[57] *de viris inlustribus* 75.

[58] See Éric Junod, 'L'auteur de l'*Apologie pour Origène* traduite par Rufin. Les témoignages contradictoires de Rufin et de Jérôme à propos de Pamphile et d'Eusèbe', *Recherches et Tradition: Mélanges patristiques offerts à Henri Crouzel*, edited by André Dupleix (Paris: Beauchesne, 1992), 165–79.

[59] Socrates Scholasticus, *HE* 4.27.

[60] Gregory of Nyssa, *de vita Gregorii Thaumaturgi*, edited by Heil. *Gregorii Nysseni sermones*, part 2, Gregorii Nysseni Opera, vol 10.1, 17–19.

[61] Luise Abramowski, 'Das Bekenntnis des Gregor Thaumaturgus bei Gregor von Nyssa und das Problem seiner Echtheit', *Zeitschrift für Kirchengeschichte* 87 (1976): 145–66. Her argument, based on many parallel passages, especially from Basil of Caesarea, that Gregory Thaumaturgus is not its source is detailed and conclusive in my view.

[62] Simonetti, 'Gregorio il Taumaturgo e Origene', 23–24, where he says that he cannot subscribe to Abramowski's conclusion wholeheartedly, and 29, where he admits that there are 'dubbi non privi di consistenza' raised against both the *Creed* and the *Address*.

this miracle with the Ten Commandments engraved on tablets of stone, but with these differences: here Gregory's soul takes the place of the tablet, and the voice of the one he saw takes the place of the graven letters.[63]

Some have thought on the basis of this passage from the *Vita* that Nyssa must mean that the text was inscribed somehow on the walls of the church at Neocaesarea where he preached this panegyric. There are several objections to that.

1 Gregory of Nyssa does not actually say that 'the inscriptions of that blessed hand' contain the *Creed* he has just recited.
2 Very few inscriptions of more than 100 words (which this one has, even if apparently parenthetical sections are omitted) have survived, and this one would presumably have been on an interior wall of a sturdy third-century church building that had survived at least one earthquake;[64] I find it difficult to imagine Gregory of Nyssa reading a very long inscription more than a century old off the wall of a dimly lit church.
3 The oriental versions of the *Vita* or of traditions on which Gregory based it have a different story and different, simpler formulas. The mystical initiation is delivered before the vision, not in it (in a Syriac text it appears on the church wall), and it is much shorter.[65] I suspect that if there was any inscription to be read in the church of Neocaesarea, it is more likely to have been in a simple form, perhaps 'One God, One Lord, One Holy Spirit, Perfect Three', which the preacher amplified to his purpose.[66] Even that would be a purely speculative addition to the corpus of Gregory Thaumaturgus' works; it seems to me safer to disregard it entirely.

The upshot of this review of the genuineness of the works attributed to Gregory Thaumaturgus is a short list, which I still believe represents the maximum list of his writings that have survived and are known to us: the *Address of Thanksgiving to Origen*; *Canonical Epistle*; *Metaphrase on Ecclesiastes*; *To Philagrius*; *To Theopompus*; and finally the fragment from the *Dialogue with Gelianus* quoted in Basil, *ep.* 210.

Details about Gregory Thaumaturgus

The *Life* of Gregory Thaumaturgus by his namesake, Gregory of Nyssa, is in great part a homily delivered in the church of Neocaesarea about a century

---

[63] *Vita* 32 (= PG 46.912D–913C, Heil 18–19), tr. Slusser 54–55.
[64] *de vita Gregorii Thaumaturgi* 48 (PG 46.924BC, Heil p. 28), tr. Slusser 62.
[65] Ilaria Ramelli, 'Gregorio il Taumaturgo nelle versione siriache della sua biografia: Alcune note', in Clausi and Milazzo, *Il giusto che fiorisce come palma*, 255–56. A Syriac version: 'Three hypostases of the Father, the Son, and the Holy Spirit, one only divine nature'; a Georgian text: 'Three hypostases of the Father, the Son, and the Holy Spirit, and one only mind of the divinity' (my translations from Ramelli's Italian).
[66] See my translation (n. 43 above), 54–55 and n. 27–28.

and a half after the earlier bishop's death.[67] It draws heavily on miracle stories of the sort that gave Gregory the epithet 'Wonderworker'; Basil of Caesarea and Rufinus of Aquileia give several of the same or similar stories from the same fund of popular accounts, which seems to have pre-existed Nyssa's homily. The historicity of those stories cannot be determined, but nonetheless the homily includes a few details that probably belong in our picture of Gregory Thaumaturgus and his life. The name of Gregory's first supporter in Neocaesarea, Musonius,[68] probably derives from an aetiological church-founding tradition;[69] Basil of Caesarea knew of a bishop of Neocaesarea named Musonius who died in the late 360s[70] and who probably came from the same leading Christian family. Gregory himself probably came from a well-to-do Pontic family; this is supported not only by Gregory's early education and the elite status of his brother-in-law[71] but also by an aside in Nyssa's homily, where he says that 'eloquence and family and other superficialities . . . were qualities of the Great Gregory'.[72] Both Gregory of Nyssa and his brother Basil of Caesarea were raised in a well-to-do land-owning household themselves, and had heard about Saint Gregory from their grandmother Macrina, as Basil testifies in a letter to the Neocaesareans.[73]

There have been various attempts to identify other historical details from the homily.[74] As we have seen, Nautin and Rizzi dispute that the Wonderworker even knew Origen, much less studied with him. At times Simonetti seems inclined to agree, but at another point he suggests that Gregory of Nyssa may have known the *Address of Thanksgiving*,[75] although he certainly does not seem to have made use of it. That Gregory Thaumaturgus knew his contemporary Firmilian of Caesarea[76] is supported by their both having attended a council at Antioch against Paul of Samosata in 264.[77] It is hard to imagine how Gregory could *not* have known Firmilian, the bishop of the principal see in Cappadocia; Origen paid a visit to Firmilian,[78] and bishops from farther away sought Firmilian out for his support, for example, Dionysius of Alexandria and Cyprian of Carthage.[79] Finally, when Nyssa tells his audience that Gregory

---

[67] The last few pages (from PG 46.956A13 and Heil 54.17 to the end) seem to be a written expansion of the oration.

[68] *Vita* 45 (= PG 46.921BC, Heil p. 26), in *St Gregory Thaumaturgus*, tr. Slusser 61.

[69] On this genre, see Gottfried Schille, *Anfänge der Kirche* (Munich: Kaiser-Verlag, 1966).

[70] Basil, *ep.* 210.3 and *ep.* 28, which is addressed to the church in Neocaesarea on the occasion of the death of their bishop, probably the same Musonius.

[71] *Address of Thanksgiving* 56–60, 65–69. Capboscq, 'Aspekte der Paideia', 286, also thinks Gregory was well-educated.

[72] *Vita* 63 (= PG 46.933C, Heil p. 36), tr. Slusser 69.

[73] Basil, *ep.* 204.6.

[74] Paul Koetschau and Henri Crouzel have differing lists; see my *St Gregory Thaumaturgus*, 4, n. 22.

[75] Simonetti, 'Gregorio il Taumaturgo e Origene', 21, n. 6.

[76] *Vita* 22 (= PG 46.905C, Heil p. 13), tr. Slusser 50.

[77] Eusebius, *HE* 7.28.1.

[78] Eusebius, *HE* 6.27.

[79] Eusebius, *HE* 6.46.3; Firmilian's reply, *ep.* 75 among Cyprian's letters.

asked not to be buried in a tomb of his own, this seems a sure indication that his tomb was not venerated locally.[80]

Gregory's theology

As I indicated above, I have taken what may be considered a 'maximalist' position in regard to the genuineness of Gregory's works. This can have the disadvantage of requiring the reader to make sense of materials which seem disparate; somewhat to my surprise, the differences among the works are not particularly great. With a writer from such a distant time and place as Gregory, difficulties are to be expected, and should not be solved by the simple expedient of inventing hypothetical figures. With that having been said once again, let us consider some characteristics of Gregory's theology as it appears in the present body of works.

Gregory of Nyssa tells the story that Gregory found only seventeen Christians in Neocaesarea upon his arrival as bishop, but by his death there were only seventeen pagans left.[81] While that is no doubt a pious legend, Gregory's experience in Caesarea must have contrasted sharply with the less-Christian and certainly less-sophisticated atmosphere from which he came and to which he returned. The challenges would have come from the old traditional religion, rather than from philosophy, Judaism,[82] or Christian heterodoxy. Certainly he would not have found the scriptural resources that existed in Palestine nor the same need to engage in detailed exegesis. When one reads the homilies of Origen, one cannot help but be struck by the knowledge of scripture which he presumes in his hearers; Gregory would not have been able to make the same presumption. Still, Gregory cites enough from both the Old and New Testaments to show that he has personal familiarity with much of scripture.

The *Metaphrase on Ecclesiastes* is a reading of Qoheleth as an argument for conversion from the world to the philosophical life, in the line of Origen's remark that Ecclesiastes 'teaches, as we said, that all visible and corporeal things are fleeting and brittle; and surely once the seeker after wisdom has grasped that these things are so, he is bound to spurn and despise them'.[83] Kenneth Noakes is very perceptive when he points out how well the *Metaphrase* 'supplement[s] the account of ascetical theology learned from Origen given in the Panegyric', that is, *Address of Thanksgiving*.[84] The most probable occasion

---

[80] *Vita* 98 (= PG 956A, Heil p. 54), tr. Slusser 84. William Telfer, 'The Cultus of St. Gregory Thaumaturgus', *Harvard Theological Review* 29 (1936): 232–324, explains this by Pontic burial practices.

[81] *Vita* 27 (= PG 26.909B, Heil, p. 16) and 97 (= PG 46.953D, Heil p. 54), tr. Slusser 52 and 84.

[82] Despite the story in Nyssa's *Vita* 73–76 (= PG 46.940C–941C, Heil pp. 41–43), tr. Slusser 73–75.

[83] Origen, *comm. in Cant.* prologue, 3, in the translation by R. P. Lawson, *Origen, The Song of Songs: Commentary and Homilies* (Westminster: Newman Press, 1957), 41.

[84] K. W. Noakes, 'The Metaphrase on Ecclesiastes of Gregory Thaumaturgus', *Studia Patristica* 15.1, edited by Elizabeth A. Livingstone (Leuven: Peeters, 1984), 196–99 (195).

for the *Metaphrase*, in my opinion, is as an exercise during Gregory's studies in Caesarea.

While the *Metaphrase* makes no direct use of other books of scripture, the *Address* employs the Bible frequently. From the gospels, we find explicit use of the incident of the widow's mite,[85] the Prodigal Son,[86] and the Good Samaritan.[87] Romans is quoted literally,[88] and the influence of the Old Testament can be sensed beyond the obvious references to the story of Jacob in Genesis, the prophecy of Isaiah, and Gregory's famous extended comparison of himself as Jonathan to Origen as David.[89] In the *Canonical Epistle*, Gregory quotes 1 Corinthians and Ephesians.[90]

On the theological front, the reader of the *Address of Thanksgiving* is struck by Gregory's vivid image of the tutelary spirit who guides him to Origen and hands him over to him. This guide is often referred to as the *logos*, and Origen himself is so closely associated with the divine Logos that Gregory says that speaking before him is like 'entering with unwashed feet (as the saying goes) into ears which the divine word itself does not visit shod in the stout leather of riddling and obscure phrases, as in the ears of most men, but entering barefoot (as it were), clear and manifest, it settles there'.[91] He has already spoken in this vein at the beginning of the *Address*: 'But now I call to mind his most godlike feature, where his inner being connaturally touches God (since although for the moment it is enclosed in what is visible and mortal, yet it is struggling with the greatest industry to become like God).'[92] Towards the end of the *Address*, he develops that praise further: 'He is the only living person whom I have either met myself or heard others tell about ... who had trained himself to receive the purity and brightness of the sayings into his own soul, and to teach others, because the Leader of them all, who speaks within God's friends the prophets and prompts every prophecy and mystical, divine discourse, so honoured him as a friend as to establish him as his spokesman.'[93]

A modern Christian reader may find this a sparse account of the economy[94] of God's dealings with us. Gregory offers a fuller theological context for it, though one that uses terms unusual in later Greek theological terminology.

---

[85] Mark 12:41–44 (*Address* 28).
[86] Luke 15:11–32 (*Address* 190–91).
[87] Luke 10:30–37 (*Address* 199).
[88] Rom 1:14 (*Address* 108).
[89] Gen 48:15 (*Address* 41); Isa 9:6 LXX (*Address* 42); and 1 Sam 18:1 (*Address* 85–92). See also Gen 2:15 and 3:14–23 (*Address* 183–88); Psalm 17:4 (*Address* 193); and Psalm 137 (*Address* 194–98). There are numerous Old Testament passages employed in Gregory's reasoning in the *Canonical Epistle*.
[90] 1 Cor 6:13 (*Canonical Epistle* 1); Eph 5:5–13 (*Canonical Epistle* 2).
[91] *Address* 18. See also *Address* 174, where one reason for the obscurities in scripture is 'so that the divine word might not come bare and unclothed into an unworthy soul'.
[92] *Address* 13.
[93] *Address* 175–76.
[94] He does use the notion of a divine economy in this regard: *Address* 40, 45, 55, 72, but also that of providence: *Address* 39, 51, 72.

The principal exposition is in the *Address* 31–39. There is the God of the universe, director and cause of all things, universal king and fountain of all good, with whom our praises begin; but we transfer them 'to one who even in this respect [i.e. offering fitting praise] heals our weakness and who alone is able to make up our shortcomings, our souls' champion and Saviour, his first-begotten Word, the Demiurge and Pilot of all things'.[95] Gregory even explains the doxology:

> The Father of the universe, who made himself one with himself, and by means of him all but self-describes himself, would both honour and be honoured, in a way, with a power entirely equal to his own; this it fell to his only-begotten to possess, first and only out of all that exists, the God-Word who is in him. All other things are able to give thanks and true worship only if, when we make our offering for all the good things the Father has given us, we attribute the power of worthy thanksgiving to him alone, confessing that the only way of true piety is to remember the cause of all things entirely through him.[96]

All of this still seems quite spiritual and even rarified, although the basic structure of Christian faith is clearly recognizable. Gregory seems to think of Christ more as the divine Logos than as the human Jesus. The incarnate Word does appear, however, as the speaker of gospel sayings,[97] and 'the Word, the Saviour of all, who protects and heals all those half-dead and robbed', is clearly a Good Samaritan, not a distant and unaffected divinity.[98]

Gregory's Christology is not docetistic but kenotic. *To Theopompus* is a ringing affirmation of the reality of God's suffering and death: 'But God, who does not need praise and is far superior to passions, came of his own volition to death, without fear or trembling disturbing him in the least.' A little later:

> when he voluntarily entered into death, he was not so contemptible as to flaunt his omnipotence when it was struck by the obstinate resistance of the power of death, but he emptied himself of the dominion which he had over all things, while the nature of God remained, even in death, without corruption, and by the powerfulness of his impassibility he subordinated the passions, in the manner of light when it is associated with darkness.[99]

It ends,

> He came, therefore, O happy one, Jesus came, who is king over all things, that he might heal the difficult passions of human beings, being the most blessed and generous one. But yet he remained what he is, and the passions were destroyed by his impassibility, as darkness is destroyed by light. He came

---

[95] There are antecedents to the term 'pilot' from Athenagoras, Theophilus of Antioch, and *Martyrdom of Polycarp* (see my translation, p. 96, n. 10), as well as to other terms in this passage.

[96] *Address* 37–38.

[97] *Canonical Epistle* 1; see also the parables mentioned in the *Address*, cited above.

[98] *Address* 200, tr. Slusser, 125.

[99] *To Theopompus* 12, tr. Slusser 166–67.

therefore, he came in haste, to make people blessed and rich in good things, immortals instead of mortals, and has renewed and recreated them blessed forever. To him who is the glorious king be glory forever. Amen.[100]

Notice that the name 'Jesus', absent from the *Address* and the *Metaphrase*, appears in that passage; it is also used once in *To Philagrius*, alongside 'Son' and 'Saviour'.[101] Gregory does not dwell much on incarnation, though for the soteriology of *To Theopompus* it is absolutely necessary or the combat with death could not take place at all. Gregory, in the writings that we have, focuses more on the Word as our heavenly guide and helper and the incarnation as instrumental in God's providence for us, less on Jesus in his earthly ministry.

The Holy Spirit appears but once each in the *Address of Thanksgiving* and the *Canonical Epistle*, and not at all in the *Metaphrase on Ecclesiastes* or *To Theopompus*. The *Address* evokes the Spirit in its classic role of the one who inspires the prophets;[102] the *Canonical Epistle* mentions the role of the Holy Spirit in the decisions taken by 'the saints'.[103] In *To Philagrius* the Holy Spirit comes up in the formal setting of a trinitarian credal affirmation. Insofar as any functional role is ascribed to the Spirit, it is coordinate with that of the Son and Saviour, Jesus, as 'the twofold ray of the Father' that 'ministers even unto us the light of truth and also is united to the Father'.[104] There is nothing here that resembles the details of the alleged creed attributed by Gregory of Nyssa to Gregory Thaumaturgus in the *Life*; if anything, the doctrine here sounds somewhat subordinationist.

Manlio Simonetti calls attention to the monarchian cast of those writings that can be attributed to Gregory with relative assurance, and he notes that he has more in common with other Asian Christian writers than with Origen and Alexandria.[105] I think that he is both perceptive and right. But, unlike Simonetti, I have no difficulty in thinking that Gregory spent all those years with Origen and still did theology in a way that contrasted with his master; he would not be the first or the last student who learned a great deal from a teacher without becoming an imitator.

The genuine works of Gregory – even *To Philagrius* – show little dogmatic development that would strain the credulity of a non-Christian who was slightly acquainted with Christian belief. There are three possible explanations of this phenomenon.

1 Gregory's own Christianity was rudimentary and reflects the kind of simplification that can be expected when a religious faith is transplanted from a cultural setting where many corollary beliefs and practices support

---

[100] *To Theopompus* 17, tr. Slusser 173.
[101] *To Philagrius* 7, tr. Slusser 177.
[102] *Address* 179.
[103] *Canonical Epistle* 7; see Acts 15:22, 28.
[104] *To Philagrius* 7, tr. Slusser 177.
[105] Simonetti, 'Gregorio il Taumaturgo e Origene', 25–27, 30.

it to the stony soil of a new territory and population. In favour of this is the evidence that a century later Neocaesarea was still something of a theological backwater whose simplistic views taxed the patience of both Gregory of Nyssa and his brother Basil.

2 The works we have are exoteric, addressed precisely to outsiders, and present quite a different theological vision from the one which would have been the theme of Gregory's preaching within Christian circles; that might explain the sparsity of argument from scripture and, in the case of the *Metaphrase*, its protreptic character.

3 Perhaps the works we have, apart from the *Canonical Epistle*, were produced by Gregory in his early enthusiasm for Christianity as a student under Origen, and document the process by which he was absorbing Christian ideas rather than the developed vision of his later years as a bishop. This suggestion has in its favour the fact that Gregory's writings were preserved in Palestine and Syria, where he had been a student. While all three explanations are defensible, I tend to think that the sophistication of Gregory's arguments in *To Theopompus* and *To Philagrius* speaks against the hypothesis that these are all works of his early years as a Christian.

Whatever the answer to that question, we are better informed about Gregory's moral teaching than about his dogmatic vision. For Gregory, the goal of moral life is 'to come to God and remain in him, having been made like him by a clean mind'. This is primarily the work of true piety, ευσέβεια, which he calls 'the mother of the virtues ... the beginning and the culmination of all the virtues'.[106] In the *Metaphrase*, he says that 'for those people who remain upon the earth there is one salvation, if their souls would recognize and attach themselves to the one who gave them birth',[107] a formulation which matches closely the *Address*'s statement of the goal of the moral life.

This true piety, in Gregory's view, calls for leading a philosophic life, and both the *Address* and the *Metaphrase* describe the urgent need for conversion to philosophy. In the *Metaphrase* he uses the experience of the futility of the unreflective life to break down the reader's resistance to philosophy, as Origen broke down Gregory's own resistance through the process so eloquently described in the *Address* 73–92. Driven to the recognition of how futile other pursuits are, he concludes, 'I saw clearly the genuine goods which face a person: the knowledge of wisdom and the possession of fortitude', accompanied by a desire for peace and quiet.[108] Here are signs not only of philosophic *otium* but also of monastic anachoresis.

Gregory's vision of the philosophic life places a high value on personal relationships. That comes through repeatedly in the *Address*, for example, in

---

[106] *Address* 149; see also *Address* 165, where he calls 'the knowledge of the divine and true piety' 'the greatest and most necessary of all'.

[107] *Metaphrase* PG 10.1017A; see also PG 10.1005C1: 'The greatest good is to lay hold of God.'

[108] *Metaphrase* PG 10.993C; compare *Address* 185: 'How profitable I learned it is to live in quietness ...!'

the famous passage where he compares the drawing power of Origen's friend-ship to David's attraction for Jonathan (*Address* 81–92), and in his appreciative remarks about the other men who form the circle around Origen (*Address* 3–4,[109] 189[110] and 196). We see the same preference for relationship over the solitary life in the way in which the *Metaphrase* develops Ecclesiastes' reflections on the isolation of the miser.[111] This passage lends some credibility to the way Gregory of Nyssa later portrayed the Wonderworker as usually accompanied by associates,[112] and may foreshadow the Cappadocians' own experiments with spiritual community.

The path of virtue to which true piety summons us includes of course the cardinal virtues so well known from earlier Greek tradition.[113] The language Gregory uses, 'mastery and understanding of the impulses themselves' (*Address* 137), is characteristic of the period and would fit well in a Stoic context,[114] as would the emphasis on doing 'what really belongs to us', rather than focus-ing on what others do (*Address* 138–39). Gregory places particular emphasis on temperance and detachment from worldly possessions. While the biblical Qoheleth says that wisdom protects a person like money (Eccl 7:12), Gregory says, 'Real life, for a human being, comes not from the precarious possession of wealth, but from wisdom' (PG 10.1005B). The strength of Gregory's feeling on the danger of excessive attachment to wealth may be reflected in the way that the *Canonical Epistle* devotes canons 2–5 and 8–10 to harsh censure of those who have taken advantage of the chaos left behind by the Goths to enrich themselves at their neighbours' expense.

Gregory introduces the notion of reward and punishment after death into his *Metaphrase* of Ecclesiastes, making it a significant ethical factor in his exhortation to take up the life of wisdom and goodness. In the *Address*, however, no such destiny after death is discussed. True, Origen is described as a man who 'has already completed most of the preparation for the reascent to the divine world' (*Address* 10), whose 'inner being connaturally touches God, though it is for the moment enclosed in what is visible and mortal' (*Address* 13). It is hard to know whether this represents a conventional type

---

[109] '. . . these wonderful men who have embraced the good philosophy'.

[110] Gregory compares life in Origen's company to paradise: '. . . the good land, where I obtained the homeland I never knew of before, and relatives, whom I finally began to know when I had them as soul-mates, and what is truly our father's house, where the father stays and is nobly honoured and celebrated by his true sons who wish to remain there'.

[111] PG 10.997CD–1000A, based on Eccl 4:7–12.

[112] *Vita* 58 (PG 46.929D); 68 (937A); 85 (948AB).

[113] *Address* 122–25. These virtues are presented in the usual way, but there is nothing wrong with that. I disagree with Crouzel's suggestion (see n. 17 above), p. 156, n. 2, that Gregory proposed a specifically Christian virtue of patience.

[114] See also *Address* 115, where virtue produces 'the calm and steady condition of the soul's impulses'. Although Crouzel (see n. 17 above: 147, n. 4) says that the 'most recent' philosophers in *Address* 124, whom Gregory derides, were Stoics, I am not convinced, nor can we be sure that Gregory divided philosophers into the same groupings which historians use today. As Crouzel notes (p. 62), one of the derided 'modern' doctrines in *Address* 124 reappears in *Address* 142, this time assigned to the ancients, and with commendation.

of praise, or whether Gregory himself thought in those terms. But in the *Address*, true piety is its own reward, and God's paradise for us today is the life of philosophy led in union with God. At the root of our capacity to lead such a life, Gregory sees 'the leader of our souls and our saviour, [God's] first-begotten word' who 'is the truth and the wisdom and the power of the father of the universe himself, and is also with and in him and united to him completely' (*Address* 35–36) – exactly the description which Gregory gives of the life of ευσέβια itself. As we have seen, however, *To Theopompus* ascribes such a saving role explicitly to Jesus.

This, as far as I can portray him, is Gregory 'the Great', who later became known as 'the Wonderworker'. We can barely discern his outline through historical documents. How many like him have vanished completely from our ken?

Bibliography

Texts and introductions

St Gregory Thaumaturgus: Life and Works, introduced and translated by Michael Slusser, Fathers of the Church 98 (Washington: Catholic University of America Press, 1998). The *Life* by Gregory of Nyssa is included.

The Works of Gregory Thaumaturgus, Dionysius of Alexandria, and Archelaus, translated by S. D. F. Salmond, Ante-Nicene Christian Library 20 (Edinburgh: T&T Clark, 1871).

Grégoire le Thaumaturge, *Remerciement à Origène, suivi de la Lettre d'Origène à Grégoire*, introduced, edited and translated by Henri Crouzel, Sources chrétiennes 148 (Paris: Éditions du Cerf, 1969).

John Jarick, *Gregory Thaumaturgos' Paraphrase of Ecclesiastes*, Septuagint and Cognate Studies 29 (Atlanta: Scholars Press, 1990).

Studies

Benedetto Clausi and Vincenza Milazzo (eds), *Il giusto che fiorisce come palma: Gregorio Taumaturgo fra storia e agiografia*, Atti del Convegno di Staletti (CZ) 9–10 Novembre 2002, Studia Ephemeridis Augustinianum 104 (Rome: Institutum Patristicum Augustinianum, 2007).

Michel van Esbroeck, 'The *Credo* of Gregory the Wonderworker and Its Influence through the Ages', *Studia Patristica* 19, edited by E. A. Livingstone (Leuven: Peeters, 1989) 255–66.

Robin Lane Fox, *Pagans and Christians* (San Francisco: Harper & Row, 1988).

William Telfer, 'The Cultus of St. Gregory Thaumaturgus', *Harvard Theological Review* 29 (1936) 225–344.

Reymond Van Dam, 'Hagiography and History: The Life of Gregory Thaumaturgus', *Classical Antiquity* 1 (1982) 272–308.

12

Eusebius of Caesarea

TIMOTHY DAVID BARNES

Introduction

Eusebius of Caesarea is one of the most misunderstood of early Christian writers. The fundamental cause of this misunderstanding, which still persists in many quarters, is simple. On the one hand, a vast amount has been written since the sixteenth century about Eusebius' *Ecclesiastical History* and his *Life of Constantine*, and historians of ancient culture, philosophy and religion have gratefully analysed the many pagan and Jewish texts that survive only because Eusebius' *Preparation for the Gospel* quotes them *in extenso*. On the other hand, most studies of Eusebius in the twentieth century neglected his biblical commentaries, even though they provide the deepest insight into his thinking and habits of mind. Admittedly, a critical edition of Eusebius' *Commentary on Isaiah* was not available until 1975, after its editor (Joseph Ziegler) had completed his life's work on the Greek text of Isaiah, while the *Commentary on the Psalms* is preserved only in part.

There have also been two serious subsidiary causes of the persistent misunderstanding. First, on the historical level, Eusebius' presentation of himself as close to the emperor in his *Life of Constantine* was accepted uncritically, even (or even especially) by those who disbelieved his depiction of Constantine, so that it was widely, perhaps even universally, assumed that in his later years Eusebius frequented the court of Constantine. Second, on the literary and intellectual level, the *Reply to Hierocles* was taken to show that Eusebius was acquainted with the so-called Second Sophistic Movement, which greatly influenced Greek literature and style in the second century and later. These two misapprehensions were only corrected quite recently: in 1981 it was demonstrated that Eusebius met Constantine on no more than four occasions, always in the company of many other bishops, and in 1992 it was shown that the *Reply to Hierocles* was written by another Eusebius and so cannot be used as a barometer of the literary culture of Eusebius of Caesarea.

Progress towards understanding both Eusebius and Constantine was, for more than a century, derailed by Jacob Burckhardt, whose classic *Die Zeit Constantin's des Grossen* was first published in 1853 and issued in a revised edition in 1880, which introduced the concept of a *Reichskirche*, absent from the first edition, under the impact of the unification of Germany in 1870 and its consequences. In flat defiance of the evidence of Lactantius and

Eusebius, both of whom he was therefore obliged to discredit by fair means or foul, Burckhardt depicted Constantine as a fourth-century Napoleon, not only a skilful politician (as he indeed was) but also essentially irreligious and amoral. Burckhardt denounced Eusebius as 'the most objectionable of all eulogists' and 'the first thoroughly dishonest historian of antiquity', for he believed that, as a habitué of the imperial court, Eusebius knew the truth about Constantine (as Burckhardt himself defined it), but deliberately misrepresented it: he praised Constantine insincerely, falsified history and indulged in 'contemptible inventions'.[1] In reality, the bishop of Caesarea lived many days' journey from Constantine's nearest imperial residences in Nicomedia and Constantinople and he met the emperor no more than four times in the dozen or so years when he was his subject.

Burckhardt renewed and added impetus to two linked and ultimately futile scholarly controversies, the one over whether the Constantinian documents in the *Life of Constantine* are authentic, the other over whether the *Life* in its present form really was written by Eusebius of Caesarea. The first controversy raged furiously in the late nineteenth century, then began to abate in the first half of the twentieth until it was completely extinguished when A. H. M. Jones, following up a suggestion by the Oxford Roman historian C. E. Stevens (who owned a copy of Montfaucon's *Athanasius*), showed that part of the text of what had always seemed to be the most dubious of all the documents in the *Life* (2.24–42) was preserved on a contemporary papyrus from Egypt.[2] The second controversy was effectively ended in 1962 when Friedhelm Winkelmann published a magisterial survey of the 'problem of the authenticity of *Life of Constantine*' since the Reformation. Winkelmann examined and disproved all the arguments ever brought against Eusebius' authorship and pointed out that, although Giorgio Pasquali had solved the literary problem of the *Life* in 1910, his solution had been grotesquely misreported by all who wrote about the *Life* for the next fifty years, including Henri Grégoire and Norman Baynes.[3] It was most unfortunate that, when Henry Chadwick ten years later supplied a preface to a second edition of Baynes's classic British Academy paper on 'Constantine the Great and the Christian

---

[1] J. Burckhardt, *The Age of Constantine the Great*, trans. M. Hadas (London: Routledge and Kegan Paul, 1949), 260, 283, 299. The original German is even sharper: 'er ist in die Hände des widerlichsten aller Lobredner gefallen, der sein Bild durch und durch verfälscht hat ... Eusebius ist nicht etwa ein Fanatiker ... er ist aber der erste durch und durch unredliche Geschichtschreiber des Altertums ... so sind dies im Munde eines Euseb, der die Wahrheit wusste, nichts als verächtliche Erfindungen' (*Die Zeit Constantins des Grossen* [2nd edn, Leipzig, 1880], 307, 334–35, 355).

[2] A. H. M. Jones and T. C. Skeat, 'Notes on the Genuineness of the Constantinian Documents in Eusebius's Life of Constantine', *JEH* 5 (1954), 196–200. The papyrus (P. Lond. 878) had received no more than a brief notice in the *Catalogue of Greek Papyri in the British Museum* 3 (London, 1907), xli; it was properly published by T. C. Skeat, 'Britain and the Papyri (P. Lond. 878)', in Siegfried Morenz (ed.), *Aus Antike und Orient. Festschrift Wilhelm Schubart zum 75. Geburtstag* (Leipzig: Harrassowitz, 1950), 126–32.

[3] F. Winkelmann, 'Zur Geschichte des Authentizitlitsproblems der Vita Constantini', *Klio* 40 (1962) 187–243, citing G. Pasquali, 'Die Composition der Vita Constantini des Eusebius', *Hermes* 46 (1910), 369–86.

Church', he implied that 'the one substantial point of fact' where Baynes needed to be corrected was his misdating of Constantine's conquest of the East to 323 instead of 324 (which was relatively trivial), and he failed to draw readers' attention to Baynes's serious error in alleging that Pasquali believed that the *Life of Constantine* contains interpolations from a later hand, when Pasquali had in fact asserted the exact opposite.[4]

The present chapter is divided into five sections: (1) Eusebius' life before he became a subject of Constantine; (2) what is known about his participation in ecclesiastical politics after Constantine's conquest of the East in 324; (3) a discussion of the date, context and contents of Eusebius' extant writings, usually with a brief bibliography of modern scholarship relevant to each work; (4) Eusebius' theological views and his interpretation of human history; (5) a bibliography.

Eusebius before 324

Eusebius was born shortly after 260. Nothing is known about his early life, but as a young man he became the pupil and later perhaps the adopted son of Pamphilus, a priest at Caesarea who devoted his wealth to building up a library which contained both the books which his patron Ambrosius had provided for Origen and Origen's writings and scholarly productions, including the Tetrapla and Hexapla with different versions of the Old Testament in parallel which Origen had devised for its scholarly study. Pamphilus and Eusebius set out to preserve the theological, scholarly and literary heritage of Origen. When the orthodoxy of Origen came under attack during the 'Great Persecution', the two men worked together on a joint *Defence of Origen and his Opinions* in five books, to which Eusebius added a sixth after Pamphilus suffered martyrdom in 310 (*HE* 6.33.4; cf. Photius, *Bibliotheca* 117, 118).[5] During the 'Great Persecution', Eusebius remained in Palestine, where he personally witnessed many martyrdoms in Caesarea, from 303 to 311, but he later visited Tyre and Upper Egypt, where he also witnessed martyrdoms after Maximinus renewed persecution towards the end of 311.

It is not known when Eusebius was ordained as a priest, but in 313 or shortly thereafter he became bishop of Caesarea, and went to Tyre, where his friend Paulinus had also become bishop after the end of the 'Great Persecution', to deliver an oration at the dedication of the new basilica there (*HE* 10.4). When Alexander, the bishop of Alexandria, excommunicated the priest Arius

---

[4] N. H. Baynes, *Constantine the Great and the Christian Church*, 2nd edn with a preface by H. Chadwick (Oxford: Oxford University Press, 1972), iii–viii. Baynes's justly famous monograph began life as a lecture read to the British Academy on 12 March 1930: it was then published in 1931 as 'Constantine the Great and the Christian Church', *PBA* 15 (1929), 341–442, with what Baynes with false modesty described as 'a few bibliographical notes', amounting to more than seventy pages (30–104).

[5] P. Nautin, *Origène. Sa vie et son œuvre* (Paris: Beauchesne, 1977), 99–153; Barnes, *Constantine and Eusebius* (Cambridge, MA: Harvard University Press, 1981), 199–201.

(either not long before or not long after 320), Arius appealed to Eusebius of Nicomedia, who had recently been translated from the see of Berytus (Opitz, *Urkunden* 1–2, 4a–6). Both Eusebius of Caesarea and Paulinus were quickly drawn into the controversy, and they convened a council of bishops in Palestine, which supported Arius against his bishop (Opitz, *Urkunden* 3, 7–10). Shortly after that, the emperor Licinius forbade the convening of further councils of bishops, and the controversy was suspended until Constantine's conquest of the East.

Eusebius and ecclesiastical politics after 324

As a metropolitan bishop, Eusebius played an important part in ecclesiastical politics until his death. As an Origenist, he was sympathetic to the theology of Arius and continued to believe that Arius had the right to propound theological views which he himself might not share, but which he did not consider heretical. Our picture of Eusebius' place in the theological constellation of his age was transformed by Eduard Schwartz's publication in 1905 of a Syriac translation of the synodical letter of a Council of Antioch which met shortly before the Council of Nicaea under the presidency of Ossius of Corduba, whom Constantine had sent to Alexandria to try to reconcile Alexander and Arius (*VC* 2.63–72): this council attempted to solve the Christological problems raised by Arius and declared a provisional excommunication on Theodotus of Laodicea, Narcissus of Neronias and Eusebius, who (the council asserted) 'were proved to have the same views as Arius' (Opitz, *Urkunden* 18).[6] When Eusebius arrived at the Council of Nicaea, therefore, he needed to have the provisional excommunication rescinded before he could participate. Eusebius' account of the Council in his *Life of Constantine* is deliberately bland and uninformative, concentrating on public ceremony and the emperor's attempt to secure unanimous agreement between those present (*VC* 3.10–16): the only document which he quotes is Constantine's letter reporting the Council's decision on the date of Easter (3.17–20 = Opitz, *Urkunden* 26). It is in this context that Eusebius' letter to his congregation in Caesarea must be interpreted (Opitz, *Urkunden* 22): he needed to explain why he had accepted the novel term *homoousios*, since it was clearly incompatible with the Christology which he had espoused before the Council. Eusebius had occasionally referred to Christ explicitly as a 'second Lord' or a 'second God' (*PE* 7.13.2; 11.14.20, quoting the latter phrase from Numenius with approval; *DE* 1.5.11; 5.pr.23, 3.3, 8.2, 16.2, 30.3) and had spoken of God the Son as a second *ousia* separate from the *ousia* of God the Father (*PE* 7.12.2; *DE* 5.1.20–24; 6.pr.1). The Council of Nicaea declared such language heretical. Hence Eusebius' complete *volte face*, which must have shocked the Christians of Caesarea, so that he felt compelled

---

[6] On this council, see esp. L. Abramowski, 'Die Synode von Antiochien 324/25 und ihr Symbol', *ZKG* 86 (1975), 356–67.

to defend himself by invoking and sheltering behind the authority of Constantine.[7]

Theological controversy continued unabated after the Council of Nicaea, with a flurry of now lost polemical works and the condemnations of eastern bishops who showed most hostility towards Arius and his views (whatever they were). Eusebius appears to have presided over the Council of Antioch which deposed Eustathius, the bishop of Antioch (the precise date is disputed),[8] and he may be presumed to have participated in the depositions of other bishops in the Syrian region who are known to have been exiled in the late 320s.[9] With Eustathius deposed, a new bishop was needed for Antioch, and both many Christians in the city and bishops who had come from elsewhere for the Council urged Eusebius to allow himself to be translated to the metropolitan see of Syria, but Eusebius wisely refused (*VC* 3.59–63). Subsequently Eusebius not only participated in the Council of Tyre which deposed Athanasius as bishop of Alexandria in 335, but was one of the leaders of the council who travelled post haste to Constantinople when they discovered that Athanasius had secretly fled there in order to appeal to the emperor against his deposition on the grounds that the council had been improperly conducted. Athanasius convinced Constantine, who annulled the decisions of the Council of Tyre, though he then sent Athanasius to Gaul as a troublemaker. In the next year Eusebius again came to Constantinople, where another council of bishops deposed Marcellus of Ancyra as a heretic, attempted to force Alexander, the bishop of Constantinople, to readmit Arius to communion, and participated in the celebrations of the emperor's *tricennalia* in July 336, just as the Council of Nicaea had joined in the celebrations of the emperor's *vicennalia* in July 325. Eusebius did not live long after Constantine died on 22 May 337: the day of his death is certified as 31 May, and the year could be either 338 or 339.

After 324 as before, Eusebius remained the metropolitan bishop of the Roman province of Palestine. He was on bad terms with Macarius, the bishop of Jerusalem, the prestige of whose see rose sharply with Constantine's construction of magnificent new churches in that city. Hence, although Eusebius attached to the *Life of Constantine* his speech at the dedication of the Church of the Holy Sepulchre in Jerusalem in September 335, he maintained a studied silence about the discovery of wood identified as the cross on which Christ had been crucified three centuries earlier, although he quotes a letter of Constantine to Macarius which refers to the discovery (*VC* 3.30.1–4). Although the *Life of Constantine* constantly insinuates and implies that its author was close to Constantine, Eusebius met the emperor only when ecclesiastical business required him to undertake the lengthy journey

---

[7] Barnes, *Constantine and Eusebius*, 226, cf. 216.
[8] R. W. Burgess, 'The Date of the Deposition of Eustathius of Antioch', *JTS*, n.s. 51 (2000), 150–60, argues strongly for late 328, between October and December.
[9] Barnes, *Constantine and Eusebius*, 227–29.

to the Bosporus. The first occasion was the Council of Nicaea in June and July 325; the second the Council which met in Nicomedia in the winter of 327/28 and readmitted Arius to communion; the third was in the autumn of 335, when Eusebius was a member of the delegation of seven bishops from the Council of Tyre who unsuccessfully requested Constantine to ratify its decisions; and the fourth and last time was in 336 during and after the Council of Constantinople. The emperor attended the councils of 325, 327/28 and 336, and it was doubtless on one of these occasions, probably the first, that he spoke to the bishops, including Eusebius and perhaps over dinner, about his vision and conversion (*VC* 1.28–30).

Eusebius' writings

The standard guide to modern editions of Eusebius' writings by M. Geerard, *Clavis Patrum Graecorum* 2 (Turnhout: Brepols, 1974), 262–75 nos 3465–507, divides them into six categories – exegetical, dogmatic, apologetic, historical, letters and doubtful or spurious. This is a flawed classification since it groups together works which are very heterogeneous in nature: of the supposedly dogmatic works (nos 3475–79), the *Defence of Origen* and the works *Against Marcellus* and *Ecclesiastical Theology* do indeed discuss theological questions, but the *General Elementary Introduction* is more an apologia for Christianity, while the work *On the Festival of Easter* concerns liturgical practice and is probably a homily.

A Works with historical content

1 Chronicle, Ecclesiastical History *and* Martyrs of Palestine[10]

These three works need to be considered together, since not only did Eusebius produce more than one edition of each of them, but they are very closely linked to one another. For the *Ecclesiastical History* presupposes and draws on the *Chronicle*, while the shorter recension of the *Martyrs* was written as the eighth book of the *History* in one of its editions.

The *Chronicle* comprises two very different parts. The first part was a *Chronography* which quoted earlier authors to establish a series of national chronologies, which the second part, the *Chronological Tables*, integrated into a universal chronology in the form of parallel columns of numbered years providing a correlation between Christian history, Jewish dates down to the Incarnation and various Greek dating systems, with important historical events

---

[10] J. Sirinelli, *Les vues historiques d'Eusèbe de Césarée durant la période prénicéenne* (Dakar: Université de Dakar, 1961); G. F. Chesnut, *First Christian Histories* (Paris: Editions Beauchesne, 1977; 2nd edn, Macon, GA: Mercer University Press, 1986); A. A. Mosshammer, *The 'Chronicle' of Eusebius and the Greek Chronographic Tradition* (Lewisburg, PA: Buchnell University Press, 1979); Barnes, *Constantine and Eusebius*, 111–63; H. Gödecke, *Geschichte als Mythos* (Frankfurt & New York: P. Lang, 1987); M. Willing, *Eusebius von Cäsarea als Häreseograph*, Patristische Texte und Studien 63 (Berlin & New York: De Gruyter, 2008).

noted between the columns. Both editions of the original *Chronicle* are lost, but an Armenian translation survives, apparently based on a Syriac intermediary, of both parts of the second edition: this concluded with the *vicennalia* of Constantine which were celebrated in both 325 and 326, and Jerome translated the *Chronici canones* into Latin when he revised and expanded Eusebius' work, continuing it down to the Battle of Adrianople in 378. The date and terminus of the first edition have been disputed. The prevalent opinion during most of the twentieth century was that it went down to the nineteenth year of Diocletian, that is, to 302/303 and hence was completed in 303 or shortly thereafter, as Schwartz argued in 1907.[11] But Rudolf Helm, the editor of Jerome's *Chronicle*, identified its endpoint as the second year of the Roman emperor Probus (276/77), where Eusebius correlated various local eras with the beginning of the 86th Jewish Jubilee, and this view was accepted by the present writer, who drew the double corollary that Eusebius composed the *Chronicle* before the end of the third century and that he composed it primarily as a work of disinterested scholarship.[12] A searching investigation of the *Chronicle* by Richard Burgess subsequently disproved both dates and established that Eusebius wrote the *Chronicle* in answer to Porphyry's *Against the Christians*, a long polemic in fifteen books, which devoted much attention to chronological matters such as the date of Moses and the date of the book of Daniel. Many of Burgess's arguments are technical, since his ultimate aim was to reconstitute the text of the second edition of Eusebius' *Chronicle* for the years 282–325; whether he has reconstituted it successfully or not, it is hard to escape his conclusion that Eusebius cannot have completed the first edition of the *Chronicle* before 306.[13] If so, then 311 is 'the most obvious choice for a concluding date'.[14]

The *Martyrs of Palestine* also survives in two versions. The long recension is preserved complete, though with several small lacunae and perhaps some interpolations by a later hand, in a Syriac translation: its publication by William Cureton in 1861 permitted the identification of sections of the original text in Greek menologia. On internal grounds, it is clear that Eusebius composed this version between Galerius' edict of toleration issued in April 311 and the resumption of persecution by Maximinus in November/December of the same year, though he may not have published it until later, since it contains passages critical of the emperor Maximinus, which cannot have been written

---

[11] E. Schwartz, 'Eusebios von Caesarea', *Realencyclopädie der classischen Altertumswissenschaft* 6 (Stuttgart, 1909), 1370–1439.

[12] R. Helm, *Eusebius' 'Chronik' und ihre Tabellenform. Abhandlungen der preussischen Akademie der Wissenschaften*, Philosophisch-historische Klasse 1923 Nr.4, 42, followed by Barnes, *Constantine and Eusebius*, 111.

[13] R. W. Burgess, 'The Dates and Editions of Eusebius' *Chronici Canones* and *Historia Ecclesiastica*', *JTS*, n.s. 48 (1997), 471–504; *Studies in Eusebian and Post-Eusebian Chronography* 1: *The* Chronici canones *of Eusebius of Caesarea: Structure, Content and Chronology, AD 282–325*, *Historia Einzelschriften* 135 (Stuttgart: Franz Steiner, 1999), esp. 59–65 ('Reconstruction and Translation').

[14] Burgess, 'Dates and Editions', 495.

before his death in summer 313 (3.6–7, 4.1, 6.1–2, 6.7, 7.7–8).[15] The short recension of the *Martyrs of Palestine* is preserved in some manuscripts of the *Ecclesiastical History* (which Schwartz identified as witnesses to an edition earlier than 324), but only in a mutilated form: it lacks any sort of preface or introduction; it ends abruptly with the statement 'The recantation also must be placed on record' (*Mart. Pal.* [S] 13.14) – a document which Eusebius quotes in full in the *Ecclesiastical History* (8.17.3–10); and its ending survives in three manuscripts of the *History* appended to Book VIII (8 app., pp. 796–797 Schwartz). It seems to be an ineluctable inference from these facts that Eusebius composed the short recension of the *Martyrs of Palestine* as an earlier version of Book VIII of the *Ecclesiastical History*, and analysis of the contents of Book VIII fully confirms the inference.[16] The two works thus have a symbiotic relationship that needs to be explained in any account of the genesis of the latter.

The *Ecclesiastical History* is not what the title of the English translation in the Penguin series proclaims it to be – 'the history of the Church from Christ to Constantine'. The first seven books are indeed a history of the Church, but only as far as the late third century. At the end of Book VII, which reached its present form no earlier than 313, Eusebius explicitly discards the chrono-logical framework of Roman emperors and bishops of Rome, Alexandria, Jerusalem and Antioch which provided a structure for his narrative for the 305 years from the Incarnation to the onset of the 'Great Persecution' (*HE* 7.30.22, 32.32). The *Ecclesiastical History* is a history of the Christian Church from its origins to *c.* 280 followed by an account of the 'Great Persecution' from 303 to 313 and the new situation of the Church after the persecution ended (8.1–10.7), with an obvious postscript on the persecution of Licinius (321–24) and his defeat by Constantine. As a result, while Eusebius notes the bishops of Rome, Alexandria, Jerusalem and Antioch down to 303, he largely omits one of the standard components of his *History* so far, that is, the achievements of Christian writers and scholars. It is true that Eusebius includes brief notices of Dorotheus, a priest of Antioch who read the Hebrew Bible with ease, Pamphilus in Caesarea, Pierius in Alexandria and the Pontic bishop Meletius (*HE* 7.32.2–4, 24–28) and a lengthy appreciation of Anato-lius, the bishop of Laodicea in Syria, who composed an Easter cycle and an *Introduction to Arithmetic* in ten books (*HE* 7.32.6–20). But there is no proper notice of the writings of Theognostus and Pierius who continued the traditions of Origen in Alexandria in the last third of the third century before the Anti-Origenist Peter became bishop; there is no mention whatever of Methodius, a bishop in Lycia who composed several important works before he died as a martyr, probably on 20 June 312; and there is no mention of

[15] Burgess, 'Dates and Editions', 502–503, arguing that the long recension was given to the world *c.* 316.
[16] Barnes, *Constantine and Eusebius*, 156–58.

the scholarship of the priest Lucian of Antioch except in the context of his martyrdom (*HE* 9.6.3; cf. 8.13.2). Eusebius' total silence about Methodius may be due to personal enmity, since Methodius attacked Origen, but Eusebius was sympathetic to Theognostus, Pierius and Lucian, who taught Eusebius of Nicomedia, his later ally in ecclesiastical politics.

The textual tradition of the *Ecclesiastical History* provides clear evidence that Eusebius published at least two editions. In particular, the manuscripts which Schwartz designated by the sigla B, D and M, together with Rufinus' Latin version and the Syriac translation, omit all the favourable references to Licinius which stand in the manuscripts A T E R, and these four manuscripts (plus M) contain a series of letters issued by Licinius in the summer or autumn of 313 (*HE* 10.5.2–18) and by Constantine in the winter of 312/13 (10.5.15–17, 6.1–5, 7.1–2), in the summer of 313 (10.5.18–20) and in the spring of 314 (10.5.21–24). From this it follows that there were at least two main editions of the *Ecclesiastical History*, one reflecting the defeat and disgrace of Licinius in 324 and at least one earlier one.

There has been serious scholarly disagreement over how many earlier editions Eusebius produced before 324 and their dates, but until recently most discussions (and especially that of Schwartz) were vitiated by incorrect imperial chronology. It was assumed that Diocletian, to whose death Eusebius refers (*HE* 8 app. 2–3), died on 3 December 316, whereas the correct date is five years earlier (3 December 311), while Constantine and Licinius, whom Eusebius presented as friends and allies in one or more early editions of the *Ecclesiastical History*, went to war in October 316, not October 314, as was universally assumed from 1665 to 1953.[17]

Schwartz posited three editions before 324, the earliest in eight books begun in 311 and completed in 312/13, while Richard Laqueur argued that the first edition was completed before the start of the 'Great Persecution', and the present writer set its date as early as *c.* 295.[18] On this view, the first edition comprised Books I–VII without the passages which obviously reflect a later date; a second edition followed *c.* 313/14, comprising (1) a revised version of I–VII, (2) the unmutilated short recension of the *Martyrs of Palestine* as Book VIII and (3) the new Book IX; and the third edition of *c.* 315 replaced the short recension of the *Martyrs of Palestine* with the present Book VIII and added as an appendix the six imperial letters of 313 and 314, five of which appear to have been sent to Eusebius by the bishop of Syracuse.[19] In a last major revision *c.* 325 Eusebius deleted all his favourable remarks about Licinius,

---

[17] For these dates, see T. D. Barnes, 'Lactantius and Constantine', *JRS* 63 (1973), 29–46 (32–38); *The New Empire of Diocletian and Constantine* (Cambridge, MA: Harvard University Press, 1982), 31–32, 73, 82.

[18] E. Schwartz, *Eusebius Werke* 9.3 (Berlin, 1909), xlvii–lxi; R. Laqueur, *Eusebius als Historiker seiner Zeit* (Leipzig, 1929); T. D. Barnes, 'The Editions of Eusebius' Ecclesiastical History', *Greek, Roman and Byzantine Studies* 21 (1980), 191–201; Barnes, *Constantine and Eusebius*, 128.

[19] T. D. Barnes, 'The Constantine Settlement', in *Eusebius, Christianity, and Judaism*, ed. H. W. Attridge and G. Hata (Leiden: Brill, 1992), 648.

removed the documents (in one of which Licinius speaks in the first person), replaced the documents with the speech which he himself had delivered in the new basilica at Tyre at the invitation and in the presence of bishop Paulinus (10.4), and added a brief account of the anti-Christian policies of Licinius and his defeat by Constantine (10.8–9). The Syriac translation derives from a copy of the *History* from which Eusebius had subsequently removed his reference to the Caesar Crispus, whom his father Constantine executed in 326, as 'an emperor most dear to God and in all respects like his father' (10.9.6–9).

The theory that Eusebius completed a first edition of the *Ecclesiastical History* before 303 has been shown to be untenable, first by Andrew Louth and then, at greater length, by Richard Burgess.[20] It must therefore be discarded. Louth concludes that the edition of 313/14 as described above was in fact the first edition, and Burgess concurs.[21] However, it remains unclear when Eusebius conceived the idea of writing a history of the Christian Church and began to assemble material. For there is an undeniable gap between Eusebius' continuous history of the Church, which peters out *c.* 280, and his narrative of the 'Great Persecution' which perforce begins with the winter of 302/303.

2 Life of Constantine

What is the *Life of Constantine*? The conventional title is a misnomer, since the title prefixed to the list of chapter headings in the manuscripts reads 'On the Life according to God of the Blessed Emperor Constantine'. It would be pedantic at this late date to attempt to replace the traditional title, but any serious analysis of the work must allow that the so-called *Life of Constantine* neither is nor claims to be a biography in the normal sense. In fact it comprises three disparate elements: (1) the *Life* itself in four books; (2) the Greek translation of a speech of Constantine addressed *To the Assembly of the Saints*, which several manuscripts present as a fifth book of the *Life*; and (3) two speeches delivered by Eusebius himself on different occasions. The authenticity of Constantine's speech has often been needlessly doubted,[22] and it should now be taken as proved beyond reasonable doubt that the emperor delivered

---

[20] A. Louth, 'The Date of Eusebius' *Historia Ecclesiastica*', *JTS*, n.s. 41 (1990), 111–23; Burgess, 'Dates and Editions', 471–504.

[21] Louth, 'Date', 123; Burgess, 'Dates and Editions', 483: 'the manuscripts reveal traces of editions completed in 313/4, 315/6 and 324/5'. The possibility that the first edition of the *Ecclesiastical History* comprised eight books and ended with the 'palinode' of Galerius, issued in April 311, as posited by Schwartz, 'Eusebios von Caesarea', 1403–1404, is excluded by the fact that the short recension of the *Martyrs of Palestine*, which on this hypothesis must have constituted the original Book VIII of the *History*, assumes that Maximinus is dead (*Mart. Pal.* [S] 4.8, 6.1, 7.8) and hence cannot have been written earlier than the second half of 313.

[22] For vindication of its authenticity, though dating the *Speech* too early, Barnes, *Constantine and Eusebius*, 73–75, 271, 323–25 nn. 115–49.

it in the main church of Nicomedia at Easter 325.[23] Some of the manuscripts have fused Eusebius' two speeches together (in reverse chronological order) into a single speech with the title 'triakonterikos' (often Latinized as *Laus/ Laudes Constantini*). Moreover, the second speech is not the speech that Eusebius promised to append (*VC* 4.46; cf. 33): an editor after his death has selected the wrong one.[24] The speech that stands first in the manuscripts is a 'Panegyric to Constantine' (*Triakont.* 1–10), which was delivered before the emperor in Constantinople on 25 July 336.[25] The second speech, 'On the Church of the Holy Sepulchre' (*Triakont.* 11–18), was delivered in the previous year, when the Council of Tyre adjourned temporarily to Jerusalem in order to dedicate Constantine's new church there in September 335. The three elements of the *Life* were designed to be read together and to establish both that Eusebius was the authoritative interpreter of Constantine and that emperor and bishop agreed on fundamental theological issues. The Constantine of the *Speech* asserts the existence of a first and a second God, 'two substances (*ousiai*) with one perfection', and that the substance of the second God derives its existence from the first (*Oratio* 9.4). Eusebius had himself used the phrase 'second *hypostasis*' of Christ (*Ecl. Proph.* 4.25 [*PG* 22.1240]), whom he also styled a 'second God' before the Council of Nicaea, though he naturally avoided such language after 325. Moreover, although the text of the *Life of Constantine* never names Arius, who died in 336 in embarrassing circumstances, it praises the emperor allusively for readmitting Arius' allies Theognis and Eusebius of Nicomedia to communion (3.66.3, echoing Opitz, *Urkunden* 30.5).

The *Life of Constantine* is not a finished literary product, as is immediately obvious from the chapter headings, which stand at the head of the work and refer to Eusebius in the third person, whereas he had always used the first person in the chapter headings of earlier works. Pasquali proved in 1910 that the *Life* in its present form is a conflation of two different drafts or concepts, which another hand, probably that of Acacius, his successor as bishop of Caesarea, published after Eusebius' death, in the same way as Philippus of Opus published Plato's unfinished *Laws*, and his proof has been amplified by Winkelmann and the present writer.[26] Every sentence of the *Life* can be assigned with ease to one of its three constituent elements, viz.: (1) an unfinished *basilikos logos* begun shortly after the death of Constantine

---

[23] See B. Bleckmann, 'Ein Kaiser als Prediger: zur Datierung der Konstantinischen "Rede an die Versammlung der Heiligen"', *Hermes* 125 (1997), 183–202; T. D. Barnes, 'Constantine's Speech to the Assembly of the Saints: Place and Date of Delivery', *JTS*, n.s. 52 (2001), 26–36.

[24] T. D. Barnes, 'Two speeches in Eusebius', *Greek, Roman and Byzantine Studies* 18 (1977), 341–45.

[25] H. A. Drake, 'When was the De laudibus Constantini delivered?', *Historia* (1975), 345–56.

[26] F. Winkelmann, *Eusebius Werke* 1.1[2] (Berlin, 1975), xlix–lvii; T. D. Barnes, 'Panegyric, history and hagiography in Eusebius' Life of Constantine', in *The Making of Orthodoxy. Essays in honour of Henry Chadwick*, ed. R. Williams (Cambridge: Cambridge University Press, 1989), 94–123, with an English translation of Pasquali's limpid closing paragraph (98).

on 22 May 337; (2) a continuation of the *Ecclesiastical History*, which Eusebius appears to have begun *c.* 325, put aside in the late 320s and resumed in the autumn of 337; and (3) the additions of the editor who published the *Life* after Eusebius' death.[27]

Although Averil Cameron and S. G. Hall in their recent commentary play down the significance of this analysis, just as Cameron had in two earlier essays, they in practice accept and apply it.[28] On the other hand, they follow the broad consensus of scholarship against the present writer in holding that Eusebius has falsified the picture of Constantine, if not quite to the same extent as Burckhardt claimed: hence they assert with confidence that the emperor 'did not actually ban pagan cult as such', even though Eusebius states categorically that Constantine forbade the setting up of new cult-objects, the practice of divination or other occult arts and sacrifice of animals as part of pagan worship (*VC* 2.45.1).[29] Such scepticism about Eusebius' reports of Constantine's religious policies after 324 has now been shown to be mistaken by Kevin Wilkinson, who has proved that the epigrammatist Palladas was not writing under Theodosius or later, as all without exception had previously believed, but earlier, in fact under Constantine.[30] Palladas lamented that 'We Greeks are men reduced to ashes,/holding to our buried hopes in the dead;/for everything has now been turned on its head' (*Anth. Pal.* 10.90). This pagan perspective on the emperor needs to be taken into account in any future account of both the author of the *Life of Constantine* and the emperor whom Eusebius celebrated.

B Apologetical works

1 *General Elementary Introduction* (Καθόλου στοιχειώδης εἰσαγωγη)

The first five books are lost except for exiguous fragments; Books VI–IX are preserved as four books of *Prophetic Extracts* ('Εκλογαὶ Προφητικαί)/ *Eclogae Propheticae*);[31] and much of Book X, which had the significant title *Second Theophany*, is preserved in the catena of Nicetas on the gospel of Luke, from which Cardinal Mai printed the extensive fragments as if they came from a lost commentary on Luke (*PG* 24.529–606, from A. Mai,

---

[27] Barnes, 'Panegyric, history and hagiography', 102–14; T. D. Barnes, *From Eusebius to Augustine. Selected Papers 1982–1993* (Aldershot: Variorum, 1994), no. XII.7–8 (not published elsewhere).

[28] Averil Cameron and S. G. Hall, *Eusebius: Life of Constantine* (Oxford: Clarendon Press, 1999), cf. Averil Cameron, '*Tria Corda. Scritti in onore di Arnaldo Momigliano*', ed. E. Gabba, *Bibliotheca di Athenaeum* 1 (Como: New Press, 1983), 82–87; *Portraits. Biographical Representation in the Greek and Latin Literature of the Roman Empire*, ed. M. J. Edwards and S. Swain (Oxford: Clarendon Press, 1997), 145–74. In the introduction to their commentary Cameron and Hall state that 'while the work certainly has biographical elements, it is better described as an uneasy mixture of panegyric and narrative history' (1); that 'Eusebius seems to have left the *VC* unfinished or unrevised when he died himself in 339' (3); and that 'the *VC* is a literary hybrid' (27).

[29] Cameron and Hall, *Eusebius: Life of Constantine*, 243.

[30] K. Wilkinson, 'Palladas and the Age of Constantine', *JRS* 99 (2009), 36–60.

[31] Edited by T. Gaisford, *Eusebii Caesariensis Eclogae Propheticae* (Oxford, 1842), whence *PG* 22.1021–262.

'Eusebii Caesariensis – Comentarii in Lucae Evangelium', *Nova Patrum Bibliotheca* 4 [Rome, 1847], 160–207).

2 *Preparation for the Gospel* (Εὐαγγελικὴ Προπαρασκευή/*Praeparatio evangelica*) and *Proof of the Gospel* (Εὐαγγελικὴ 'Απόδειξις/*Demonstratio evangelica*)[32] Eusebius composed this double work in refutation of Porphyry, *Against the Christians*, between 314 and *c.* 321. It originally had thirty-five books in all (15 + 20), but the last ten books survive only in fragments.

3 *Theophany* in five books, of which the full text survives only in a Syriac translation.

The *Theophany* repeats the positive arguments of the *Preparation for the Gospel* and the *Proof of the Gospel* in an abbreviated and simplified form. Eusebius probably composed the work shortly after 324, perhaps as early as 325/26, though it has often been dated a decade or more later.[33]

C Biblical scholarship and exegesis

1 *On the Place-Names in Holy Scripture* (Περὶ τῶν τοπικῶν ὀνομάτων τῶν ἐν τῇ θείᾳ γραφῇ/ *Onomasticon*)[34] The *Onomasticon*, the fourth and only surviving part of a larger work, is a biblical gazetteer, which has long been recognized as an important source for the historical geography of the Holy Land during the Roman period.[35] It shows no awareness of Constantine's building activities in Palestine, but that does not necessarily prove that it must have been written before 324.[36]

2 *Gospel Canons* (sometimes misleadingly styled *Ammonian Sections*)[37] Ammonius of Alexandria had produced a primitive concordance to the gospels in which the four gospels were copied in four columns with their texts rearranged so that parallel passages stood opposite one another. With Ammonius' work before him, Eusebius produced a more sophisticated concordance by dividing the text of each gospel into sections numbered consecutively and then drawing up ten tables or canons. Eusebius explained

---

[32] Barnes, *Constantine and Eusebius*, 71–72, 178–86; J. Ulrich, *Euseb von Caesarea und die Juden. Studien zur Rolle der Juden in der Theologie des Eusebius von Caesarea*, Patristische Texte und Studien 49 (Berlin & New York: De Gruyter, 1999); A. Kofsky, *Eusebius of Caesarea against Paganism* (Boston & Leiden: Brill, 2002); A. J. Carriker, *The Library of Eusebius of Caesarea*, Supplements to Vigiliae Christianae 67 (Leiden & Boston: Brill, 2003); S. Inowlocki, *Eusebius and the Jewish Authors. His Citation Technique in an Apologetic Context*, Ancient Judaism and Early Christianity 64 (Leiden and Boston: Brill, 2006); A. P. Johnson, *Ethnicity and Argument in Eusebius'* Praeparatio Evangelica (Oxford: Oxford University Press, 2006).

[33] Barnes, *Constantine and Eusebius*, 186–88, 367 n. 176.

[34] For a recent text of both Eusebius' version and Jerome's, together with an introduction, notes, and translation (unfortunately not entirely trustworthy), R. S. Notley and Z. Safrai, *Eusebius' Onomasticon. The Place Names of Divine Scripture*, Jewish and Christian Perspectives Series 9 (Boston & Leiden: Brill, 2005).

[35] P. Thomsen, 'Palästina nach dem Onomasticon des Eusebius', *ZDPV* 26 (1903), 97–141, 145–88; Barnes, *Constantine and Eusebius*, 106–11; D. E. Groh, 'The Onomasticon of Eusebius and the Rise of Christian Palestine', *Studia Patristica* 18.1 (1989), 23–31.

[36] T. D. Barnes, 'Eusebius and Legio', *Scripta Classica Israelica* 27 (2008), 59–66.

[37] C. H. Nordenfalk, 'The Eusebian Canon-Tables: Some Textual Problems', *JTS*, n.s. 35 (1984), 96–104.

how to use them in an introductory letter to one Carpianus: 'The first contains numbers in which the four, Matthew, Mark, Luke and John have said similar things' and so on until 'the tenth in which each of them wrote about something in an individual manner'.

3 *Problems and Solutions* or *Questions and Answers* (Ζητήματα καὶ λύσεις; cf. *DE* 7.3.18)[38]

The original is lost, but a Greek epitome survives which indicates that there were two series of *Problems and Solutions*: (a) *To Stephanus on the Genealogy of our Saviour* and (b) *To Marinus on the Resurrection of our Saviour addressed to Marinus*.[39] The problems to which Eusebius provided what he thought were solutions are familiar to any attentive reader of the gospels, the first question being the obvious:'why do the evangelists give the genealogy of Joseph and not of Mary?' If Jesus really was 'begotten of the Holy Ghost by the Virgin Mary', then he had no blood relationship with Joseph and his ascendants. Modern students of the New Testament still wrestle with the same problem.

4 *Commentary on the Psalms* and *Commentary on Isaiah*[40]

While the larger part of Eusebius' *Commentary on Isaiah* has survived as a continuous text written in the margins of a LXX manuscript, the greater part of his *Commentary on the Psalms* is lost. Although the complete text of Eusebius' exegesis of Psalms 51–95.3 (*PG* 23.441–1221) is preserved, only two other commentaries on complete psalms survive: on Psalm 37 among the doubtful works of Basil of Caesarea (*PG* 30.81–104)[41] and on Psalm 49 (R. Devreesse, 'La Chaîne sur les Psaumes de Daniele Barbaro', *Revue Biblique* 33 [1924], 65–81, 498–521). In addition, however, much of Eusebius' commentary on Psalm 118 is quoted in a catena manuscript, which permits his exegesis of particular passages to be compared with that of Origen, Didymus, Apollinarius, Athanasius and Theodoret (M. Harl, with G. Dorival, *La chaîne palestinienne sur le Psaume 118*, Sources chrétiennes 189–90 [Paris, 1972]). The *Commentary on the Psalms* was certainly completed after

---

38 A. E. Johnson, 'Rhetorical criticism in Eusebius' Gospel Questions', *Studia Patristica* 18.1 (1989), 3–39.

39 On the Syriac versions published by G. Beyer, 'Die evangelischen Fragen und Lösungen des Eusebius in jakobitischer Überlieferung und deren nestorianische Parallelen. Syrische Texte, herausgegeben, übersetzt und untersucht', *Oriens Christianus*, n.s. 12–14 (1925), 30–70; 3rd Series 1 (1927), 80–97, 284–92; 2 (1927), 57–69, see C. Zamagni, *Eusèbe de Césarée: Questions évangéliques*, SC 523 (2008), 16–18.

40 Barnes, *Constantine and Eusebius*, 95–105; M. Simonetti, 'Esegesi e ideologia nel Commento a Isaia di Eusebio', *Rivista di Storia Letteratura Religiosa* 19 (1983), 3–44; C. Curti, *Eusebiana I, Commentari in Psalmos, Saggi e Testi Classici, Cristiani e Medievali* 1 (Catania: Centro di studi sull'antico cristianesimo [dell'] Università di Catania, 1987), 193–213; M. J. Hollerich, *Eusebius of Caesarea's* Commentary on Isaiah: *Christian Exegesis in the Age of Constantine* (Oxford: Clarendon Press, 1999).

41 For the attribution to Eusebius, M. Richard, 'Les premières chaînes sur le Psautier', *Bulletin d'Information de l'Institut de Recherche et d'Histoire des Textes* 5 (1956), 88–98, citing the arguments of the Benedictine editor of Basil, Julien Garnier, reproduced by Migne, *PG* 29.ccii–cciii.

324, though it may have been substantially written much earlier, but Eusebius probably composed the whole of his *Commentary on Isaiah* after 324, since it so consistently interprets the Hebrew prophet as foretelling not only the Incarnation, Crucifixion and Resurrection of the Saviour and the persecutions, but also the emergence of a Christian Roman Empire under Constantine.[42]

5 Short exegetical fragments on thirteen other books of the Old and New Testaments are listed as *CPG* 3469.

D Theological treatises

1 Against Marcellus *and* Ecclesiastical Theology

Eusebius wrote his two primarily theological works at the end of his life in order to convict Marcellus of Ancyra of Sabellianism: the first justifies the deposition of Marcellus by the Council of Constantinople in 336, while the second prepares the ground for his deposition by a Council of Antioch in 338/39 after his return from exile in 337. In both treatises Eusebius argues that his own theological views and those of other political supporters of Arius fall within the boundaries of what he calls 'the orthodoxy of the Church', while those of Marcellus do not. The final paragraph of *Against Marcellus* was clearly written after the death of Constantine (2.4.29–31), but the bulk of the work may well have been written earlier and presented to Constantine before the Council of Constantinople as proof of Marcellus' heresy.[43] The *Ecclesiastical Theology* is a diffuse reworking of the same theme and material, preceded by a letter to Flacillus, the bishop of Antioch, who presided over the council which deposed Marcellus for the second time.

E Letters and sermons

1 Letter to Euphrantion, bishop of Balaneae (Opitz, *Urkunden* 3)
2 Letter to the Church of Caesarea explaining his acceptance of the creed adopted at the Council of Nicaea in 325 (Opitz, *Urkunden* 22)
3 *On the Festival of Easter* (Περὶ τῆς τοῦ Πάσχα ἑορτῆς/ *De sollemnitate paschali*): A. Mai, *Nova Patrum Bibliotheca* 4 (Rome, 1847), 207–16, whence *PG* 24.693–706

What survives is commonly identified as part of the 'mystical explanation of the account of the festival' that Eusebius addressed to Constantine and the emperor acknowledged (*VC* 4.34–35).[44] But the work reads more like a homily than a learned treatise, and its main purpose appears to be to explain and justify the decision of the Council of Nicaea on the date of Easter (Opitz, *Urkunden* 26). If that is the case, then Eusebius' references to

---

[42] Barnes, *Constantine and Eusebius*, 249; Barnes, 'The Constantine Settlement', 651–53.
[43] S. Parvis, *Marcellus of Ancyra and the Lost Years of the Arian Controversy 325–345* (Oxford: Oxford University Press, 2006), 127–32.
[44] J. Quasten, *Patrology* 3, *The Golden Age of Greek Patristic Literature from the Council of Nicaea to the Council of Chalcedon* (Utrecht: Spectrum; Westminster, MD: Newman Press, 1960), 339–40.

a forty-day fast before Easter prompt the inference that it was Constantine who introduced the originally western custom of Lent into the East in 325.[45]

F Lost works

1 Collection of ancient martyrdoms (*HE* 4.15.47; 5.4.3; 5.21.5: *BHG* 3, *Auct.* 1182)[46]
2 Eusebius assisted Pamphilus in the composition of his *Defence of Origen and his Opinions* while he was in prison in Caesarea, and he added a sixth book after Pamphilus' death (*HE* 6.23.4, 33.4, 36.4).[47]

The contents of most of the work must be reconstructed from Photius' brief summaries of what appear to be both the five-book and the six-book versions of the *Defence* (*Bibliotheca* 117, 118), but the preface and Book 1 survive in a Latin translation made by Rufinus in 397 (*PG* 17.541–616), whose complicated textual tradition has now been sorted out in the excellent edition by R. Amacker and É. Junod, *Pamphile et Eusèbe de Césarée: Apologie pour Origène, suivi de Rufin d'Aquilée: Sur la falsification des livres d'Origène, Sources chrétiennes* 464, 465 (Paris: Le Cerf, 2002).

3 *The Life of Pamphilus* (*HE* 6.33.3; 7.32.25; *Mart. Pal.* 11.3; Jerome, *De viris illustribus* 81; *Contra Rufinum* 1.9) contained a catalogue of the library in Caesarea built up by Pamphilus which Eusebius constantly used.
4 *Against Porphyry in 25 books*: A. Harnack, *Porphyrius 'Gegen die Christen,' 15 Bücher. Zeugnisse, Fragmente und Referate. Abhandlungen der königlich preussischen Akademie der Wissenschaften*, Phil.-hist. Kl. 1916, Nr. 1 (Berlin, 1916), 30–31
5 *On the Polygamy and Large Progeny of the Patriarchs* (*DE* 1.9.20, cf. *PE* 7.8.29): all that survives is a brief quotation in Basil, *De spiritu sancto* 29.72 (*PG* 32.204).

G Two works of disputed authenticity[48]

1 Letter to Constantia (*PG 20.1545–1550*)[49]

This letter, which first surfaced at the iconoclastic council of 754, contains both distinctively Eusebian language and apparent anachronisms, such as a painted portrait of Christ and an allusion to the human nature of Christ. The most plausible hypothesis is that the letter quoted in 754 was a

---

[45] T. D. Barnes, Review of A. Camplani, *Le lettere festali di Atanasio di Alessandria, Studio Storicocritico* (Unione Accademica Nazionale: Corpus dei Manoscritti Copti Letterari) (Rome: CIM, 1989), *JTS*, n.s. 41 (1990), 261–62.
[46] The collection of fragments printed by Migne, *PG* 20.1519–1534 is unreliable: the last comprises abbreviated excerpts from *HE* 8.5–12, which belong to an edition of the *Ecclesiastical History* later than the first.
[47] Barnes, *Constantine and Eusebius*, 199–201.
[48] Works generally acknowledged to be spurious are listed at *CPG* 3505–507. I have deliberately ignored both *CPG* 3493 = *BHO* 700 and the *Panegyric of Ten Holy Egyptian Martyrs* (*PG* 20.1533–1536: *BHG*[3] 1194 = *CPG* 3492), which seem certainly spurious to me.
[49] The known fragments are re-edited with an introduction and brief commentary by A. von Stockhausen in T. Krannich, C. Schubert and C. Sode, *Die ikonoklastische Synode von Hiereia 754. Einleitung, Text, Übersetzung und Kommentar ihres Horos, Studien und Texte zu Antike und Christentum* 15 (Tübingen, 2002), 92–112.

genuine letter of Eusebius with interpolations from a later hand. Specifically, it has been proposed that shortly after either 313 or 325, Constantia, a half-sister of Constantine who was the wife of Constantine's imperial colleague Licinius from 313 until his death in 325, wrote to Eusebius requesting a painted portrait of Christ and that Eusebius, in accordance with the views set out in the third book of his *Preparation for the Gospel*, wrote back explaining that he could not fulfil her request because it was inappropriate; a fair copy of Eusebius' letter was preserved in the episcopal archives in Caesarea, and at some date after *c.* 450 parts of the letter were rewritten to intensify and sharpen its arguments against the propriety of attempting to represent Christ at all, perhaps by someone who wished to impugn the status and authority of the picture of Christ on show in Edessa.[50]

2 Reply to Hierocles[51]

This work, which is a reply to the comparison made between Apollonius of Tyana and Christ in the anti-Christian polemic which Sossianus Hierocles recited in Nicomedia in 303 (Lactantius, *Divine Institutes* 5.2.2, 2.12–17, 4.1) was probably written by a Christian sophist in northern Asia Minor who happened to be called Eusebius. At some date it was misattributed to the author's homonym Eusebius of Caesarea, who never refers to it despite his many cross-references to his own writings and who shows no literary or lexical influence of the Second Sophistic Movement anywhere in any of his indubitably authentic works.[52]

Eusebius on God in history[53]

Eusebius is an inelegant and repetitious writer, and he was neither a precise thinker nor a theologian of any significance during his lifetime. He regarded

---

[50] T. D. Barnes, 'Notes on the Letter of Eusebius to Constantia (*CPG* 3503)', *Studia Patristica* 41 (2010), 313–17. For earlier discussions, see C. Murray, 'Art and the Early Church', *JTS*, n.s. 28 (1977), 303–45; S. Gero, 'The True Image of Christ: Eusebius' Letter to Constantia Reconsidered', *JTS*, n.s. 32 (1981) 460–70; H. G. Thümmel, 'Eusebios' Brief an Kaiserin Konstantia', *Klio* 66 (1984), 210–22: these three scholars argued, respectively, that the quotations which first surfaced in 754 were forged, probably authentic and certainly from a genuine letter of 313.

[51] Edited and translated into English by C. P. Jones, *Philostratus: Apollonius of Tyana* 3 (Cambridge, MA and London: Harvard University Press, 2006), 154–257; edited by É. Des Places with an introduction, French translation and notes by M. Forrat (*SC* 333, 1986).

[52] T. Hägg, 'Hierocles the lover of truth and Eusebius the sophist', *Symbolae Osloenses* 67 (1992), 138–50; T. D. Barnes, 'Monotheists All?', *Phoenix* 55 (2001), 151–52. In the introduction to his recent edition and translation, Jones stoutly defends the traditional attribution of the work and avers that Hägg's hypothesis 'strains credulity beyond the limit' (*Philostratus* 3, 152).

[53] See, in general, M. Weis, *Die Stellung des Eusebius im arianischen Streit: Kirchen- und dogmengeschichtliche Studie* (Freiburg im Breisgau 1920); H.-G. Opitz, 'Euseb von Caesarea als Theologe', *Zeitschrift für die neutestamentliche Wissenschaft* 34 (1935), 1–19; H. Berkhof, *Die Theologie des Eusebius* (Amsterdam, 1939); Barnes, *Constantine and Eusebius*, 126–27, 167–88; F. M. Young, *From Nicaea to Chalcedon* (London: SCM Press, 1983), 8–23; R. P. C. Hanson, *The Search for the Christian Doctrine of God: The Arian Controversy 318–381* (Edinburgh: T&T Clark, 1988), 46–59, 159–72.

himself as an intellectual heir of Origen, which led him to found his theology on the assumption that God the Son is in some way inferior or secondary to God the Father. Origen himself put the three persons of the Trinity on a level of equality, but he also asserted that the Father and the Son do not have a single *ousia* or *hypostasis*, but 'are two distinct existences' (*Against Celsus* 8.12, trans. H. Chadwick).[54] Eusebius took this as the starting point of his Christology, so that he was fundamentally sympathetic to the views of Arius when these provoked his bishop to excommunicate him. Eusebius drew a sharp distinction between the unoriginated Father and the Son who had an origin. He thought of God the Son as secondary to the Father, as a second God, the second cause, whose substance (*ousia*/οὐσία) derives its source from the Father and is fashioned in his image: after the ineffable and infinitely great power of the God of the universe, he believed that there comes 'next after the Father the power, both creative and illuminating, of the divine Logos' (*PE* 7.15.1–3). Eusebius did not change his basic Christological assumptions as a result of the controversy over the views of Arius; he was merely careful after 325 to avoid openly calling Christ a 'second God' or asserting that Christ had a different *ousia* from the Father, lest he lay himself open to a charge of heresy as defined by the creed of the Council of Nicaea and its anathemas (Opitz, *Urkunden* 24). From his earliest writings onwards, Eusebius construed the LXX version of Proverbs 8.22 as the Son or Logos stating: 'The Lord created me the beginning of his ways' (κύριος ἔκτισέν με ἀρχὴν ὁδῶν αὐτοῦ εἰς ἔργα αὐτοῦ). It is significant that his last work, the *Ecclesiastical Theology*, quoted this favourite proof-text of the 'Arians' no fewer than twenty-one times.[55] Eusebius was not interested in speculative theology or philosophical subtleties. But he wrote voluminously and often to show how his conception of a subordinate Logos explained the course of human history from the creation of Adam to the end of time, and his chosen form of argument even in his apologetical works was normally close textual analysis of biblical texts.

Eusebius had an idiosyncratic interpretation of human history. He believed that Christianity, so far from being a new religion with its origins in the reign of the emperor Tiberius, was the primeval religion of the human race. He asserted the virtual identity of Christianity with the religion of the Old Testament patriarchs, who despite appearances were not Jews. The divine Logos had revealed himself to Abraham and the rest, who were Christians in all but name. Before Moses the human race was divided between these ancient Hebrews who worshipped God and the rest of the descendants of Adam, who lived no better than beasts. Moses introduced Jewish customs as images and symbols of the truth which Christ later revealed to all through the divine theophany of the Incarnation. Greek philosophy was inspired by and derived from Moses, who lived before the Trojan War and

---

[54] For other relevant passages, see Barnes, *Constantine and Eusebius*, 88, 331 n. 62.

[55] Fourth-century interpretations of this ambiguous text, which comes first in his list of 'Arian' proof-texts, are summarized briefly by Hanson, *Search*, 832.

whose laws began to civilize the world and to prepare gentiles to receive knowledge of God. Both the traditional religions of the Greco-Roman world and Judaism, therefore, represented in Eusebius' eyes declensions from true religion. The Mosaic dispensation replaced the religion of the patriarchs, but God intended it only as a temporary measure until it was superseded by Christ's coming. Hence, when the Jews killed the promised Messiah (Eusebius perpetuates this anti-semitic version of the Passion story), God punished them with political extinction, while ensuring that the Christian Church, the repository of His truth, prospered – and continues to prosper.

Eusebius read the Bible as foretelling the whole course of human history. The Old Testament foretold not only the Incarnation, Crucifixion and Resurrection of Christ, but also the destruction of the Jewish Temple and polity, the persecutions and the eventual triumph of the Christian Church, and even the Christian Roman Empire of Constantine. What of the New Testament? For Eusebius it foretold the future, especially Christ's second theophany at the Last Judgement, which, during the 'Great Persecution', he appears to have believed to be imminent.

Bibliography

Critical editions of Eusebius' principal works and English translations

1 Eusebius Werke *in the series* Die Griechischen Christlichen Schriftsteller der ersten (drei) Jahrhunderte *(Leipzig, 1897–1918; Berlin, 1954–)*

EW I = GCS 7

Life of Constantine including the three appended speeches: I. A. Heikel (1902)

EW I.1[2] *Life of Constantine* without the three appended speeches: F. Winkelmann (1975; revised edition, Berlin, 2008)

There is a generally reliable translation of the four books of the *Life* accompanied by an introduction and historical commentary by Averil Cameron and S. G. Hall, *Eusebius: Life of Constantine* (Oxford: Clarendon Press, 1999) and a translation of Eusebius' two speeches by H. A. Drake, *In Praise of Constantine: A Historical Study and New Translation of Eusebius' Tricennial Orations* (Berkeley: University of California Press, 1976), 83–127, which rarely goes badly astray, even though Drake fails to recognize the main verb of the first sentence (the jussive θελγόντων, which he construes as a participle). Unfortunately, the translation of Constantine's speech by M. J. Edwards, *Constantine and Christendom. The Oration to the Saints; The Greek and Latin Accounts of the Discovery of the Cross. The Edict of Constantine to Pope Silvester*, Translated Texts for Historians 39 (Liverpool: Liverpool University Press, 2003), 1–62, is untrustworthy.[56]

---

[56] On these three translations, see briefly T. D. Barnes, Review of Averil Cameron and S. G. Hall, *Eusebius: Life of Constantine* (2001), *Classical Review*, n.s. 51 (2001), 39–41; Review: Mark Julian Edwards, *Constantine and Christendom. The Oration to the Saints. The Greek and Latin Accounts of the Discovery of the Cross. The Edict of Constantine to Pope Silvester.* Translated Texts for Historians 39 (Liverpool: Liverpool University Press, 2003), *JTS*, n.s. 55 (2004), 351–54. Edwards ignores the

EW II.1–3 = *GCS* 9.1–3
Ecclesiastical History, the short recension of the *Martyrs of Palestine* with the Greek fragments of the long recension, Rufinus' translation of *HE* 1–9 and his continuation of Eusebius down to 395: E. Schwartz and T. Mommsen, *EW* II.1–3 (1903, 1908, 1909); 2nd edn revised by F. Winkelmann, *GCS*, N. F. 6.1–3 (1999).

The English translation by G. A. Williamson, *The History of the Church from Christ to Constantine* (Harmondsworth: Penguin, 1963), is not completely reliable, even in the version revised by A. Louth (1989). Better are the translations by K. Lake and J. E. L. Oulton in the Loeb series (London and Cambridge, MA: Heinemann, 1926, 1932) and R. J. Deferrari, *Fathers of the Church* 19 (Washington: Catholic University of America Press, 1953), 29 (1955), but the best and most helpful translation is the accurate, if somewhat old-fashioned, version of both the *Ecclesiastical History* and both recensions of the *Martyrs of Palestine* by H. J. Lawlor and J. E. L. Oulton (London: SPCK, 1927) with an accompanying volume of notes (1928).

EW III.1 = *GCS* 11.1
Onomasticon, with Jerome's Latin version *en face*: E. Klostermann (1904)
The translation in G. S. P. Freeman-Grenville, R. L. Chapman III and J. E. Taylor, *Palestine in the Fourth Century A. D. The Onomasticon by Eusebius of Caesarea* (Jerusalem: Carta, 2003), 9–98, is more reliable than the later translation by R. S. Notley and Z. Safrai, *Eusebius'* Onomasticon. *The Place Names of Divine Scripture*, Jewish and Christian Perspectives Series 9 (Boston & Leiden: Brill, 2005).

EW III.2 = *GCS* 11.2
Theophany: German translation of Syriac translation with the Greek fragments: H. Gressmann (1911); 2nd edn revised by A. Laminski (1991, pub. 1992)
The translation by S. Lee, *Eusebius Bishop of Caesarea on the Theophaneia or Divine Manifestation of our Lord and Saviour Jesus Christ* (Cambridge, 1843), is based on his *editio princeps* of the Syriac text (London, 1842).

EW IV = *GCS* 14
Against Marcellus and *Ecclesiastical Theology*: E. Klostermann (1906; 3rd edn revised by G. C. Hansen (1991)

EW V = *GCS* 20
Chronicle: annotated German translation of the Armenian version: J. Karst (1911)

EW VI = *GCS* 23
Proof of the Gospel: I. A. Heikel (1913)
W. J. Ferrar, *The Proof of the Gospel, being the Demonstratio Evangelica of Eusebius of Caesarea* (London: SPCK, 1920)

EW VII = *GCS* 47 (replacing *GCS* 24 + 34)
Jerome's Latin version of the *Chronicle*: R. Helm (1956)

EW VIII.1–2 = *GCS* 43.1–2
Preparation for the Gospel: K. Mras (1954, 1956)

---

improvements to Heikel's notoriously inadequate edition noted by F. Winkelmann, 'Annotationes zu einer neuen Edition der Tricennatsreden Eusebs und der *Oratio ad sanctorum coetum* in *GCS* (*CPG* 3498.3987)', *ANTIDORON. Hommages à Maurits Geerard pour célébrer l'achèvement de la Clavis Patrum Graecorum* I (Wetteren: Cultura, 1984), 1–7.

E. H. Gifford, *Eusebii Pamphili Evangelicae Praeparationis libri xv* (Oxford, 1903): edition, translation and commentary

2 Texts with French translations in the series Sources chrétiennes
(Lyon and Paris, 1941–45; Paris, 1946–)

Ecclesiastical History and the short recension of the *Martyrs of Palestine*: G. Bardy, SC 31, 41, 55, 71

Preparation for the Gospel: various editors

I: J. Sirinelli and É. Des Places (206, 1974); II-III: É. Des Places (228, 1976); IV, V.1–17: O. Zink and É. Des Places (262, 1979); V.18–36, VI: É. Des Places (266, 1980); VII: G. Schroeder and É. Des Places (215, 1975); VIII-X: G. Schroeder and É. Des Places (369, 1991); XI: G. Favrelle and É. Des Places (292, 1982); XII-XIII: É. Des Places (307, 1983); XIV–XV: É. Des Places (338, 1987)

Problems and Solutions: C. Zamagni, *Eusèbe de Césarée: Questions évangéliques* (SC 523, 2008)
For other works, see the individual discussions above.

Selection of modern works

H. W. Attridge and G. Hata, eds, *Eusebius, Christianity, and Judaism* (Leiden: Brill, 1992).

T. D. Barnes, *Constantine and Eusebius* (Cambridge, MA: Harvard University Press, 1981).

T. D. Barnes, *Early Christianity and the Roman Empire*, Variorum Collected Studies Series 207 (London: Variorum Reprints, 1984).

T. D. Barnes, *From Eusebius to Augustine. Selected Papers 1982–1993*, Variorum Collected Studies Series 438 (London: Variorum Reprints, 1994).

H. C. Brennecke, U. Heil, A. von Stockhausen and A. Wintjes, *Athanasius Werke Dokumente zur Geschichte des arianischen Streites* 3 (Berlin and New York: De Gruyter, 2007), xix–xxxvi, 77–136.

D. S. Wallace Hadrill, *Eusebius of Caesarea* (London: Mowbray, 1960).

A. Harnack, *Geschichte des altchristlichen Literatur bis Eusebius* 2 1.2 (Leipzig, 1893) 551–86 (by E. Preuschen); 2.2 (1904), 106–27.

F. J. Foakes Jackson, *Eusebius Pamphili. A Study of the Man and his Writings. Five Essays* (Cambridge: Heffer & Sons, 1933).

J. B. Lightfoot, 'Eusebius of Caesarea', *Dictionary of Christian Biography* 2 (London, 1880), 308–48.

H.-G. Opitz, *Athanasius Werke 3.1. Urkunden zur Geschichte des aranischen Streites (318–28)* 1 (Berlin and Leipzig, 1934); 2 (1935).

J. Quasten, *Patrology 3, The Golden Age of Greek Patristic Literature from the Council of Nicaea to the Council of Chalcedon* (Utrecht: Spectrum; Westminster, MD: Newman Press, 1960), 309–45.

E. Schwartz, 'Eusebios von Caesarea', *RE* 6 (1909: the first half of the volume was published in 1907), 1370–439, reprinted in his *Griechische Geschichtschreiber* (2nd edn, Leipzig: Koehler & Amelang, 1959), 495–598.

J. Stevenson, *Studies in Eusebius* (Cambridge: Cambridge University Press, 1929).

Index of ancient and biblical texts

Index of names and subjects

Abraham 9, 190
Adam xiv, 43, 45, 47, 48, 49, 61, 62, 65, 190
Alexandria xiv, 68, 81, 111, 112, 113, 116, 142
Antoninus Pius 2, 18
apostolic tradition 148–50
Aquila xiv
Arian controversy 124
Aristides 19
Aristotle 2, 58, 76
Arius 176, 177, 178, 183, 190
Assyria 15, 17
Athanasius 177
Athenagoras 13, 52, 66
Augustine 50, 86, 123, 125, 139

baptism 49, 88, 92, 129, 130, 132, 133, 134, 135, 136, 138
Bar Kokhba revolt 1, 4
Basil of Caesarea 154, 156, 164, 170, 186
Basilides 71, 119
Bauer, W. 33, 70
Bellinzoni, A. J. 4 n. 9, 27 n. 36
Birley, A. R. 16
bishops 127, 128, 131, 132, 134, 137, 144
Burckhardt, J. 174, 174 n. 1

Caesarea 111, 114
Calixtus xvii
cannibalism 6
Caracalla 86
Carthage xvii, 85, 86, 100, 101, 105, 106, 109, 127, 129, 132, 135
Celsus 118–19
Chadwick, H. 111, 125 n. 57, 174, 190
christology 48, 49, 61, 62, 65, 90, 98, 124, 152, 152 n. 40, 168, 169, 190
Clement of Alexandria xiv–xv, 68–84, 111
Constantine 173, 174, 182, 183, 184
cosmology 114, 117, 120, 121
Council of Antioch 177, 187

Council of Nicaea 176, 177, 178, 183, 187, 190
Council of Tyre 177
Crescens 16, 19
Cyprian xvi–xvii, 96, 127–40, 165

Decius xvii, 114, 127
DeConick, A. D. 31 n. 42
Demetrius 113
demiurge 119, 168
Didache 148
Didymus the Blind 81
Diocletian 138, 154, 179
Docetism xviii
Donatism xvii, 139
Dura Europas 23, 27

early catholicism 49
education 73, 78, 79, 86, 109, 111, 112, 113, 114, 123
Edwards, M. 117, 120
Eleutherus 36, 37
Encratism 15, 18, 23, 30, 33
Ephesus 4
Ephrem 23, 27–30
Epicureans 76
Epiphanius 17, 112, 113, 143
Erasmus 49, 125
eschatology 118, 120
eucharist 49, 92, 107, 132, 134, 135
Eusebius of Caesarea xi, xvii, xviii–xix, 13, 30, 33, 52, 54, 60, 66, 69, 105, 106, 111, 112, 113, 154, 156, 157, 158, 173–93
Eusebius of Nicomedia 175, 181
Evagrius 81, 124, 162
Eve 43, 45, 47, 48

fall 46, 63–4
Felicity 86, 100
Flavia Neapolis 1–2, 4

Galerius 179
gnostic 30, 38–9, 45, 71, 71 n. 8, 76, 80, 111, 114, 117, 120, 141